European Coordination Centre fo
and Documentation in Social S

D1543655

INTERNATIONAL
COMPARATIVE RESEARCH

Problems of Theory, Methodology
and Organisation in Eastern and
Western Europe

Other Publications of the Vienna Centre

AMANN, A
Open Care for the Elderly in Seven European Countries

BERTING, J., MILLS, S. C. & WINTERSBERGER, H.
The Socio-Economic Impact of Microelectronics

CAO-PINNA, V. & SHATALIN, S.
Consumption Patterns in Eastern and Western Europe

DURAND-DROUHIN, J-L. & SZWENGRUB, L-M.
Rural Community Studies in Europe, Volumes 1 & 2

FORSLIN, J., SARAPATA, A. & WHITEHILL, A.
Automation and Industrial Workers, Volume 1, Parts 1 & 2 and Volume 2

GABROVSKA, S. *et al.*
European Guide to Social Science Information and Documentation Services

HERFURTH, M. & HOGEWEG-DE HAART, H.
Social Integration of Migrant Workers and Other Ethnic Minorities:
A Documentation of Current Research

MENDRAS, H. & MIHAILESCU, I.
Theories and Methods in Rural Community Studies

SZALAI, A. & PETRELLA, R.
Cross-National Comparative Survey Research: Theory and Practice

NOTICE TO READERS

Dear Reader

If your library is not already a standing/continuation order customer to this series, may we recommend that you place a standing/continuation order to receive immediately upon publication all new volumes. Should you find that these volumes no longer serve your needs, your order can be cancelled at any time without notice

ROBERT MAXWELL
Publisher at Pergamon Press

WITHDRAWN

WITHDRAWN

3 0700 10088 4153

INTERNATIONAL COMPARATIVE RESEARCH

Problems of Theory, Methodology
and Organisation in Eastern and
Western Europe

Edited by

MANFRED NIESSEN

and

JULES PESCHAR

*for the European Coordination Centre for Research and Documentation
in Social Sciences*

PERGAMON PRESS

OXFORD · NEW YORK · TORONTO · SYDNEY · PARIS · FRANKFURT

U.K.	Pergamon Press Ltd., Headington Hill Hall, Oxford OX3 0BW, England
U.S.A.	Pergamon Press Inc., Maxwell House, Fairview Park, Elmsford, New York 10523, U.S.A.
CANADA	Pergamon Press Canada Ltd., Suite 104, 150 Consumers Rd., Willowdale, Ontario M2J 1P9, Canada
AUSTRALIA	Pergamon Press (Aust.) Pty. Ltd., P.O. Box 544, Potts Point, N.S.W. 2011, Australia
FRANCE	Pergamon Press SARL, 24 rue des Ecoles, 75240 Paris, Cedex 05, France
FEDERAL REPUBLIC OF GERMANY	Pergamon Press GmbH, 6242 Kronberg-Taunus, Hammerweg 6, Federal Republic of Germany

Copyright © 1982 The European Coordination Centre
for Research and Documentation
in Social Sciences

All Rights Reserved. No part of this publication may be reproduced, stored in a retrieval system or transmitted in any form or by any means: electronic, electrostatic, magnetic tape, mechanical, photocopying, recording or otherwise, without permission in writing from the copyright holders.

First edition 1982

Library of Congress Cataloging in Publication Data

Main entry under title:
International comparative research.
Contributions to the First International Seminar
on Cross-National Comparative Research, held in
Warsaw, Poland, Sept. 21-26, 1980.
Bibliography: p.
1. Social sciences—Comparative method—Congresses.
2. Social sciences—Research—Europe—International
cooperation—Congresses. I. Niessen, Manfred.
II. Peschar, J. L., 1944-   . III. European Centre
for the Co-ordination of Research and Documentation in
Social Sciences. IV. International Seminar on Cross-
National Comparative Research (1st : 1980 : Warsaw,
Poland)
H62.A315 1982   300'.72   82-16519
ISBN 0-08-027960-0

British Library Cataloguing in Publication Data

International comparative research.
1. Sociology—Methodology
I. Niessen, Manfred II. Peschar, Jules
301'.018   HM24
ISBN 0-08-027960-0

Printed in Great Britain by A. Wheaton & Co. Ltd., Exeter

Contents

Part Three

Organisation and Cooperation in International Comparative Research

Part Four

Case Studies

Appendix

List of Contributors

JAN BERTING is Professor of theoretical sociology and the history of sociology at the Erasmus University in Rotterdam, the Netherlands, Member of the Board of Directors and Programme Committee of the Vienna Centre.

JOHAN GALTUNG is Founder and former Director of the International Peace Research Institute in Oslo, Norway. Presently Professor at the Institut Universitaire d'Etudes du Developpement and Director of a United Nations University Project, both in Geneva, Switzerland.

TORSTEN HUSÉN is Professor of Education and Director of the Institute of International Education at the University of Stockholm, Sweden. Former Chairman and now President of the International Association for the Evaluation of Educational Achievement (IEA).

CHANTAL KOURILSKY is Researcher at the Institut de Recherches Juridiques Comparatives of the Centre National de la Recherche Scientifique (CNRS) in Paris, France. Lecturer in Soviet legal terminology at the Institute of Comparative Law, University of Paris I. Presently on leave and seconded to the Vienna Centre as Scientific Secretary for projects in the field of comparative law.

MICHEL LESAGE is Professor of Public Law and Political Science at the University of Paris I and Director of the Institut de Recherches Juridiques Comparatives of the Centre National de la Recherche Scientifique (CNRS) in Paris, France.

MANFRED LOETSCH is Professor of Sociology at the Institute for Marxist-Leninist Sociology at the Academy of Social Sciences in Berlin, German Democratic Republic.

STEPHEN C. MILLS was Research Fellow at the Manchester Business School and has been Director of the Vienna Centre since 1976.

EDMUND MOKRZYCKI is Researcher at the Institute for Philosophy and Sociology of the Polish Academy of Sciences, Warsaw, Poland.

MANFRED NIEßEN is Researcher and Lecturer in the Education Department at the University of Trier, Federal Republic of Germany. Presently on leave and seconded to the Vienna Centre as Scientific Secretary for projects in the field of comparative education and training.

JULES PESCHAR is Researcher and Lecturer in educational sociology and methodology at the Department of Sociology of the University of Groningen, the Netherlands. Presently on leave and seconded to the Vienna Centre as Scientific Secretary for projects in the field of comparative labour studies and training.

OSKAR VOGEL is a rural sociologist and Chairman of the Head Office for Sociological Information and Documentation in the German Democratic Republic. Presently on leave and seconded to the Vienna Centre as Scientific Secretary for projects in the field of comparative rural sociology.

Acknowledgements

The chapters of this book were specially prepared for the Seminar on Cross-National Comparative Research. The seminar, however, could not have been organised and carried out without the help of many institutes and persons.

In the first place UNESCO in Paris provided a financial foundation for the whole enterprise by allocating a special grant from their training programme to the Vienna Centre. In the second place, the Polish Academy of Sciences was willing to host the seminar in Miedzeszyn near Warsaw and supported it in its usual generous way.

The seminar would of course not have been possible without the dedication of the invited lecturers: Jan Berting, Johan Galtung, Torsten Husén, Michel Lesage, Manfred Loetsch and Edmund Mokrzycki. In the preparatory stage most of them spent a day with us in Vienna to discuss the seminar plans (one of them even stayed for a weekend to help us solve problems). Of particular value was their willingness to discuss their experiences in comparative research with the participants of the seminar inside and outside the "official" sessions. The often expressed feeling of the participants that they benefited very much from frequent "informal" talks must to a great extent be credited to those lecturers who could manage to be present during the whole seminar.

Furthermore, we want to thank Jan Berting for his willingness to chair the two panel discussions which took place at the seminar and in particular Andrzej Sicinski from the Polish Academy of Sciences who joined these panels.

The plan of the seminar was of course also discussed with the Vienna Centre's scientific staff. Stephen Mills, Chantal Kourilsky, Oskar Vogel and Jens Qvortrup were especially involved and presented papers which stimulated the discussions. From the participants Jens Dangschat, Hussein Fahim, Nicole Gain, Vladimir Gaskov and Oskar Niedermayer presented projects in which they are engaged. We thank all of them for their valuable contributions to the seminar.

Finally, but certainly not the least important, were the participants in the seminar coming from 17 countries. It was conceived as a training for young social scientists engaged in or planning to participate in international comparative research. However, the many discussions within and outside the programme proved that they also contributed much to the seminar. Its final success was to a large extent dependent on them as well as many other persons not mentioned by name here. Two exceptions must be made: Gaby Beck and Péter Tamási (Vienna Centre) carefully edited the papers from a linguistic point of view.

Preface

The European Coordination Centre for Research and Documentation in Social Sciences, in short called the Vienna Centre, was established in 1963 by UNESCO. It had the aim of forming a common ground for cooperation between social scientists from countries with different economic and political systems.

In the 17 years behind us some 25 comparative projects were started and carried out under the auspices of the Vienna Centre, and some 15 projects are now in different stages of completion. Therefore, it would be an understatement to say that the Vienna Centre staff as well as its project participants have only gained some experience with regard to the execution and management of comparative research projects. Of course, it cannot be denied that not all efforts were completely successful, but this is the fate of almost any ambitious enterprise. On the other hand, we, as the Vienna Centre, can be proud of the enormous progress being made in the substantive cooperation between social scientists coming from different socio-economic systems and working together in scientific projects. After all these years of experience the Board of Directors of the Vienna Centre agreed with a proposal to make the experiences in East–West cooperation available to a wider scientific public and to organise *Training Seminars* for young scientists in the European Region. When organised on a regular basis, the competence in cross-national comparative research and coordination could be increased, to the benefit of all projects in this field.

Moreover, the importance of the Vienna Centre's seminar programme can also be seen in a broader perspective. It is in line with one of the conclusions adopted by the "Scientific Forum" of the Conference on Security and Co-operation in Europe held in Hamburg in 1980. It says that "appropriate support should be given to arrange advanced seminars and training courses for young scientists from participating and other States that would enable them to study new scientific methods for shorter or longer periods. Information about these activities and arrangements should be disseminated as widely as possible."

When I look at the experiences and the papers of the first of these seminars as they are presented in this book, I can be very optimistic about the future of cooperation in comparative research. The seminar proved to be successful and the many contributions were very stimulating. At the same time it is clear that still much can be done and that the Vienna Centre can play a very important role in the field of comparative research.

That this first seminar could be so successful is to a large extent due to the many persons involved. The invited lecturers — from inside and outside the Vienna Centre projects — cooperated in a very generous way. They were stimulated by the two Vienna Centre scientific staff members, M. Nießen and J. Peschar, who managed to organise the seminar in a way that it could reach its difficult goals: give insight into and understanding of the problems of comparative research. May I express, on behalf of the Vienna Centre, our thanks to all those involved in this important enterprise.

Professor Adam Schaff
President of the Board of Directors of the Vienna Centre

Vienna, November 1980

Introduction

by Manfred Nießen and Jules Peschar

THE INTERNATIONAL SEMINAR ON CROSS-NATIONAL COMPARATIVE RESEARCH

The European Coordination Centre for Research and Documentation in Social Sciences (Vienna Centre) was established by the International Social Science Council in 1963 as a result of a unanimous decision of the UNESCO General Assembly. Its special task was, in a period of political "détente", to facilitate scientific cooperation and exchange through the coordination of concrete comparative research projects in both Eastern and Western Europe. During its existence for some 17 years now many research projects have been started and carried out simultaneously in a varying number of socialist and non-socialist countries.[1]

Already in 1972 both the International Social Science Council and the Vienna Centre took the initiative to organise a Round Table on the cumulative experiences with regard to international comparative research. This conference in Budapest was especially devoted to problems in comparative survey research. Three Vienna Centre and two non-Vienna Centre projects were carefully monitored and analysed on theory, methodology and practical problems in the research process. It appeared then – of course – that international cooperative comparative research is a rather complicated and time-consuming enterprise, mainly because of its multi-lateral information and decision structure. Many persons are involved with different theoretical and methodological backgrounds and it is not always possible to find consensus. It is not surprising, therefore, that besides problems of theory and method, also problems of organisation were discussed in Budapest. A full account of the conference is presented in Szalai and Petrella (1977).

Especially in the field of coordination and organisation, not much experience is cumulated and even less dispersed. This led a reviewer of the field of cross-national methodology to the conclusion that essentially no good solution for international research coordination is available (Elder 1976). We do not suggest the contrary, but want to stress the availability of information sources and quite a number of relevant experiences waiting for evaluation.[2]

---

[1] An overview of the current Vienna Centre activities is presented in this book by Mills. The history of the Vienna Centre is more extensively documented in Petrella & Schaff (1974).

[2] This is apparently studied at this very moment by the East–West Centre in Honolulu, Hawaii, which evaluates management competences in international cooperative research and development projects (Dr. Kathleen Wilson, project coordinator). The International Institute for Management Sciences in Moscow undertakes similar screenings of problems in international cooperation, mainly in the technical-scientific domain.

Therefore, when a decision was taken to hold an International Seminar on Cross-National Comparative Research, three arguments played a major role:

1. The Budapest conference reflected on the state of the art in cross-national research at the beginning of the seventies. It was confined to survey techniques, i.e. to one main approach only. Already within this realm, an important part of the techniques, namely, statistical analysis by means of computer packages, was only in its initial stage, mainly available in some big countries. In between we have experienced an enormous growth in social sciences, and not exclusively on the basis of survey techniques. The emphasis on large-scale research has somewhat diminished and other paradigms have come into the picture. In short: the situation has changed and it is on the basis of an assessment of the changed situation that a seminar became useful.

2. To solve the problems of organisation and coordination is vital for every cooperative international project. As mentioned above, these aspects have already entered the discussion. Their interrelationship with the way scientific problems are solved is, however, not given enough attention in our view.

Within Vienna Centre projects an additional facet enters the picture, namely, the fact that scholars from Eastern and Western Europe cooperate. All these problems have to be included in a seminar on cross-national research.

3. Comparative research and cooperation between national teams in such an enterprise confronts us with differences in competence. The need for international training activities becomes obvious and has been mentioned frequently (for instance Rokkan 1968, Gadourek 1977). Wiatr brought up the argument again during the Budapest ISSC/Vienna Centre conference and suggested that the Vienna Centre would take the initiative for training activities (Wiatr 1977, p. 364). In doing so, there was no intention to double the tradition of the International Social Science Council seminars which are devoted to problems of data analysis in various specific fields.

Against the background of these considerations, the Vienna Centre organised the first International Seminar on Cross-National Comparative Research. It was held in Warsaw, Poland, from 21–26 September, 1980, with some 45 persons – lecturers and participants – coming from 17 countries in East and West participating. The idea was to hold a training seminar for young social scientists, where at the same time the "state of the art" and typical problems should be presented and discussed. One goal was to disseminate experience from Vienna Centre projects, where researchers from Eastern and Western Europe cooperate. But by no means was the seminar restricted to these experiences. In fact we thought it better to include a wide variety of evidence from other – non Vienna Centre – projects as well, to serve the goals of the seminar: training in the problems of cross-national comparative research.

At the end of the seminar a general evaluation showed that most of the participants were quite satisfied with such an approach. This supports the Vienna Centre in its intention to continue in this way and schedule other seminars in this domain for the next years.[3]

[3] As a logical step, the next seminar (summer 1981) is planned to be a substantive evaluation of comparative research in some specified areas.

THE CONTENT OF THE SEMINAR AND THIS BOOK

This book is a collection of the contributions to the seminar in Warsaw. Three topics were on the agenda: theory, methodology and organisation of international comparative research with special emphasis on the cooperation in social sciences between Eastern and Western Europe. The evaluation of substantive results was left outside this framework on purpose (this should be the topic of another seminar to follow), but on the other hand it could not be avoided that substantive matters were also touched upon.[4] The seminar concentrated on the following problem areas:

First it dealt with the *theory of comparative research*. The complaints about lacking theory in social sciences in general have their counterpart in comparative research. There is a large gap between what the handbooks prescribe and what happens in reality in cross-national research.

The *strategy in comparative research* to collect empirical information to be used for descriptive, explanatory or analytical purposes is a second major issue which includes methodological problems. Especially in multi-national research, problems of effectiveness and parsimony with regard to the research goals have not attracted much attention.

The *organisation and coordination* of international research is a dimension that is often forgotten (Framhein & Mills 1979). As already mentioned, there are not many publications available in this domain (except for instance Mihailescu 1977); however, it is quite obvious that although good organisation cannot save a "poor" project, improper organisation can almost ruin every relevant research.

Of special interest for the seminar was the *interplay* between matters of organisation and coordination on the one hand and the scientific strategies on the other.

---

[4]During the seminar two panel discussions were organised to deal with substantive findings as well as with policy implications of comparative research. The following questions were to structure the discussions:

1. Comparison of Results from Comparative Research

This panel discussion was to follow the question of whether there are common or divergent dimensions to which the results of different comparative projects can be related, for instance:
− East−West. Are there consistent differences between. Eastern and Western countries? Is the within-system variation smaller or greater than the between-system variation?
− North−South. Are there consistent differences between countries in different stages of economic development? Do these differences dominate those in other dimensions, e. g. East−West?
− Within-countries−Between-countries. Are the between-countries variations still informative when compared to the within-countries variations?

2. Policy Implications of Comparative Research

This panel discussion was to deal with questions such as the following:
− Are there findings of comparative research which are relevant for policy-making? On what level: national, international? In what way are they relevant?
− Are there findings which have been used in policy formulation?
− Did considerations of policy-relevance influence the planning and conducting of research projects?
− Which discussions did this have for the project (e. g. when representatives of non-scientific organisations such as trade unions, firms, public administration were participating)?
− Can results of comparative social research be relevant at all for policy matters on the national and/or international level? If yes, what conditions have to be fulfilled?

The contributions to the seminar – and to this book – are structured into four sections:

Part 1. A set of four lectures was chosen to approach in a systematic way the "Theory and Strategy of Comparative Research". The following questions are discussed:
- "Why compare?"
- "What to compare?"
- "How to compare?"
- "What to take into account when comparing?"

Part 2. Following this systematic approach, two contributions deal with "Selected Methodological Issues in Comparative Research". The first paper gives an overview on problems in the quantitative domain, the second one focusses on methodological considerations of qualitative issues in comparative research.

Part 3. Problems of "Organisation and Cooperation in International Comparative Research" are treated in the next three contributions. The first paper systematically elaborates such problems under the perspective of cooperative research between Eastern and Western Europe. The second one presents a specific outstanding venture in the international comparative field and is, thirdly, followed by the case of the Vienna Centre.

Part 4. The final two "Case Studies" were originally designed to serve as sources for and stimulation of discussions in the working groups during the seminar. Each of them therefore presents, as concretely as possible, a specific methodological problem out of a Vienna Centre project.

A more comprehensive introduction is placed before each of the parts, in order to stress the coherence of the four parts of the book.

REFERENCES

Elder, J. W. (1976) Comparative Cross-National Methodology. In: *Annual Review of Sociology,* 2; 209–230.

Framhein, G. & S. C. Mills (1979) Infrastructure – the Third Element in International Comparative Research. In: J. Berting, F. Geyer & R. Jurkovich (eds.). *Problems in International Comparative Research in the Social Sciences;* 123–135. Oxford: Pergamon Press.

Gadourek, I. (1977) The Impact of Technology and the Growth of Knowledge upon some Current Pitfalls of the Methodology of Sociology. In: *Methodology and Science,* 10, 222–239.

Mihailescu, Ioan (1977) Possibilités et limites de la recherche comparative transnationale. In: *Information des Sciences Sociales,* 16, 213–229.

Petrella, R. & A. Schaff (1974) *A European Experiment in Cooperation in the Social Sciences: Ten Years Activities at the Centre, 1963–1973.* Vienna: European Coordination Centre for Research and Documentation in Social Sciences.

Rokkan, S. (ed.) (1968) *Comparative Research Across Cultures and Nations.* Paris: Mouton.

Szalai, A. & R. Petrella (eds.) (1977) *Cross-National Comparative Survey Research: Theory and Practice.* Oxford: Pergamon Press.

Wiatr, J. (1977) The Role of Theory in the Process of Cross-National Survey Research. In: A. Szalai & R. Petrella (eds.) *Cross-National Comparative Survey Research: Theory and Practice;* 347–372. Oxford: Pergamon Press.

Part One

THEORY AND STRATEGY
OF COMPARATIVE RESEARCH

The contributions of this part attempt at a systematic approach to the problems of theory and strategy of comparative research.

In the first one *Jan Berting* elaborates on the question of why and in what case comparative research is necessary. This is a rather intricate question because, as pointed out at the beginning of the chapter, the "state of the art" of comparative studies does not lead very easily to a positive answer. The author also discusses shortcomings of alternative approaches and introduces various dimensions as part of a typology of comparative studies. On the basis of these deliberations, criteria are elaborated as a guideline to decide whether cooperative comparative research is appropriate and what design might be useful.

Johan Galtung addresses the meaning of "nation" as a variable, thus directly embarking on the question "What to compare?" He concentrates on two interpretations — "nation" in the sense of country on the one hand and of ethnic group on the other — and discusses various levels of analysis for both cases as well as classifications of variables for each. Directly referring to the process of comparative research itself is the elaboration on one variable of "nation" in the sense of ethnic group — knowledge as characterised by intellectual styles. This contribution challenges some of the hidden background assumptions of mainstream comparative research.

Manfred Loetsch begins his contribution with considering some reasons for the apparent difficulties that comparative studies meet in relating their findings to differences between socio-economic and cultural systems. In so doing, he taps one of the major dimensions of East—West cooperative research. The attempt to explain these difficulties includes the analysis of some basic features of "how" comparisons are made. On the basis of the analysis, proposals for achieving comparability are formulated which concern the selection of the research object as well as the research strategy.

Edmund Mokrzycki identifies as *the* problem of comparative research the fact that its objects are bound to different contexts. He illustrates this by reference to a specific comparative study, and he also raises the question what distinguishes comparative from non-comparative research. He then turns to a discussion of strategies how to cope with the outlined basic problem, i. e. what strategic position should be taken with regard to the context-boundness of phenomena.

Why Compare in International Research? Theoretical and Practical Limitations of International Research

by Jan Berting

1. INTRODUCTION

Before we start with a discussion on specific problems within the field of international comparative research it may be useful to put forward two general questions: "Why do we engage in this type of research? (What are our goals?)" and "Have we been successful as social scientists in reaching our goals?"

To begin with the last question: generally speaking, international comparative research does not seem to have been very successful in contributing to the development of the social sciences.

One of the conclusions of an international seminar on this topic, held in 1978 in the Netherlands, stated that during the last few decades international comparative research scarcely resulted in any accumulation of scientific knowledge.[1] Although this conclusion also applies to other types of sociological knowledge, this lack of accumulation of knowledge appears to be somewhat more obvious in international comparative research, provided we make an exception for some types of macro-sociological research. At least when we go further back in time, the contributions in the field of macro-sociological comparative studies were evident. I only have to refer to the works of Marx, Weber, Tocqueville and Durkheim.

Even when we turn to a field in which the number of international comparative studies is relatively numerous and in which the methodological problems do not seem to be very complicated in comparison to many other fields, the same rather gloomy picture arises. Treiman remarks in his *Problems of Concept and Measurement in the Comparative Study of Occupational Mobility:* "Despite this enormous interest and effort, however, our knowledge about societal differences and similarities in rates, patterns, and processes of mobility remains surprisingly shaky. Indeed, very little has been firmly established beyond what we find in Sorokin. We can agree with him (1927, pp. 139–141) that in no society is there perfect mobility and in no society is there perfect inheritance of status. In all societies, the transmission of advantage from one generation to the next, and the conversion of one form of advantage into another, is partial and imperfect. Apart from this we have really established nothing. In particular, claims regarding systematic societal

---

[1] J. Berting, "What is the Use of International Comparative Research?", in: J. Berting et al. (editors), *Problems in International Comparative Research in the Social Sciences.* Oxford: Pergamon Press, 1979, pp. 159 ff.

5

variations in mobility rates, patterns, and processes are no better supported now than they were when Sorokin wrote." Treiman continues: "It has been asserted, for example, that the rate or amount of intergenerational mobility is roughly comparable in all industrialized societies (Lipset and Bendix, 1959, p. 13, Svalastoga, 1965). But it has also been asserted that even among industrialized nations the rate of mobility is positively correlated with the degree of industrial *development* (Fox and Miller, 1965; Cutright, 1968). Obviously, both of these claims cannot be true, and there are no technical grounds for choosing between them. On other questions, there is no evidence at all."[2]

Not only have our achievements in international comparative research been rather modest during the recent decades — I refer especially to the achievements in American and Western European sociology — but also rather one-sided. Only a few studies are devoted to *the comparison of nations as a whole* or to *the comparison of major societal institutions in different societies.* An important exception must be made, however, for the contributions of those political scientists who are engaged in comparing political systems.[3] It is odd that in international comparative sociological research not the macro-sociological studies are dominating, but studies that direct the attention to individuals and to the relationships between individuals. A further restriction in this type of research can be observed, caused by the emphasis on attitudes, motivations and opinions of individuals. This individualistic and psychologistic trend is strongly connected with a predilection for national samples, for the use of surveys and questionnaires. Finally, an explicit theoretical base is often lacking or only superficially treated. Most empirical research seems to be descriptive and not directed to test hypotheses that are derived from theory. Of course, there are a lot of reasons that can "explain" this one-sidedness in most of the international comparative research designs.

The purpose of this seminar was to investigate the circumstances that cause the above-mentioned trends and to ponder about the possibilities of changes in a direction that is more fruitful for the development of the social sciences in the long run.

The problems we are confronted with are often considerable. I will give some examples.

In a recent study of S. Barnes et al.,[4] research teams from eight countries worked together on political participation in democracies, emphasising non-institutionalised, non-electoral political action. This emphasis reflects, as the authors emphasise, the prominence of protest in mass politics of Western democracies during the 1960s (cf. p. 27). Here I do not discuss the study — although I think this study earns our attention

[2]J. Treiman, "Problems of Concept and Measurement in the Comparative Study of Occupational Mobility", in: W. Wesolowski et al. (editors), *Social Mobility in Comparative Perspective.* The Polish Academy of Sciences Press, 1978, p. 37.
Treiman refers in this quotation to P. A. Sorokin, *Social and Cultural Mobility.* New York: The Free Press of Glencoe (Expanded reprint of *Social Mobility.* New York: Harper, 1927); K. Svalastoga, "Social Mobility: The Western European Model", *Acta Sociologica,* Vol. 9, pp. 175–182; S. M. Lipset and R. Bendix, *Social Mobility in Industrial Society.* Berkeley: University of California Press, 1959; T. G. Fox and S. M. Miller, "Economic, Political and Social Determinants of Mobility: An International Cross-Sectional Analysis". *Acta Sociologica,* Vol. 9, pp. 76–93; P. Cutright, "Occupational Inheritance: A Cross-national Analysis". *American Journal of Sociology,* Vol. 73, pp. 400–416.
[3]See e.g. A. Lijphart, *The Politics of Accommodation: Pluralism and Democracy in the Netherlands.* Berkeley and Los Angeles: University of California Press, 1968.
[4]S. Barnes et al., *Political Action. Mass Participation in the Western Democracies.* Beverly Hills/London: Sage Publications, 1979.

as such —, but only select the arguments for the adoption of a research design that illustrates the above-mentioned bias. In the first place, the authors complain about a lack of theory that may guide their research. "A major problem that we faced was the poverty of available theory for guiding research. As we looked for guidance we found theoretical fragments, often deriving from other times and places, instead of operation-alizable theory. While none of these fragments turned out to form a theoretical core for our research, several have influenced our thinking."[5]

Of course this problem is not only characteristic of comparative research but of all research that tries to explain a specific social phenomenon. In international comparative research with several national teams working together, it will generally be very difficult to reach a consensus on the specific theory to be adopted (this problem is similar to that we confront when engaged in interdisciplinary research). If the international comparative research had started with the intention to test hypotheses, derived from a sociological theory (say exchange theory, or class theory) this part of the cooperation would have been much easier, of course. The study "... concentrates heavily on attitudinal and other data derived from individuals. We are aware of the very large impact that political structures have on individual attitudes and actions. By studying countries with relatively similar political structures we minimize the impact of systemic factors and amplify the importance of individual level factors."[6] I wonder, however, what the meaning of "similar" is, with reference to the political systems (and the societal structures) of the FRG, UK, USA, Netherlands, Switzerland, Finland, Italy, Austria.

The authors state, moreover: "Compared with the more obviously political variables such as party organization, electoral laws, and institutional structure, psychological processes can be expected to be *relatively* invariate across political systems ... we focus on measures at the individual level, regardless of their possible origins in group and other nonindividual sources."[7] The goal of the research "is to explore relationships among our independent and dependent variables that form similar patterns in all or most of the countries. We recognize that important country differences exist". However, besides these arguments for the selection of the research design, another one is mentioned: "We would have liked to have had data for treating contextual effects ... But the implementation of a truly contextual design would have necessitated extensive aggregate data on the level of some meaningful contextual unit. These were not available and could not be collected within the constraints of a limited sutdy, if at all."[8]

These citations nicely illustrate the drift to individualistic, psychologistic, survey research in international comparative research in the social sciences that is undertaken by a combination of national teams. Note, by the way, the inconsistency of the arguments given: "selection of countries with relatively similar political structures ... to minimize the impact of systemic factors" and "the argument that party organization, electoral laws, institutional structures are relatively variate compared with psychological processes."

When a social scientist decides to undertake an international comparative study without being part of an international team, he has, generally speaking, far better opportunities for the selection of a research design that fits macro-sociological problems.

[5] S. Barnes et al., op.cit., p. 15.
[6] S. Barnes et al., op.cit., p. 18.
[7] S. Barnes et al., op.cit., pp. 20–21.
[8] S. Barnes et al., op.cit., p. 22.

Moreover, he has better opportunities to formulate his problem in a theoretically meaningful way. The main drawback of this type of research is the extensive difficulty the researcher is confronted with when he is trying to gather the relevant data from different countries. Often, data available in one country do not exist in another, or when they exist, they are not really comparable (e.g. different breakdowns in census data, differences with regard to the definition of the units, the statistics do not cover the same period, etc.), or the accessibility of data banks is poor. The greatest difficulty is perhaps to assess in an adequate way the quality of information on the social structure or system of the societies that is being compared. Take, for instance, the very interesting study of Harold Wilensky, *The Welfare State and Equality*.[9] In this study he tries to explain the reluctance of the United States to join such affluent countries as Sweden, the Netherlands, Federal Republic of Germany, France and Belgium in the provision of health and welfare benefits and services as a matter of social right. He is, as he says, aware that the public welfare effort of such affluent countries as Switzerland, Australia, Canada, and Japan was not very different from that of the United States. This is a macro-sociological problem, as he wants to study "first, the interplay of affluence, economic system, political system, and ideology; second, the effect of social organization on the behavior of political elites."[10]

Of course, Wilensky has to rely mostly on secondary sources concerning the social structures of the countries he wants to compare, and only those that give the information in a language that is accessible to him. So he sometimes has to rely on only one sentence from a study to characterise a whole system. I shall give an example. One of his hypotheses is that: "Social heterogeneity and internal cleavages slow down welfare-state development only when they are given sharp expression by a decentralized, if not fragmented, policy."[11] Then he refers to the Netherlands, a country that in his opinion is an extreme case, both in spending on welfare expenditures and in the degree of social heterogeneity (religious cleavages). Of course, this case does not fit into his hypothesis, unless it could be proven that the Netherlands are strongly politically centralised. And indeed, using one sentence from a study that describes in a rather global way the Dutch society he concludes, that "A strong government, however, is able to channel their expression and dampen the cleavages. The provinces and municipalities are weak; their heads are appointed at the Hague; government integrates the confessional-political blocs at the top in a complex network of advisory bodies, public and semi-public. The welfare state flourishes."[12] The sharp rise in spending on welfare expenditures, however, took place *after* the publication of this study[13] and *after* the disintegration of the pillarisation system.

Also Belgium, with its strong ethnic—linguistic struggles, is regarded as having a strong, centralised government. Also in this case the political developments that accompany the rise of the welfare state do not corroborate his hypothesis. Wilensky did a very good job in trying to find the structural and ideological roots of public expenditure, using an international comparative design. Nevertheless, this study illustrates

[9] H. Wilensky, *The Welfare State and Equality*. Berkeley: University of California Press, 1975.

[10] H. Wilensky, op.cit., p. xi.

[11] H. Wilensky, op.cit., p. 53.

[12] H. Wilensky, op.cit., p. 54.

[13] J. Goudsblom, *Dutch Society*. New York: Random House, 1967.

in a vivid way the necessity to enhance the quality of international macro-sociological studies. Even when one has good access to the data available when there are no language barriers, when one has a good overall knowledge of the national cultures involved, the problems of a macro-sociological comparison are plentiful, as I experienced the last few months when I was engaged in a macro-sociological analysis of two countries, the Netherlands and my neighbour country Belgium. Although I have a lot of census data, historical sources, analyses of specific macro-sociological prboblems etc. at my disposal, I did not realy succeed in unravelling the nature of the social heterogeneity of Belgium in comparison to the Netherlands, using data on the class structure, the religious divisions of cleavages, the ethno-linguistic cleavages and the orginisation of political life. On very strategic topics, information is often lacking (i.e. on the nature of relationships between business elites and political elites, on the composition of the economic elites, on the changing market opportunities of different economic classes etc.).

In my opinion, we have to undertake a series of studies in several countries that *may be the base of future macro-sociological international comparative studies.* Those studies must have a rather similar design and must give information on the main *structural cleavages and divisions in the societies.* Such a design was proposed by Runciman[14] in relationship with social stratification studies. I will not replicate his scheme although I use it as the starting point for the enumeration of themes that have to be included in a comparative macro-sociological study of a very limited number of countries.

1. *Societal elites:* description of those minorities in which the members have relatively much power or influence. We need information about the size of such elites in different societal areas (politics, bureaucracy, economy, religious organisations, media, science, etc.), the degree of centralisation in decision-making, the rate of inflow/outflow, the internal cohesion of the elites (nature of internal networks and of selection procedures, degree of solidarity, types of conflicts between sub-elites), the nature of networks between elites (say between the political system and the economic system) both within and between nations, power distributions between elites and the legitimacy of the power concerned.

2. *The market opportunities of important societal categories:* the market opportunities of societal categories are heavily dependent on the type of schooling and training, on property, social origin and on economic and technological developments. When we engage in international comparative macro-sociological studies we have to direct our attention to the main interest groups in society, their present market position and the ways these market positions are changing. So we need information about the size of important societal categories, such as unskilled workers, independent middle classes, white collar workers, professionals, technicians, etc. Then the following questions can be answered:

What is the size of those categories, how much increase or decrease of positions within those categories as a consequence of technological innovation, and changing market relationships takes place, what are the opportunities for the amelioration of the market positions of those societal categories, is there a dual labour market, how are the participants defending their interests on a collective and individual level and what is the position of the unemployed? etc.

---

[14]W.G. Runciman, "Towards a Theory of Social Stratification". In: F. Parkin (editor), *The Social Analysis of Class Structure.* London: Tavistock Publications, 1974, pp. 55–101.

3. *Differential remuneration of labour:* the scale of differentials allocated to occupational categories. What is the role played by education, training, seniority, market fluctuations in supply of labour, power of (professional) organisations, traditional distinctions etc.? In what ways are the distributions influenced by government policies that have as their objective the redistribution of opportunities (e. g. rental allowances, scholarships)? Which are the opportunities for different occupational groups for tax evasion and accumulation of functions?

4. *Differences in style of life:* this component directs the attention to differences in value orientations, consumption styles, leisure activities, language differences, aspirations and to the evaluations of life styles (e. g. prestige gradings, hierarchical differences). In what ways do these life styles influence the market opportunities (e. g. selection of individuals on life-style characteristics, life-style effects on the belief in opportunities).

5. *Group consciousness of interests:* collective representations about the social order, ideas about the legitimacy of social differences and about social justice. Images of society are not only a reflection of the social structure, but also contain ideas about alternative societies, and about the role of classes or groups in societal change. In relation to this component we are interested in the acceptance or rejection of cultural pluralism (religious and ethno-linguistic differences), of the means to regulate conflicts (strikes, consultation, etc.), and in the degree of trust in the state as the central organisation for the resolution of major social problems as well as in the awareness of antagonism between producers and consumers, between workers and management, between individual life chances and collective ones, etc.

When we start an international comparative macro-sociological study we often do have at our disposal several studies on the topics mentioned. The information these studies contain has to be rearranged in such a way that it becomes evident where the important lacunae are to be found that hinder a thorough analysis of the interrelationships between class positions, ethnic—linguistic and religious divisions, life styles and political organisation. On this footing we can continue the international comparative study of social institutions and organisations of social movements and attitudes of populations towards certain social changes. Moreover, we will be in a better position to test in a more definite way important hypotheses about the meaning of certain societal characteristics and developments (e.g. does the logic of industrialism lead to a lessening of class differences within advanced societies and to a convergence between those advanced societies as far as the main characteristics are concerned.[15] What are the exact consequences of the size of nation on the internal differentiation?).

We started our discussion with the question: "Have we been successful as social scientists in reaching our goals by engaging in international comparative research?" The answer is that the accumulation of knowledge, flowing from this type of research, is not very impressive in most fields. Many data have been gathered and processed, many similarities and differences have been described. We are, however, confronted with many problems when we try to explain or to interpret these (dis)similarities between social phenomena in different societies as we often lack knowledge about the societies concerned as a whole. This knowledge is of paramount importance in the explanation or

[15]M. S. Archer and S. Giner, *Contemporary Europe. Class, Status and Power.* London: Weidenfeld and Nicholson, 1971, pp. 2 ff.

10

interpretation of social phenomena that are always context-bound,[16] at least in several respects.

2. TYPES OF INTERNATIONAL COMPARATIVE RESEARCH IN THE SOCIAL SCIENCES

Until now I have only implicitly referred to different types of international comparative research in the social sciences. My introductory remarks have already illustrated the relevance of the type of international cooperation for the research design and for the goals that can be reached by adopting international comparative research. We start with the presentation of a classification of types of international research that was proposed by Stein Rokkan.[17]

After the presentation of this classification, we will discuss the goals of international cooperation.

Rokkan's classification (Table 1) is based on (a) stages in the research process and (b) the degree of international cooperation.

Table 1. Cross-national research: levels of internationalisation

Types	I	II	III	IV	V	VI
Criteria	National research into several states	"Imperialist" research	"Repeated" research	Regressive research	Cooperative research	
Conception	N	N	N	I	I	I
Data collection	N	I	I	I	I	I
Analysis	N	N	I	N	I	I
Interpretation	N	N	N	N	N	I

N = predominantly "national"
I = predominantly "international"

Studies such as those of Wilensky[18] or of Lipset and Bendix[19] are Type I. The authors use data that have been collected and published independently in the countries

---

[16]E. Mokrzycki, "On the Adequacy of Comparative Methodology". In: J. Berting et al. (editors), *Problems in International Comparative Research in the Social Sciences.* Oxford: Pergamon Press, 1979, pp. 93 ff.

[17]S. Rokkan, "Cross-cultural, cross-societal and cross-national research". In: UNESCO (ed.), *Main Trends of Research in the Social and Human Sciences* (Part I: Social Sciences). The Hague: Mouton, 1970.

[18]H. Wilensky, op. cit.

[19]S. Lipset and R. Bendix, *Social Mobility in Industrial Society.* Berkeley and Los Angeles: University of California Press, 1963.

11

concerned. This type of research can be undertaken with a very restricted contribution from international networks.

Going to the left hand part of Table 1, the amount of international cooperation increases, although in Type II research, the international aspect consists only of the technical assistance of local people during the data collection stage. Here, there is no international team at work at all.

As far as the organisation of the research is concerned, Types V and VI are not more complicated research types than I or II. When, to take an example, two or three social scientists from different countries would set up an international comparative study on a macro-sociological level (e.g. the type of research that was described earlier), the organisational relationships would be very simple. It is somewhat curious that these types of studies are not rather abundant, as only a rather close cooperation between a few scientists from different countries seems to be an important necessary condition. An example of this type is the famous study of Thomas and Znaniecki, *The Polish Peasant in Europe and America.*[20]

Often, however, there are several national teams at stake that are interdependent in very complicated ways. Collaboration within a loosely-knitted network of national teams is confronted with huge problems. Generally it is very difficult to get a research-design adopted that satisfies the majority of the participants. Because of these problems chances are rather high that individuals or even teams drop out long before the final research stage is reached or that the international collaboration comes to an end after the data collection stage (Type IV: Regressive research).

3. THE GOALS OF INTERNATIONAL COMPARATIVE RESEARCH: WHY DO WE COMPARE?

These types of international comparative research are connected in several ways with the scientific goals we try to reach. Generally international comparative research in the social sciences requires bigger investments than research that is done within the boundaries of a single country. These investments pertain to the budget, the duration of the research process, the loss of autonomy of the researchers (especially in those cases where national teams are collaborating), the costs of coordination of the researchers and/or research teams, the costs of "tension management" and the energy necessary to develop tools that are required by this job, to mention just a few of the important costs of international research.

International comparative research must have a sizable surplus value in comparison to national research to compensate these higher investments. Part of this surplus value may not be related to the manifest scientific goals of international comparative research, but to other more latent goals that may be, nevertheless, of the utmost importance. One of this second type goals may be the contribution to international understanding and peace. International comparative research may also serve nationalistic goals primarily e. g. when data are collected that do not serve a scientific goal but the aims of governmental services: statistical comparisons that present results that are flattering for

---

[20]W. I. Thomas and F. Znaniecki, *The Polish Peasant in Europe and America* (Two Volumes). New York: Dower Publications, 1927.

12

some nations ("cosmetic" comparisons: "We are doing better than other nations") or that are used to urge the population to do better ["We are lagging behind in comparison to (some) other nations"].

In this contribution we are interested in the scientific goals in the first place. The scientific goal or objective of a comparative study may be primarily of a theoretical or a descriptive nature.

A theoretical objective means according to Wiatr:[21]

a. The selection of topics with an eye to the potential theory-confirming or falsifying function of the study (replication of studies under different conditions). We may want to know whether relationships observed in earlier studies and formulated as theoretical generalisations hold true under new circumstances.

b. Selection of topics because of their potential importance for formulating new hypotheses and, eventually, theoretical propositions. The selection of topics in survey-research is a-theoretical or based on other than theoretical considerations if none of the above-mentioned situations occurs.

The theoretical goal may also be tested on the basis of (a) the hypotheses that are formulated in the study (i.e. whether they are derived from a general theory); (b) the construction of the sample (e.g. in survey-research) and (c) the interpretation of the research-findings.

Descriptive research is defined as the opposite of theoretical research. Wiatr points out explicitly that he does not regard this pair of concepts as a dichotomy but as the extreme points of a continuum. Descriptive research tries to answer questions like "What are the differences and similarities between certain units, how large are those differences etc.". "Projects are, therefore, defined as *descriptive* if their objectives are stated in terms of establishing similarities between countries, rather than formulating, verifying and modifying general hypotheses." "The distinction is based on the goal of the study and not on the use made of the information . . ."[22]

A second distinction that I wish to make is between *discipline-oriented research* and *policy-oriented research*.

Discipline-oriented research tries to contribute to the solution of problems that are connected with the main sociological themes (or the main themes of other social sciences). These main sociological themes or *Problemstellungen* are defined in the paradigms of the discipline[23] [e.g. (neo-)Marxism, the Frankfurt School, structural-functionalism, symbolic interactionism, individualistic exchange theory, "socio-biology"].

Policy-oriented research tries to answer the questions that are raised by policy-makers (governments, labour unions, representatives of social movements, etc.). The primary objective of this type of research is not to contribute to the development of science but to the clarification of the problems policy-makers are confronted with. This type of research tries to indicate which social variables may be manipulated, and what the

[21] J. Wiatr, "The Role of Theory in the Process of Cross-national Survey Research". In: A. Szalai et al. (eds.), *Cross-national Comparative Survey Research: Theory and Practice*. Oxford: Pergamon Press, 1977, p. 347.

[22] J. Wiatr, op.cit., p. 357.

[23] Cf. J. Berting, "A Framework for the Discussion of Theoretical and Methodological Problems in the Field of International Comparative Research in the Social Sciences. In: J. Berting, et al., op. cit., pp. 150–151.

consequences of this manipulation (policy) will be, to evaluate the consequences of some policy or to provide the policy-makers with a description of complicated social situations. Like the first distinction, this one must not be regarded as a dichotomy, but as the extremes of a continuum.

The combination of these two criteria leads to four research types; the following differentiation may be useful:

a. *Theoretical–discipline-oriented* research: development of sociological theory; explanation of important social phenomena (social inequality, social change, division of labour etc.).

b. *Theoretical–policy-oriented* research: selection of variables that can be part of policy-measures; elucidation of policy-problems; evaluation of effects of policy.

c. *Descriptive–discipline-oriented* research: ideographic studies (e.g. historico-sociological descriptions of complex phenomena); description of phenomena within the field indicated by the main themes (exploration).

d. *Descriptive–policy-oriented* research: collection of data that are primarily useful for policy-makers (data that have no *prima facie* relevance to the major sociological themes).

Although we do not have at our disposal statistics that give us an indication of the relative frequency of occurrence of the four above-mentioned types of research, the descriptive type of research seems to be dominant in international comparative studies that are based on the cooperation of several national teams. In many of those studies, the technical problems of description are emphasised, such as scaling problems, the functional equivalence of phenomena, social indicators for important social processes, sampling problems, etc.

At the beginning of this contribution we stated that international comparative research is characterised by a strong predilection for the use of questionnaires and survey-techniques and by the fact that an explicit theoretical base is often lacking. The field of descriptive studies seems to be regarded by many social scientists who are engaged in international comparative research as relatively neutral. This idea of neutrality affords a common meeting ground for cooperation between researchers with quite differing theoretical, political and policy aims. Convergency on the descriptive level can be regarded as the result of compromising between policy-oriented and discipline-oriented social scientists who are aware of the huge difficulties they will be confronted with when the theoretical and political orientations are made explicit. By sticking to the descriptive level, the discipline-oriented scientists may hope that they can test – *malgré tout* – some hypotheses that are theoretically relevant, hypotheses that need international investigations to be falsified or verified. The policy-oriented scientists may hope that they will get data and some elucidation of problems that fit into the frame of reference of policy-makers.

A really worthwhile pay-off of international comparative research in the social sciences is possible *when the research design enables the researchers to test* hypotheses that can only be tested in international (cross-national or cross-cultural) research.

International comparative research in the social sciences is a necessity when the researcher wants:

a. to ascertain which are the common components of cultural and social systems or wants to prove that different cultural phenomena can be related to some structure or model (see, e.g. the studies of M. Levy Jr., and C. Lévi-Strauss);

14

b. to verify whether a certain observation can be formulated as an empirical generalisation. For example: "Is a specified type of social inequality a characteristic of all known societies?" This kind of question is primarily related to descriptive research, while questions referred to under (a) are related to theoretical—discipline-oriented research.

In contradistinction to the questions mentioned above, there are research questions that highlight characteristics that are system-specific. In these cases the researcher wants:

c. to ascertain whether one or more specified characteristics occur under definite social conditions (e.g. "To what extent is the development of production techniques related to the development of specific types of social inequality?");

d. to know to what extent a social or cultural phenomenon, which is relatively constant within a specific society or culture, has a broader range of variability when a number of different societal types are compared (e.g. family structures, specific types of social mobility, value systems).[24]

The answer to the question "Why do we engage in international comparative research?" might follow from an analysis of the problems posed in social science research and the research designs selected to answer those problems. This analysis could enable us to differentiate between studies that:

a. try to answer questions that only have a slight relevance to the development of the social sciences; this does not mean that those studies are without any merit, because they may be a contribution to policy-oriented research, on a theoretical and/or a descriptive level;

b. apply an international comparative design to research problems for which the design is not a necessary condition; it may be that other motives than scientific ones lead to the adoption of international comparative research designs;

c. apply an international comparative design to research problems requiring such a design, but pose research problems which, however, fail on the methodological or organisational levels;

d. do not apply an international comparative design while it appears obvious that the problems posed would benefit from such a design; it may be that in those cases the researchers have avoided this type of research because they were confronted with important obstacles (e.g. language problems, lacunae in their research training).

The selection of a research design in international comparative research in the social sciences, that is based on the international cooperation of national teams, is dependent on a number of conditions and circumstances. Some of those conditions and circumstances were discussed in this contribution, others are treated in the following papers.

The nature of the research design to be adopted by a network of national teams is dependent on:

a. The primary research goal. Often theoretical—policy-oriented or descriptive—policy-oriented research is not manifestly connected with international comparative research. Policy-problems require a rather quick answer — say within one year or even within a shorter period — while international comparative research that is based on the cooperation of national teams often takes 6—7 years. Moreover, policy-oriented research requires an interdisciplinary research design and concentrates on problems that are

---

[24] Further conclusions are presented in: J. Berting, "What is the Use of International Comparative Research?" In: J. Berting, et al., op. cit., pp. 171 ff.

strongly tied to the specific social and economic conditions that prevail in one nation-state or a specific area within the nation-state;

b. The type of cooperation and organisation (centralised—decentralised; network of national teams or an international team etc.);

c. The degree of (implicit) consensus on the underlying "paradigm";

d. The nature of the methodological and technical problems that are connected with the topic selected for investigation (e.g. functional equivalence of the same phenomenon in different countries);

e. The available infrastructure (e.g. presence or absence of international organisations for the coordination of social research on an international level or of reliable statistics and data banks);

f. Considerations of a political and/or individual nature.

Our task is to find solutions to these problems, solutions that will probably be different when we are working with a network of national teams from the so-called "advanced societies" from those solutions that will come up when we are working in networks of teams from developed *and* developing countries.

On the Meaning of "Nation" as a Variable*

by Johan Galtung

1. INTRODUCTION

For several reasons, the word "nation" has attained two, even three, very different meanings, all of them relevant for the general subject of comparative studies (meaning studies comparing nations). The three meanings are:

1. "Nation" in the sense of *country*, a political entity in territorial space, autonomous in the sense that ultimate legitimate control over internal power relations is inside the country (e.g. with the particular organisation referred to as the "state"). A country is also often called a *state*.

2. "Nation" in the sense of *ethnic group,* a socio-cultural entity in non-territorial space (as it may be scattered anywhere), characterised by some kind of shared culture, for instance, carried by language, religion, way of life, shared history and/or racial (anatomical) characteristics.

3. "Nation" in the sense of a *nation-state,* meaning a "state" (country) populated (almost) only by members of the same "nation" (ethnic group).

To give some rough orders of magnitude: there are about 150 nations in the first sense of the term in the world today (although the autonomy of many of them is a matter of dispute), about 1500 nations in the second sense of the word, whereas the number of nation-states must be in the order of magnitude of 15. Most countries are today multi-ethnic, and the "minorities" may even, singly or combined, be majorities – "minority" being a power term (meaning powerless), not a statistical, numerical expression. Obviously, if the programme of organising the world as a set of nation-states is to be implemented (the Herder programme) the result would be a world divided into 1500 nation-states after an average of nine independence struggles within each of today's countries has been accompanied by unification processes for divided nations. Hopefully some other programme or some other process will be invented in the meantime.

In the following, we shall pick up the first two meanings of the term "nation", in the sense of country or state, and in the sense of ethnic group. They are both important, among other reasons because of the implicit nation-state programme guiding the political

*Paper presented at the Vienna Centre training seminar, Warsaw, 21–26 September, 1980. I am grateful to the Vienna Centre for the invitation to the seminar and for an occasion to return to the fascinating experience of coordinating the Vienna Centre study *Images of the World in the Year 2000* (published as a book with that title, Ornauer, Wiberg, Sicinski, Galtung eds., Mouton 1976; below referred to as *IM 2000*), with some reflections. The points of view expressed in this paper, however, are not necessarily those of the other participants in that ten-nation study.

process in many places in the world. No doubt the world is to a large extent an inter-state system, ambiguously referred to as an "international" system. But it is also an international system in the other sense, an inter-ethnic system, with dialogues and confrontations between civilizations, linguistic and religious groups, ways of life, racial groupings. (And in addition, it is a system divided by class, age and sex — the function of the state being to mediate not only ethnic divisions, but also these three.) As a matter of fact, it may be argued that the salience of nation in the sense of ethnic group has become increasingly evident in recent years with all the intra-state conflicts for "minority" autonomy (meaning protection against the majority), and the rise of fundamentalist religious groupings (Islam) across state borders, at the same time when Western civilization in general is challenged everywhere, including in the West.

Thus, to interpret "nation" only in the sense of a territorial polity is to give too much prominence to one way of dividing and organising human kind, the Westphalia system, at the expense of the other way, the ethnic division (not to mention the additional three: class, age and sex).

Comparative analysis in this limited sense is indispensable, and one basic conclusion from the *Images of the World in the Year 2000* study was precisely how salient this division is,[1] meaning how inter-state differences tend to prevail over intra-state differences. But if the task of social science is to make the world more transparent, then transparency in one direction may make us less sensitive to other directions or cuts — as in a crystal. Hence, discussing "nation" as a variable, we should at least pick up both, not only one, of the major meanings of that term.

2. THE PROBLEM OF LEVELS

Regardless of how "nation" is interpreted, there is a Chinese boxes or *matrushka* aspect in it. Within the nation as a state, a political actor at the international level, there are districts/provinces/departments/municipalities, organisations and associations, and so on; political actors at the local level.[2] Inside that, there is the primary group of families, friends, peers surrounding individuals, and inside that again the individual level. Let us refer to them as *macro*(national), *meso*, *micro* and *inner* levels, respectively. The same can now be said about nation in the cultural sense: there are subcultures, sub-sub-cultures and individual culture — the latter perhaps best referred to as personality (deeply rooted attitudes and beliefs and behaviour patterns). And there are also other things, non-human beings, man made or not, inside nations.

Hence, a comparative study is not merely a problem of choosing nations. It is in general a multi-stage operation where the first stage is the selection of a set of nations,

---

[1]*IM 2000*, pp. 574—78 are about this. Two formulations, very much backed up by the data:
"When it comes to the great issues of space, peace and war, our data indicate that the nation will probably continue to be the salient actor for a long time to come." "When it comes to the great issues of time, development and national goal-setting, the nation will probably also be a salient actor for a long time to come."
It may be objected that if a study is designed to compare nations, the nations will show up as important. This objection is discussed and rejected, among other reasons because other cleavages, such as age, sex and class, were also explored.
[2]See Johan Galtung, "A Structural Theory of Integration", *Essays in Peace Research*, Vol. IV, Ejlers, Copenhagen 1980, Ch. 11.

then from each nation a set at the meso level, then at the micro level, then at the individual level, then at the non-human level. Some of these levels may be dropped, and one may reduce the operation to the single stage of selecting nations only, studying them as if they were billiard balls, homogeneous inside. For some types of international studies this macro approach would be satisfactory. But for social scientists operating at the meso, micro or inner levels constitutes the *raison d'être* of the study. The macro level being introduced to provide variations in contexts would make it possible to better understand and interpret the findings at the other levels.

Thus, the typical "comparative study" arising out of social science methodology and concerns of the 1950s would involve a two-stage operation: first a selection of nations, then a selection of individuals for interviewing, survey style, is undertaken. The first stage is usually not random, e.g. based on pre-existing networks of research institutes with whom research cooperation of this type is possible; the second stage usually random (simple or stratified). But this is only one example of what could be done. Thus, a random selection of individuals from a random selection of micro units (e.g. families) from a random selection of meso units (e.g. municipalities of a certain type) from a random selection of macro units (e.g. countries) would be entirely sensible. And there is no reason why one should end up with individuals; one could end up with museums, with written sources of law, with road networks, with anything. What remains as common element would be the twin ideas of *Chinese boxes of units* starting with the nation, and *multi-stage sampling* from these levels, or layers, starting with a sample of nations. Where one ends up is less important.

3. VARIABLES FOR NATIONS AS COUNTRIES/STATES

A nation at the same time exists in and by itself, is a part of a super-system of nations, and has an inside, subsystem. It is like an atom which can be understood in its own right, in terms of how it relates to other atoms, and in terms of its composition. But systems can be described in many ways. The following classification of variables for countries/states, in five types, seems useful:[3]

Nation by itself	1.	*Absolute variables,* such as size, population, continental belongingness, or to other groups.
Nation as part of a super-system	2.	*Relative variables,* such as "big" (which makes no sense except by comparison) or any kind of variable on which nations may be ranked.
Nation as part of a super-system	3.	*Relational variables*, based on interaction of nations in pairs, dyads, bilaterally.
Nation as part of a super-system	4.	*Structural variables,* based on interaction of nations in *n*-tuples, *n*-ads, multilaterally.
Nation as having subsystems	5.	*Inside variables,* with the same four types.

The absolute variables are relatively unproblematic but also relatively uninteresting. They are classificatory only. All nominal scale variables, such as grouping nations according to continents, or the alphabet, which is analytically about equally useful as using

[3]See Johan Galtung, *Theory and Methods of Social Research*, Columbia University Press, Allen & Unwin 1967, pp. 40–41 (below referred to as TMSR).

"Asia" as a category,[4] belong here. But this also applies to variables at higher levels of measurement: categories of size (area, population, GNP, whatever) can be used as absolute properties, their capacity for ordering the units (meaning the countries/states) may simply not be made use of. The only aspect used is whether two nations belong to the same or different categories, and the only type of statement one can arrive at is the rather uninteresting "Nations of Category I show Pattern A whereas nations of Category II show Pattern B". There is no sense of co-variation, whether in the causal, or even in the correlational sense. But this means that the "nation"-variable is not really made use of for the basic point in using the nation *as a variable,* so that some idea of how the nation as a context affects "lower levels" (or better, using the Chinese boxes/*matrushka* metaphor and not the hierarchy/pyramid metaphor: more "inside layers") can be arrived at. One should be able to formulate statements of the type "the higher the nation is on variable X, the higher the tendency to show Pattern A and the lower the tendency to show Pattern B".

The relative variables do this job for us: they are, by definition, at least ordinal level variables. They are variables on which nations can be *ranked* in terms of more or less. If in addition they can be *rated* (interval or ratio scales), that is useful for those who believe in "measurement", among other reasons because they believe in interval scale statistics.[5] As rating implies ranking (but not vice versa) there is no problem from the point of view of arriving at statements of the type indicated — and the additional refinement brought in by interval scale properties is probably much more useful in the physical than in the social sciences. Another point, however, is that in order to explore hypotheses of the "the more X, the more Y" type, there must be at least three values of the variable X represented in the sample of nations so as to know whether the relation is roughly linear or more curvilinear (simply meaning that the nations that are in between have the highest, or lowest, values on Y). Example: is "aggressiveness" highest among countries that are low, medium or high on "level of development" — a rather important problem almost regardless of how the two highly ambiguous variables are defined, or, not to mention, operationalised.[6]

Thus, *rank variables* will be crucial in the use of nation as a variable, and one should have at least three rank levels (for instance capitalist, socialist and in-between; not

[4] Asia is simply too diverse, comprising Islamic, Hindu, Buddhist, Chinese and Japanese civilisations (see Section 4 in the text); very many languages, different political/economic systems, and so on. Europe has at least a certain Christian common cultural heritage and languages with certain similarities, not to mention histories with many points of intersection, given that much expansionism in so little space. There is something "European" in general about Europe, but there is hardly anything "Asian", except in the broad sense of human in general.

[5] See TMSR, II 4.4, pp. 358–89 for a warning against this faith.

[6] After the Second World War most wars have been fought in the Third World, on the territory of poor countries; the major belligerents over time, however, being (former) colonial powers defending their control over those territories. That control was challenged, a challenge that can well be referred to as "aggressive" in the broad sense of the word. But is it highest for the poorest, or for the richest, or for the in-betweens? Important question, as much of the motivation behind "technical assistance" was based on the first of these three hypotheses — and hence on the idea that with decreasing poverty there will be decreasing aggressiveness. Actually, the third hypothesis may come closest to empirical reality: the poorest are too apathetic, the richest too easily coopted, it is the in-between that has both capability and motivation to rebel. All this just to indicate the importance of trichotomies rather than dichotomies for analysis of social science data, also at the level of the nation — with dichotomies so much of this gets lost.

merely the classificatory "capitalist" versus "socialist"). Preferably these should include variables that are important politically in the sense that it matters much to countries whether they are high, low or medium; top dog, middle dog or underdog to use that terminology (T, M or U).[7] Such variables relate directly to power: if nations want to be high on them then there is power at that point: resources, big population, economic potential, military destructive capacity, etc.

From knowledge of where a nation stands on a set of such variables, composite variables or indices of different kinds can be constructed. On the one hand there are the equilibrated profiles, upwards (TTT...T) and downwards (UUU...U) — on the other hand the disequilibrated profiles, high on some, low on others of these rank dimensions (e. g. high on GNP/capita, low on schooling/capita). Often such composite variables may give much more information of analytical value than the sum of the insights derived from the simple variables — there is an interaction effect, in other words.[8]

Then, there are the *relation variables*. They are variables characterising relations between nations rather than the nations themselves, in other words, characterising *interaction,* concrete relations with something passing back and forth, not abstract relations like "bigger than", "better than" (they belong to the relative variables). How, then, does one characterise interaction? Just to give two examples: in terms of level of *symbiosis,* and level of *exploitation*. A symbiotic interaction is one which is so important to both of them that by hurting the other they also hurt themselves. An exploitative interaction is one where the net benefits from the interaction relation are much higher to one than to the other. If the exploitative interaction is not symbiotic, then it may simply be broken by the party that benefits least if it has opportunity costs (e.g. could benefit more by entering other deals). But if it is both exploitative and symbiotic, the relation is often referred to as one of *dependency* and it is very difficult to break out of it. The party at the top is dependent but benefits much from it; the party at the bottom benefits little, not at all or loses, but may lose even more by breaking the relation. And so on, and so forth: the point is that dyads may be characterised, and nations may be characterised in terms of how they enter such dyads, or what types of dyads they are in.

Then, the *structural variables*. They are ways of summarising how a nation is located in multilateral interaction patterns, like a commercial network, airline network, or the web of international organisations, governmental or nongovernmental. Interaction networks can be represented by graphs, and as such they can be parameterised in many ways known in the theory of graphs.[9] Each nation can, for instance, be given an "associated number", which would be length of the longest path to any other nation (well-known to airline passengers: how many times do you have to change planes in order to reach the nation furthest away from your own). The nations with the highest

[7]For a number of studies using this terminology and approach, see Johan Galtung, *Essays in Peace Research*, Vol. III, Ejlers, Copenhagen 1978, Parts I, II and III — Social Position Theory, Rank Disequilibrium Theory and Social Structure Theory, pp. 29–314. Chapter I develops the idea of "Center–Periphery" in some detail.

[8]See TMSR, pp. 414 ff for some ideas about the type of analysis.

[9]The theory of graphs bridges the world of geometry and the world of arithmetics in attributing numbers to certain geometrical configurations and, consequently, is rather ideal for making indices out of geometrical configurations that represent structures. For one exercise in this see Johan Galtung, *The True Worlds,* The Free Press/MacMillan, New York 1980, sections on "Operationalisation of Structure-oriented Goals", pp. 455–58.

associated number constitute the periphery of the system, those with the lowest number the centre. And, correspondingly, for organisations: the simple number of intergovernmental (and also inter-nongovernmental) organisations of which a nation is a member is not a bad indicator of what the situation is for that nation. In the same vein, the number of embassies in the capital of a country also says something about the importance accorded to that country by the rest of the international system.

Combining the information given by the relative, relational and structural variables, not in a composite index but in a profile, gives us rich information. The profile of the rank situation is already a rich picture, with its equilibrated top dogs, disequilibrated in-betweens and equilibrated underdogs.[10] That the former tend to be the exploiters in more or less symbiotic relations and at the same time in central positions of the structure of multilateral patterns, the latter the exploited in the periphery and the in-betweens those that struggle to change their own position (and sometimes also to change the whole structure) belongs to the picture — *grosso modo*.[11] In this, all kinds of power relations come into play — economic, political, military, cultural, social, communicational — the international system being a relatively brutal place.

Let us then move to the fifth category of variables, the *inside variables*. We are now looking inside the country/state, it is no longer a billiard ball in the international system, it is a universe in its own right. To characterise that inside, however, we would like to have variables that facilitate comparison between and among nations, not changing inside variables when we move from one country to the other. We often hear the expression "you cannot compare Nation I and Nation II" — a not very fortunate expression. One can compare anything with anything, an apple with a camel for that matter (the latter weighs more, for instance) — but whether the comparison is fruitful is another matter, and that depends on the choice of variables.

Take as examples two rather important inside variables: capitalist/socialist and democratic/non-democratic. It is very difficult to reduce these rich dichotomies to one dimension that can be operationalised.[12] But if one tried, then "the proportion of the economic surplus controlled by those who produce the surplus" might not be the worst approach to understanding socialism (clearly ruling out state capitalism) and "the degree of control over decision-making concerning oneself" not the worst approach to understanding democracy (clearly ruling out the bland and highly abused term "participation" — *control* is the point, not merely participation). In both examples we are, incidentally, clearly dealing with structural variables, with patterns of interaction involving power relations — economic and political power, respectively. Thus, one escapes the flat dichotomy.

To take another example: countries can be characterised in terms of how centralised they are, starting with such important trivialities as communication and transportation networks (just look at the road map of France, for instance), working one's way towards administrative networks and other types of power networks. They can be characterised

---

[10] See Chapters 4, 5 and 6, footnote 7 above.

[11] See Ch. 4. "A Structural Theory of Aggression", and Ch. 8, "A Structural Theory of Revolution", footnote 7 above.

[12] See the whole Appendix, "World Social Indicators", pp. 431—465 of *The True Worlds* for a number of efforts at operationalisation of concepts not always considered operationalisable.

in terms of what proportion of the total, or the urban, population lives in the biggest city, and so on. In short, the possibilities are numerous.

Conclusion: comparative research is not merely a question of having a set of nations in which to do the inside level study. The set has to be well drawn and one has to know which dimension(s) one wants to use in making comparisons, using nations as contexts. For this, inside level expertise (psychology, social psychology, sociology) is insufficient; political science and international relations knowledge is indispensable.

4. VARIABLES FOR NATIONS AS ETHNIC GROUPS

In the preceding section nations were seen as actors, and their subsystem also, essentially as actors, down to the level of the individual. The key word for conceiving of nations was *structure,* and underlying structure: *power.* The key word for understanding ethnic groups would be *culture,* and underlying culture: *meaning.* Again, there is the levels problem, touched upon in Section 2 above:

The level of the *human species*	Basic human needs					
The level of *civilisation* (cosmologies)	OCCIDENTAL			HINDU	ORIENTAL	
The level of *subcivilisations* (religious ideologies)	sacred: Christian, Islam	secular: liberal, Marxist			Daoist, Shinto Confucian, Buddhist	
The level of *national culture*	Saxonic	Teutonic	Gallic	Indic	Sinic	Nipponic
The level of *national subculture*						
The level of *individuals* (personalities)						

No effort will be made here to go into the intricate problems offered by the chart;[13] it should only be emphasised that the terms given are for illustration only, there is certainly no pretence at completeness. Cosmologies, religions/ideologies, culture and subcultures are seen as *programmes,* usually only partly known to those holding them, calling for implementation. Moreover, all personalities in a given national culture have specificities but they also have something in common, the national culture (although it may come out very differently in its interaction with more individual personality traits). And correspondingly for nations: all nations in a given civilisation have specificities but they also have something in common, the cosmology of that civilisation (although it may come out very differently in its interaction with more specific national traits). Needless to say,

---

[13] For details, see "Five Cosmologies: An Impressionistic Presentation", *GPID Papers,* Geneva 1980.

23

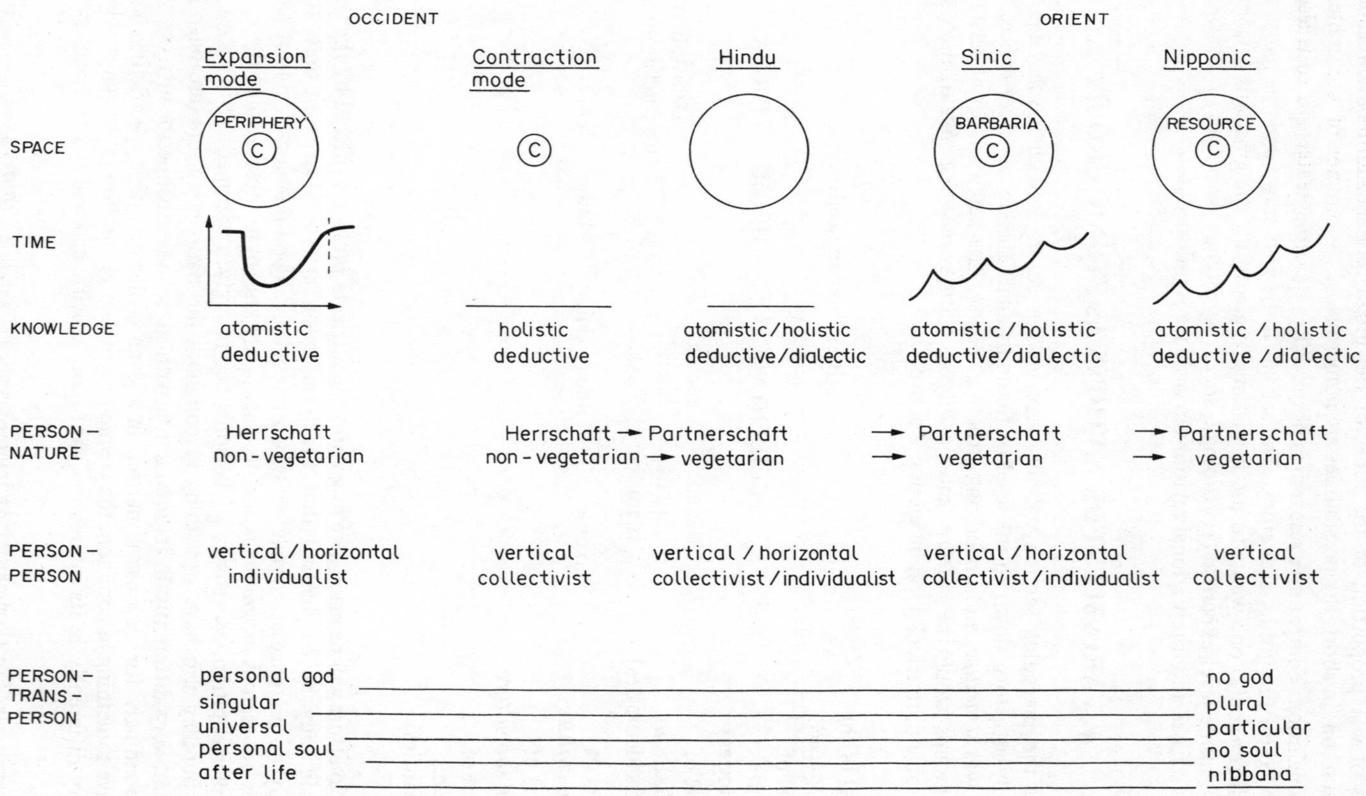

Figure 1. *Five cosmologies: some positions*

a concrete nation in the sense of a country/state may be located at the cross-beam between the cultural radiations from several centres.[14] If it is multi-ethnic, it may itself be a very complex amalgam, if not at the personal so at least at the national level.

How does one characterise a nation in this sense of the word? Which are the variables that can be used to characterise cultures? One approach would be in terms of what meaning that culture gives to categories, such as Space, Time, Person—Nature, Person—Person and Person—Transpersonal relations. Other categories at the same level of importance are certainly conceivable, but we let this do just as an indication. In Figure 1 some indications are given of how five civilizations (in other words, not nations but "macro-nations" or "macro-cultures" since "nation" here refers to culture) can be characterised, as one set of hypotheses, on these six categories. It should be noted that "occidental" is here divided into "expansionist" and "contracting" — roughly corresponding to Antiquity/Modern Age on the one hand and the Middle Ages on the other — assuming that Christianity, Islam, liberalism and Marxism all come in expansionist, and more modern, contracting, versions.

Carriers of meaning, of culture, and particularly of deep culture (such as the deep ideology shared by liberalism and Marxism and deep religion shared by Christianity and Islam) are religions, myths, languages, cultural artefacts, material (man-made) and social structures — only very superficially and partially attitudes and beliefs. Methodologies would be different from the methodologies used to study actors and structures: more aimed at meaning and *Verstehen,* perhaps using content analysis in the search for patterns of themes, but in general intensive rather than extensive.

5. A NOTE ON INTELLECTUAL STYLES

In the preceding section something was said, in very general terms, about cosmologies as ways of characterising macro—nations or macro—cultures. Let us spell out a little more one particular aspect of cosmology, the characterisation of knowledge — also known as epistemology: the basic assumptions about the nature of knowledge.[15] In the figure on the preceding page something is already said about (expansionist) Occidental, Sinic and Nipponic epistemology. For those who live in the Occident, like the present author, "Occident" is a slightly too gross category: it calls for some specifications. Three national cultures are indicated: the *Saxonic,* the *Teutonic* and the *Gallic.* They are used here to refer to intellectual styles.[16] Why these strange words, why not simply say Anglo-American, German and French? Because these are words referring to nations in the sense of countries, and it is very obvious that inside a country like, say, France, many intellectual styles may be found, even inside the same person. Hence, what we are after may be seen as ideal types in the Weberian sense, and for that we need other terms.

We shall assume that intellectuals anywhere are engaged, roughly speaking, in four tasks: (1) exploring *paradigms* (*what* kinds of things are there?), (2) a *descriptive* or empirical task (*how* are these things), (3) *explanatory* or theoretical tasks (*why* are these

[14]For details, see "Structure, Culture and Intellectual Styles", *GPID Papers,* Geneva 1980.

[15]For details, see "In Defense of Epistemological Eclecticism", *GPID Papers,* Geneva 1980.

[16]Footnote 14 above; later efforts will include attempts at characterising the Indic (India) and the Sinic (China).

things the way they are, covering not only empirical but also potential reality) and, finally, (4) *commentary* − on how other intellectuals perform (1), (2) and (3). The latter one has as its subject of enquiry not reality in general, but reality as reflected by intellectuals, usually books and articles − and it is perfectly possible to become a professor/ academician on the basis of that kind of exploration alone, never touching "real" reality.

Intellectual styles would then differ in their relative emphasis on these four fields, roughly speaking as follows:

	Saxonic	Teutonic	Gallic	Nipponic
Paradigm exploration	weak	strong	strong	weak
Description empirical, data	very strong	weak	weak	strong
Explanation theoretical	weak	very strong	very strong	weak
Commentary	strong	strong	strong	very strong

The common element among intellectuals of all kinds is the tendency to engage in commentary of each other − although the nature of that commentary may be highly different. Beyond this common element there are two types in the table, at this level of gross characterisation: the Saxonic−Nipponic, strong on data and facts, weaker on the philosophical basis and theory-formation; and the Teutonic−Gallic, with the opposite profile, strong on the philosophical basis and theory-formation, weaker on the data.

Within the Saxonic, there is, of course, the more American tendency in the direction of extensive data-collection (statistical, many units but not so much information on each) as opposed to the more British intensive data collection (the case study, ideographic history and social anthropology as opposed to the more nomothetic social sciences of the US tradition).[17] In other words, what passes for a fact differs from one place to the other, but they share a conviction that knowledge rests on documentation, one way or the other. The Nipponic style also has this, but the commentary aspect is so strongly developed, especially taking the form of characterising researchers by classifying them into schools, that the descriptive task looms less high.

Both the Teutonic and the Gallic are more *cerebral*. But in so being, they differ: the Teutonic more based on the search for the axiomatic pyramid that facilitates the much honoured pursuits of *Zurückführung* and *Ableitung,* the Gallic more complex with pyramidal exercises couched in highly embroidered, artistic forms of expression where *elegance* plays a key role as a carrier of conviction power (including *jeux de mots, double-entendre,* euphony, alliterations, etc.). Data serve the purpose of illustration rather than. confirmation. Just as there is a Saxonic sense of vertigo once the intellectual activity starts constructing theories more than a couple of centimetres above the empirical base,

[17]See TMSR, 1.2, particularly p. 15 for an elaboration of this distinction.

26

there is a shared Teutonic/Gallic fatigue with the unstructured empirical dust on level ground, however solidly one's feet are planted, or precisely because the feet are so solidly planted that one is not permitted to fly, or at least to float above the ground.

Let us now try to introduce one explanatory variable into this effort to describe the ideal types — in other words, applying more aspects of intellectual activity to this meta commentary on intellectual activity. Only two assumptions will be used:

1. Data unite whereas theories divide: data facilitate a dialogue whereas theories become a question of "believe or not".

2. The Saxonic and Nipponic are consensus, even harmony seeking cultures, whereas the Teutonic/Gallic relish dissent/disharmony.

The British researchers cherish impassioned discussions of data "as gentlemen"; for the Japanese, social harmony must be retained; for the Germans as also for the French, to have strong stands and to be attacked is considered perfectly normal. Hence the profiles for intellectual activity hinted at in the table above, seen as underlying patterns defining the epistemologies of these intellectual styles, directing their research activity in ways usually unknown to themselves. They themselves, with the possible exception of the Japanese, will tend to see what they do as natural and normal, even as universal, as *the* way of doing science.

The reason why I have mentioned all this in this connection is because of a particular feature of comparative research. Nations are not only "variables" in the sense of being contexts in analysis of data, more or less well understood, more or less well integrated into the study itself. They also enter very concretely as research teams because of the unwritten rules:

1. if a nation is represented as an object of study, it should also be present in the research team as a subject of the study;

2. the ultimate expert on a nation as an object is that nation as a subject.

Clearly, these are the social science counterparts of such important principles in international politics as "no taxation without representation" (translation: data collection instead of money collection = taxation), and "non-intervention in internal affairs" (intellectually instead of politically). But this means that a comparative study might involve researchers coming from highly different, even discrepant, intellectual styles. This is, of course, also possible for research teams from the same nation, even for a "team" consisting of one (complex) person — but if comparative research is to span an international spectrum of any scope then diversity in intellectual style is likely, and a challenge!

Imagine now that the spectrum spanned is a conflict spectrum, e.g. an East—West or a North—South spectrum — not merely a comparison of countries in North-Western Europe. Imagine further that the research cooperation is seen as a goal in itself. The predictable outcome is obvious: there will be a focus on description, on data collection and data processing and low level data analysis; not on theory formation. The technicalities, including the trivialities, of the first three will unite, at the expense of the boredom among the more Teutonically or Gallically inclined; there will be an instinctive, collectively shared, tendency to shun theory formation. This will play the comparative game into the hands of those who in advance are the carriers of this type of intellectual style: the Saxons on either side of the Atlantic; some of them, of course, also found in such places as France and Germany. In short, what we are saying is simply this: the very nature of comparative research, where it is so important to keep the teams together, will tend to favour a Saxonic approach because it favours a least common denominator on which one can agree: data-collection and the lower levels of data analysis. This is a well-known phenomenon in the United Nations system but there, also for the simple reason that there is a division of labour between the staff assembling data, on a comparative basis, and the policy-making bodies making decisions more or less on the basis of the data etc. collected by the staff. A Saxonic approach maintains this division.[18]

6. ON THE THEORETICAL IMPLICATIONS
OF COMPARATIVE STUDIES

Imagine now that we have obtained a good sample of nations and of inner layers, what next? For simplicity, let the nations be of the first type, countries, and with only one inner layer, individuals whose opinions on the development of their own country and the relations among countries are explored — like in the *Images of the World in the Year 2000*. In other words, a completely conventional design, but for that reason not necessarily to be put only to conventional uses.

The thing to be avoided, in a sense the saddest possible outcome of this type of study (but a rather frequent one) is a set of uninterpreted "marginals" tabulating all responses by country, but never using the nation-variable analytically. As (bad) social science prose, it reads something like this: "As we see, in Country A there were X% with an optimistic view whereas in country B there were Y%."[19] Full stop. The word "whereas" substitutes for analysis. When pressed, for instance, by their own inner urges to go one step further, such authors will often escape through the apparent wisdom of invoking non-comparability: "It might be tempting to draw some conclusions from these differences but as we do not really know whether the words mean the same in A and B it would be hazardous to enter into such speculations." The next sentence is sometimes a call for a follow-up study, which then will end pretty much in the same way.

Against this line of thinking there are some important arguments:

1. *Semantic differences:* of course there are. But they should be taken into consideration during the construction of the questionnaire and not only be the usual translation back into the language in which the questionnaire was first drafted, but the translation both ways for all pairs of languages to be used in the study.[20] Then, semantic differences would, of course, be one basis for interpretation of statistical differences, as one source of insight, usually among several. But this presupposes some idea of the direction of the difference, not merely the idea that there are differences.

2. *National differences:* of course there are. It would be extremely strange if the averages (and percentages are averages on a 0.1 scale) in two different nations should not differ, given how differently nations treat their citizens. Some people are afraid of

---

[18] See *Processes in the UN System: An Issues Paper,* Volker Rittberger, ed. GPID, Tübingen 1980.

[19] It also belongs to the picture that the percentages are often given with two digits behind the decimal point, a spurious precision indeed when sampling and other errors render even the second digit before the decimal point dubious!

[20] In a ten-language study this means a total of 90 translation jobs to be carried out, from each one to each one. But this should be doubled, for not only should Dutch be translated into Hindi; the Hindi translation into Dutch should also be (back)translated into Hindi. Taken seriously, this would be an incentive to limit the number of languages included in a study.

elaborating such differences beyond the purely numerical, lest this should lead to racist or nationalist sentiments/prejudices. But to this the objections would be that

— nations are not races, they are often cross-cut by races;
— even if they were there is no basis for inferring that differences would have a biological basis, as all human beings seem capable of being socialised into any power-system or meaning-system;
— it is not the role of a social scientist to shun away from differences but to explore them and also give to them another sense than the prejudicial and the destructive.

3. *Differences in intellectual style:* of course there are. There are those who can have the data in front of them for years, with huge percentage differences in the same direction screaming for an interpretation, without ever going beyond stating the finding. And there are those who with no intersubjective data basis at all arrive at the most startling insight, sometimes tenable, sometimes not — the Gallic and Teutonic being more in this direction, the Saxonic and Nipponic more in the other. The task of good social science would seem to be to bridge this gap, well knowing that the data dug up by the empiricists and the interpretations by the theoreticians constitute basic parts of this edifice. Why do only partial social science when one might do the whole thing... .

Of course, he who shuns away from analysis in a multi-nation study might also do so in a single-nation study, but we are concerned with the multi-nation study. And the first condition to get out of the non-interpretation predicament is, of course, to make use of variables for nations, and preferably variables with at least three values and at least one nation for each value. The task, then, is to relate variables characterising nations to variables characterising individuals, and this can be done at several levels of complexity.

At the most elementary level this is rather simple, for what we are dealing with is usually not individuals but aggregates, samples of individuals, from a nation. An average of those aggregates is also a variable characterising a nation, in a sense, only "from below"; a variable characterising the nation as such (e. g. in terms of political or economic system) or relative to the international system "from above" is not that different. A nation may be characterised, using the system in Section 3 above, as technically-economically developed and its population as "development-sceptical/pessimist" (variables of types 1 and 5 respectively). Of course, these two variables can be related to each other, and the finding, "the more developed the country, the more sceptical the population" may emerge. To do this, however, it is indispensable that the countries really distribute well on a sufficient range of technical-economic development. And one should also be able to test the importance of some third variable, such as capitalist/socialist: could it be that all the developed countries are capitalist and (for that reason) pessimist? The finding should hold also within a set of capitalist countries and within a set of socialist countries, as in fact, it does.[21]

Still another way of linking the individual and the national levels would be by testing an individual level finding to see whether it holds in nations which are so different that it looks like a relatively "universal" finding (we put it in quotation marks for it is a little ludicrous of us humans to refer to our little planet as the universe). Of course, it

[21] Thus, for the findings about "science scepticism", "development pessimism" and "development fatigue", "the dividing line was generally in terms of level of development, *not* in terms of capitalist vs. socialist" (*IM 2000*, p. 116).

does not have to hold in all, there could be a marked tendency as when in the *Images of the World in the Year 2000* study we found that "the periphery (inside the countries) hopes for change, but does not think there will be much of it. The center thinks there will be change, but does not hope for much of it".[22] In other words, the periphery is in a more evaluative, the centre in a more predictive mood. In a sense obvious: the centre is satisfied with the status quo, the periphery is not, so the centre controls through prediction, the periphery hopes to translate evaluation into facts that the centre may be able to predict but not to control.

Still another, and in an analytical sense "higher" level of analysis would look for more complex relations between national and individual levels. More precisely, the hypothesis would be of the form "if the absolute/relative/relational/structural variables characterizing a nation are at level A, then the inside variables are at level a, but if they are at level B then the inside variables are at level b". All of this could in additon be made issue-specific, as in the statement "when it comes to problems of development and science the . . . centers are closer together than the nations. When it comes to problems of peace philosophy the centers are even further apart".[23]

There is also another type of proposition that could be explored tying nation level variables not only to individual level variables but to individuals as such: could it be that the more an individual has the same characteristics, the same profile on a set of variables, as the nation, the more will he/she tend to identify, even act on behalf of that nation? Imagine a nation high on education and low on income, slated to be "aggressive" in the sense of being self-assertive, wanting changes in the total system. Imagine an individual within this nation with the same profile: would he not tend to recognise himself in the nation and vice versa?[24] Or in a nation slated for status quo behaviour, high on all possible rank dimensions, would not an individual inside that nation with the same status-set be the ideal carrier of such inclinations? In short, the possibilities are numerous, mildly speaking. In a sense one may even say that only through comparative studies do we really start doing *social science* in the sense of attempts to link together levels of analysis, from the psychological individual level via micro level (social psychology), meso level (sociology), to macro level (political science, international relations). But there are two branches in this level/layer list: one that picks up structure and power and appeals more to sociologists and political scientists, and one that picks up culture and meaning and would appeal more to anthropologists, humanists, perhaps also to many historians although they are certainly also pursuing the first branch. In a class for and by themselves are the economists who certainly will have to tie better together theories of micro- and macro-economics, but have a tendency to do so without considering individual psychology, small group phenomena, structure, power, culture, meaning, history and international politics in their belief that economics is *sui generis,* a phenomenon closed to other fields, sufficiently described by economic parameters.

Thus, the comparative study is not only *inter-national* in the composition of the research team, it also has to be *interdisciplinary* if the study really is to make use of a multi-nation design. One reason why so few studies do so, independent of intellectual

[22]*IM 2000*, p. 392.
[23]*IM 2000*, p. 397.
[24]"A Structural Theory of Revolution", (footnote 7 above), p. 302.

style, is hinted at above: simply because inner/micro/meso level specialists know too little about the macro/regional/global levels of analysis. And a simple reason why culture/meaning aspects usually do not enter is that the specialists in these fields are not very strong on the more entrepreneurial aspects of comparative research. The entrepreneurs, for obvious reasons, come more out of the statistical or nomothetically oriented sciences, and these people, in turn, are not very conversant with culture and meaning. But sooner or later the way in which comparative research, using nation as a variable (but also lower territorial levels like districts and municipalities, and also higher units like regions) is done, corresponds to the way in which so much else in our world is organised (like international scientific associations and transnational corporations, for instance). This structure of research itself will prevail, forcing changes in the way of doing social science. Thus, it is only logical that the United Nations also has a United Nations University with a Human and Social Development Programme pursuing the development "problématique" around the world, of course using its structure to build networks that are cooperative and in some cases can do comparative research.[25]

One may, however, safely say that the whole story of comparative research is not one of social scientists filled with interesting ideas to be tested or at least explored, forcing a new international and interdisciplinary research structure into action, or at least into existence. It is rather the other way round: the structure is there, for instance, in the form of the Vienna Centre ("for research and documentation in social sciences") but far from being fully utilised for its scientific potential.[26]

A typical example of this is the underutilisation of the second interpretation given to "nation", in terms of culture. Why should the social scientists leave so much to the specialists in the humanities to explore such important aspects of culture as the different meanings of *time,* in different cultures, even in macro-cultures = civilizations? Of course, those specialists have their own approach which leads them to attribute great importance to culture expressed in cultural products, of art and literature, and little significance to the attitudes and beliefs and the patters of behaviour of people in general. This is where anthropologists enter, and increasingly so as they no longer limit their approach to non-industrial cultures. To study the deep ideology underlying attitudes and beliefs, and the deep structure underlying patterns of behaviour using nations in the second sense as the unit of study, open to internal variations particularly along class, sex and age lines, should be entirely feasible, using survey designs of the types indicated above.

This way one might also open for a more fruitful study of the old topic of national character, of *Völkerpsychologie,* much maligned and for good reasons, but a phenomenon that hardly disappears by not being studied. And one might get away from some of the "elitism" in culture studies, e.g. defining philosophy as the products of philosophers, not of people.

Is it necessary or advisable to have a complete theoretical framework made up in advance, before a comparative study is launched? The answer is probably to avoid the two extremes of having no theory at all, and of having a very complete, deductive theory.

---

[25] For some views on how this is working in practice, see Johan Galtung, "The United Nations University as a Research Organization", and "Towards Synergy in Networks of People with Networks of Problems", *GPID Papers,* Geneva 1979.

[26] And even for the Vienna Centre, a pioneer in the field of bridging East—West gaps in social sciences, the theoretical results tend to be meager, and the comparison of their many comparative studies, looking for similarities and differences, has still to come.

With no theory at all the comparative study becomes a fishing expedition for data in search of theory and there is the risk of not getting much in return for the considerable costs incurred simply because questions asked of the empirical world have not been sufficiently precise to elicit precise answers. But if these questions are very precise there is the opposite risk: that only answers already contained in the questions, in the trite form "confirmed/disconfirmed" (the question being whether a set of hypotheses can be confirmed) will emerge. In other words, the danger is that the theory freezes the paradigm, the set of variables and set of units of analysis and the basic relations among them so that the researcher will not be sufficiently open to new signals, to new questions and, even more basically, to new paradigms because he is only looking for new answers (and sometimes not even for that, he is only looking for old answers, for confirmation of old hypotheses).

To steer a middle course between the Scylla of too little and the Charybdis of too much theory is not easy. There is no clear middle position where a cluster of methodological rules can emerge; it is rather a question of intuition and perhaps also experience, and fatigue or at least dissatisfaction with the two extremes. What matters is to have a good grasp of the general direction of a study and some view of the total span of units from the various levels/layers and variables from the various disciplines that enter into the study. There have to be theory-elements, theory-islands so to speak, but not a well-knitted theory-continent leaving no blank spots on the map — for only maps with blank spots on them are the really useful ones in research.

7. ON THE PRACTICAL IMPLICATIONS OF COMPARATIVE STUDIES

Let us look for a moment at three conclusions that came out of the *Images of the World in the Year 2000* study:[27]

"1. When it comes to *domestic perspectives* the organizing axis is the level of technical-economic development. Nations high on this dimension are pessimistic, bewildered and uncertain, probably a) because they see the negative effects of this type of development, b) *because they feel they have exhausted the program of their societies and that the future is without challenging and clear goals.* Nations low on that dimensions do not have this vision and may even reject it. They follow in the same footpaths but with the optimism stemming partly from the ignorance of the adverse effects, partly from the feeling of having a program. *And this seems to be the program defined and developed by countries that are already disillusioned by it.*

2. When it comes to *international perspectives* the organizing axis is the international role behaviour: East—West as opposed to the North—South axis that seemed to prevail for the domestic perspectives. The distinction between socialist and capitalist nations is activated: The population samples seem to have internalized, even to a remarkable extent, the *ethos* of the policies pursued by their governments on the international scene. To belong to a pact, or at least to live in the field of forces defined by the East—West conflict, seems somehow to give people a sense of identity. The overwhelming

[27]*IM 2000*, p. 118.

impression, however, is not one of a humanity divided by national borders, but of a humanity united in a desire for peace and in an almost surprising consensus when it comes to how it could be obtained. And at this point, one may even talk about a people-government contradiction, cutting across the East—West and North—South axes.

3. *Finally and basically,* the two preceding points notwithstanding, these are not data reflecting an innovating humanity exploring and facing a fascinating open-ended future. These seem rather to be data reflecting a humanity with its back to the future, looking at the past, and the present — and projecting from that experience into the future. In a sense these are the data one would expect at the end of a phase in human history, not at the beginning of a new one."

Obviously, this has something to do with politics, with highly practical matters for individuals and nations and groups of individuals and groups of nations. Is there any reason why social scientists should abstain from drawing implications of a more practical nature, as opposed to theoretical implications, for theory-building only?

It is obvious that there are implications. Thus, in the field of *development* one would explore whether the pessimistic views held in the most developed countries are realistic, and in case they are, it might serve as a warning for people in the less developed countries. And in the field of *peace,* if attitudes are so entrenched, maybe the best would be to get around the East—West issues and focus on something else, in a cooperative endeavour, in discussing joint problems of development and future, running enterprises (from joint ventures to transnational universities) together, and so on.[28] Of course, these are broad *policy* implications, very general guidelines, not precise *political* implications for concrete action, here and now. For that, such studies might be inadequate, but for policy implications, they may yield quite a lot. As a matter of fact, the whole *IM 2000* study shows, in my view, relatively convincingly that public opinion may be a very good indicator simply because people may see problems and report on them before the elites do.

But how much and what such studies yield also depends on how the social scientists conceive of their own role. In a nation, in the first sense of that word, there are people and there is also the *Obrigkeit,* the state/corporate/intelligentsia elites. Let us refer to it all as the state, for simplicity. Obviously, the social scientists are somewhere in between, studying the "people", being paid by the state, usually reporting to those who pay more than to those who are studied. It should be noted that there is also another organisation in society that does this: the police. The danger always exists that what social science essentially amounts to is to spy on the population on behalf of the state, sensing the mood of the populace better than a state organ such as the police can really do it.

This kind of reflection is particularly important in studies using nation as a variable for the simple reason that states are also basing themselves on comparisons. Statesmen want to know how they stand relative to other nations; social scientists engaged in comparative studies can answer many of their questions and give rise to even more. Through this process, and through the simple mechanism of "who pays", governments and inter-governmental organisations may gain too much influence over comparative studies.

---

[28]One may say that the "spirit of Helsinki" was an exercise in this direction. However, for that effort to be peace-building it should not add too many new bones of contention to the already existing ones. And one may say that the New International Economic Order, in its UN version also dating from the mid-1970s, was and is an exercise in how to "follow in the same footpaths but with the optimism stemming partly from the ignorance of the adverse effects, partly from the feeling of having a program" (this was actually written in July 1970).

To this, there are at least two simple answers: that social scientists see themselves more as the spokesmen/women of the people in general, articulating their concerns, defining social problems as they are seen by people; or else that social scientists join other social scientists, in universities and in international social science organisations, and — in the name of academic freedom — study what can be studied for its more pure social science interest without practical implications drawn or even approached in any meaningful sense. This latter possibility is the more frequently found, the more is the position, more or less, of the social scientists referred to as "critical" or "engagé", and working for elite interests is in a sense compatible with both of these positions.[29] The latter ones tend to be surprise-free social scientists, producing within the paradigm of thinking used by the elites themselves predictable findings with acceptable recommendations — thereby reinforcing the tendency for elites to be badly informed.

As international politics become more intense, among other reasons due to the way in which economic conflicts of interests will blend with cultural differences and even with incompatibilities (for instance in the religious sphere), comparative studies will become even more important, not only as policy but also as political instruments — as witnessed by the tendency of countries like the US and Japan to make use of such studies. This means that there will be more pressure on social scientists to deliver the kind of goods that can be used for governmental decision-making. Some will do this, others will go in the other two directions — the polarisation of the social science communtiy will continue. And all of this because of the tremendous salience of the nation as a unit in the international system, along all kinds of axes and cleavages, and hence the salience of the nation as a variable in comparative studies. And yet we social scientists are only at the very beginning of trying to come to grips with all these problems — some of which have been indicated in this paper. Maybe it is better that social scientists themselves come to a clear recognition of their duties and responsibilities, to science and to the world, than having others dictate the conditions after the problems emerge as confrontations.[30]

[29] For more on this see Johan Galtung, "Dialogue as Development", *GPID Papers*, Geneva 1979.

[30] The present author has a number of experiences with policy-related comparative studies, from the utterly unpleasant such as the Camelot story (see "After Camelot" in *Papers on Methodology*, Eljers, Copenhagen 1979, pp. 161–179) to the quite pleasant such as the efforts of the European peace research community in the 1960s to promote a spirit of cooperation rather than deterrence and confrontation as a basis for security (*Co-operation in Europe*, Universitetsforlaget, Oslo 1970, particularly pp. 9–20).

How to Achieve Comparability?

by Manfred Loetsch

1. INTRODUCTION

International comparative investigations are possible in different ways. Their empirical basis can be especially very different: national and international statistics; national research, on the basis of which the comparison is made in a secondary analysis; national reports on investigations, in which similar but not identical research instruments have been used etc.

In my contribution I *exclusively* deal with international comparative investigations of a certain type. They are based on studies:

– of sociological character, in which the most important data are obtained by sociological research methods,

– and in which identical research instruments are used in all countries that are to be involved in the comparison.

The problems I want to deal with are mainly connected with experiences made during my participation in the Vienna Centre's research project on "Automation and Industrial Workers". At the same time certain experiences of another international comparative study – not belonging to the activities of the Vienna Centre – will also be included. It is a comparative research study on social structure being carried out in the framework of the multilateral problem commission of socialist countries "Development of Social Structure", an organ of the Academies of Sciences, in which the Soviet Union, Hungary, Poland, Bulgaria, the CSSR and the GDR are participating.

2. THE PROBLEM OF DIFFERENT LEVELS. PRIMARY EMPIRICAL DATA AND THEIR GENERALISATION

It is self-evident that international comparative investigations will lead to insight into essential relationships and processes in the relevant countries. In particular when scholars from countries of different social and political systems are participating, it is very clear that the intentions of the researchers are to get elucidation of the character of these systems, their deeply rooted differences and possible similarities.

This is obvious for several reasons. Firstly, it is just the raison d'être of sciences to obtain insight into internal essential relationships. The international reputation which a research project and its participants intend to obtain seems to depend very directly on the profundity and complexity of the investigated problems; if you take the burden and the risk of such an undertaking, an insight is to be obtained that can claim a higher scientific level.

Secondly, studies of such dimensions are conducted in relation to theoretical frameworks. Independently of the position of the individual participant one should ask, whether the idea of convergence of systems can be derived from the research findings, whether theorems of technological determinism can be confirmed, whether features of the so-called post-industrial society emerge, whether (in the case that social structures are researched) decisive empirical relevance can be assigned to classes, etc. Thus there are good reasons for an international comparative research to be drafted in such a way that it results in statements which are situated on the level of generalisation just presented. But it is exactly here that the problem is located. I think I do not exaggerate in saying that basic differences of opinion regarding the interpretation of the data in the Automation research were to be found here.

First I would like to describe the situation. The so-called "central hypothesis" of the whole study was, that between different socio-economic systems greater, more deeply rooted differences were to be expected than between different technological (automated and non-automated) systems. With this hypothesis the whole investigation was raised to a level where the final question was to put the difference of socio-economic systems to an empirical test. If the socio-economic systems "capitalism" and "socialism" were in fact as different as was considered above all by the Marxist side, then — so it could be heard by different participants of the project — the results of the research should in the end be presented in such a way, that the data of the capitalist countries form one "bloc" and those of the socialist countries another. If this were not the case and if, at the same time, no adequately sharp differences between the automated and non-automated units could be proved, then both the explanation model "system" and the explanation model "technological determination" should be rejected.

As shown by Liisa Rantalaiho,[1] the data of socialist countries on the one hand and capitalist countries on the other were different enough, but not *so* different that *each* socialist country basically differed from *each* capitalist country in *every* respect. Rather, the essential differences in the profile of data were parallel to similarities that can be described in the following way: according to the degree of similarity of the data, there appeared pairs or groups of countries to which belonged both socialist and non-socialist countries.

My issue here is not the result of the research itself; this has been and will be published and can be read.[2] Here the issue is the methodological problem hidden behind the outlined situation. On the immediate level of the empirical data, similarities *must* appear — regardless of how different the countries from which the data stem may be.

Firstly, reality itself shows similarities; the systems are not different in *every* respect. In the case of the automation research this concerns, above all, those aspects of work content which are determined by the type of technique. Because there is neither a socialist nor a capitalist technology, working conditions having their basis in technological conditions must be characterised by certain similarities: so, for example, heavy physical work, certain functionally determined qualification requirements, principles of division of labour etc.

---

[1] (Note by the editors). The author refers to a paper presented by Liisa Rantalaiho of Tampere University (Finland) at the 9th World Congress of Sociology in Uppsala, Sweden in 1978.

[2] Forslin, J., A. Sarapata and A. M. Whitehill (1979) *Automation and Industrial Workers. A Fifteen Nation Study*. Vol. 1, Part 1. Oxford, Pergamon Press.

Secondly, and in particular, we can start from the assumption, that decisive differences between countries of different socio-economic systems cannot be shown at all by empirical instruments as they are used in sociological investigations. In the case of automation, this concerns above all the mechanisms by which the principal *aims* are set and means for reaching these aims are determined. Which branches are automated and which not, which variants are given preference over others, how the decision-making processes in which all this is fixed are organised – these are aspects which can be grasped neither through questionnaires nor through other sociological instruments used for obtaining primary data.

Here we have to deal with the basic problem of every science: the relation between essence and appearance. If – as in the case of the mentioned "central hypothesis" – the quality of socio-economic systems is asked for, then one is looking for essential relationships, which only become empirically manifest in a mediated way. Here we encounter problems such as the character of the property relations, the power structures including the relevant decision-making processes, the system of class forces, the basic mechanisms of distribution and other things. On the other hand, it is characteristic of empirical research methods, e.g. of a questionnaire, to reflect outward *manifestations:* the work content at the concrete work place, the work satisfaction or dissatisfaction of the individual worker, his concrete participation or non-participation in decision-making concerning the introduction of new technology, concrete forms of his remuneration, etc. The assumption, that the different character of socio-economic systems should become immediately visible in data of this kind, respectively, the assumption that, if this is not the case, one cannot speak of a different character of systems regarding the investigated circumstances, is based on the idea, that the essence immediately becomes visible in the appearance or even that both are one and the same. This, however, is – and certainly needs no further proof – nonsense from the point of view of cognition theory.

Thirdly one effect must be added which may be called the unifying effect of the set of instruments. It concerns the following: If – which was my presupposition – a research is carried through with uniform instruments, there must not be any differences between the instruments used in the individual countries. Now this means, however, that circumstances which are *different* in the individual countries must be inquired in the *same* way.

In other words: The formulation of the test questions – e.g. of a sociological questionnaire – is in its essence a process of *abstraction.* Step by step the concrete conditions of the relevant countries are eliminated till formulations are finally found, which can be assumed to be applicable in the same way to all the countries involved in the investigation. Particularities of the individual countries here must be ignored, they must be abstracted of.

To give an example, it is self-evident that in 15 investigated countries forms, mechanisms and contents of participation are different; furthermore it can be assumed that the *basic* differences do not result from partial particularities of enterprise organisation but from principal social conditions: the class relations, the degree of influence on social processes obtained by the working class, of political organisation of the working class, etc. *Principally* different, even contrary, is the content of participation if, on the one hand, a certain influence of the working class is imposed on another class having qualitatively different class interests, or if, on the other hand, the question is to achieve the influence of the working class as a leading class in society also in the organisation of

37

decision-making processes within the firm. "Participation" in the first case is a form of struggle between two opposite classes, in the second case a form of exerting power through the leading class in society.

The identical questionnaire, however, must abstract from this; it would not be uniform anymore, if it tried to integrate the specific character of one or the other system. Thus, phenomena whose content is not only different but even contrary appear in the instruments as uniform — and consequently also in the results. The process of abstraction from particularities which is inevitable in the elaboration of instruments pushes aside the socio-economic background.

Thus in international comparative studies, between countries of different socio-economic systems, the basic problem in the sense of cognition theory in connection with questionnaire inquiries is multiplied. As is well known this problem generally consists in the fact that in the formulation of the questionnaire, a process of translation of "programme questions" into "test questions" takes place — i.e. a process of transformation of an inquiry situated on a certain level of theoretical abstraction into questions that are empirically concrete and try to grasp the general in the concrete. International comparative investigations are faced with the same problem; this problem however is aggravated by the abstraction from socio-economic and national peculiarities, it is extended by a new dimension of complexity. Consequently the problem which is hidden behind this translation of programme questions into test questions obtains a new dimension of complexity: the problem of re-translation.

It is almost trivial to refer to the fact that the evaluation of research findings does not only take place on the level of test questions. The translation of programme questions into test questions in only the smaller part of this general problem of cognition theory; the decisive part lies in the procedures necessary to *return* in the statement to the level of programme questions. In other words: If general theoretical inquiries form the starting point of the research, then the empirical findings must — by *generalisation* — be brought back to this level; the process of translation from the theoretical "programme question" into the empirical "test question" is now to be carried out in the "backward" direction: as a generalisation of the empirical result to the level of abstraction of the starting point.

If one can formulate the following rule for national investigations, one can do so all the more for international ones: This process of transformation and re-transformation is all the more difficult, the greater the distance between the two levels is. The more general, abstract and comprehansive the theoretical questions from which one starts are, the more difficult it is to translate them into adequate empirical test questions, and the more difficult it is to return from the level of the test question to the level of the theoretical starting point. And exactly this was the case in an exemplary way in the automation research. I am sure that Phil Jacob,[3] my main opponent in many controversial issues, would agree with me in *this* point: The question of how socio-economic systems are involved and work in the transition from non-automated to automated production processes exceeds the possibilities of a single empirical study; the *distance* (in the sense of cognition theory, i.e. here in the sense of the levels of abstraction) between *this*

---

[3] (Note by the editors). The author refers to the discussion on workers' participation in the automation project, to be published in *Automation and Industrial Workers*. Volume 2, Oxford, Pergamon Press (in press).

question and the questions which can be asked by empirical instruments is too great and — as showed itself ultimately — cannot be bridged in a satisfactory way.

What has been disregarded in the mentioned process of abstraction? There is first and foremost the problem of *interests:* Which basic class forces are the bearers of the essential decisions about the development of modern technology? Whose class interests determine the target criteria of technological progress? Do the principal goals result from profit interests or from the efforts to better satisfy the essential needs of the working people? Which decision-making processes are typical for these, which ones for those main social relations? In which economic mechanism — e. g. market economy or planned economy — does the transition to automation take place? Which basic forms of political organisation are operating — so for example concerning the realisation of different interests? This enumeration could be arbitrarily extended — but it may be sufficient to illustrate the statement that counts here: *These* are the circumstances in which the different character of socio-economic systems reveals itself — and they are at the same time those, which *cannot* be contained in the concrete instruments. What distinguishes the USA from the Soviet Union, the Federal Republic of Germany from the German Democratic Republic above all other things, are just the basically different class relations in the framework of which the transition to automation is taking place — and exactly this must disappear from the questionnaires, which have to "work" in both cases in the same way.

It seems to me that from these experiences of the automation research conclusions can be derived that are important for any other comparative study. In my opinion there are above all two of them.

Firstly, it is inevitable that in the process of interpretation of the data and their theoretical generalisation and evaluation, those things be re-integrated which were eliminated during the process of translation into the test questions. If differences and particularities — be it between socio-economic systems, be it on the national level — have been eliminated on the way from the theoretical to the empirical question, this cannot mean disregarding these things henceforth too. Rather, it becomes a problem of interpretation to re-integrate the empirical data into the context, from which they had been separated with the formulation and application of instruments. This, however, cannot be done otherwise than by bringing back the individual empirical result into the frame of social and national system conditions and by evaluating it within this framework. Even if in Countries A and B (be it the German Democratic Republic and the Federal Republic of Germany) equal percentages of workers report on having the possibility of participation, the text being written on the basis of this result must take into account the situation, that participation *is* in the two cases something different. This is not, as Jacob claims, a false ideologisation of empirical data, but an inevitable requirement of their re-translation to the level of abstraction of the starting questions.

Secondly, the problem can at least be reduced, as follows from the epistemological distance between the two levels. From the rule that the difficulties of bridging this distance are all the greater, the greater the distance itself is, it follows that this distance itself should be kept as small as possible.

This means: already during the formulation of theoretical starting points of the problems to be investigated, the possibilities of empirical realisation must be involved. If, returning to the automation research, it is not possible to plan a study in a way, that a variable "system" can be determined as *empirical* variable and measured as such, no other way remains than to renounce, from the very beginning, a comprehensive question like this.

This leads back to my starting point. Understandable as it may be to aspire to results of a high theoretical level in the drafting of a research project, the main danger also lies here. The *exaggerated* theoretical intention can lead to questions that cannot be pursued empirically, to pretensions that cannot be fulfilled. Once such intentions have been fixed, the further work is oriented at them — in the case of the automation project with the result of contents which stem from the fact that efforts were made to answer a question which *cannot,* in a satisfactory way, be empirically answered by an empirical study like the one carried out. In this sense, theoretical modesty in the formulation of the problems to be investigated is the condition for scientific quality of an investigation.

3. DIFFERENT TYPES OF DATA:
"HARD" AND "SOFT" DATA

Strangely enough, the differences of opinion in the automation project arose exclusively on the basis of empirical *questionnaire* data and their evaluation. Data from other instruments (statistical data and data from the work place analysis) were not subject to differences in opinion. This is astonishing, however, only at first sight. Basic problems of the survey method lie behind this effect.

As successful as the translation into test questions may be, every questionnaire always "works" in a concrete context. The respondent always transforms the question he is going to answer into the sphere of his concrete and immediate experience. He always interprets the formulation by referring to concrete experiences and environment conditions. Whatever one may try to do, there is no way of avoiding it. This brings about, however, an effect of unsharpness and uncertainty: the researcher who interprets the data never knows exactly which concrete content has been added to the relevant test question by the respondent.

To give an example: The answer "participation is not possible" can indicate different things: the actual lack of co-determination in the social system as a whole, authoritarian management style in the individual firm, but also the individual experience with one chief. In international projects there are at least *three* overlapping levels:

— the level of the country and its peculiarities according to which the uniform questionnaire is subjectively interpreted by the respondents;

— the level of the firm (up to the respective work team), the particularities of which modify the respondents' understanding of the test question;

— the level of the individual, his value system and experiences which are a third source influencing the understanding of the questions and thus also the obtained data.

These uncertainties can certainly be reduced by a high degree of sophistication in formulating questionnaires — but they cannot be eliminated entirely because they are rooted in the method itself.

But this is a different problem. While the distance between levels of abstraction can be bridged through additional interpretations, the effect mentioned here cannot be compensated in the stage of data evaluation: the interpretations of the questions take place in the consciousness of the respondent and cannot be decoded subsequently.

40

This is equally true for national studies; it has, however, an additional dimension in international comparative investigations: the difference in character of the context in which the questionnaire is conceived and interpreted is much greater and so is also the uncertainty of the obtained data.

From this it does not follow that questionnaires should be rejected; the consequences are more differentiated.

Firstly, all possibilities of the questionnaire should be exhausted to concentrate on relevant *circumstances* with regard to which a shift in meaning in the interpretations of the respondents is excluded; in general: facts are more reliable and *more comparable* than opinions. The more the questionnaire is used to grasp objective circumstances (data about the person, his income, his real material living conditions, unambiguous patterns of behaviour, etc.), the greater their comparability. The more a questionnaire aims at the respondents' opinions (interests, needs, value orientations, aims, assessments, etc.), the greater the uncertainty of the data and the more restricted their comparability. I call this latter type of data "soft data" and I think that studies which work mainly with this type of data are with regard to comparability based on an unsettled ground. From this follows *secondly:* preference is to be given to the research instruments leading to "harder" data, i.e. data in which the danger of a shift in meaning by unmeasurable interpretations of the respondents is excluded.

Here I do not only — and not even primarily — refer to information from official statistics, which for other reasons (e. g. because of ways of assessment) can be difficult — if at all possible — to compare. In the automation project as well as in the above-mentioned comparative research on social structure, a research instrument was used, the basic idea of which seems to be applicable to other studies, too. An essential social component of the scientific—technological progress and automation lies in the development of the objective working conditions. In an analogous way, the study on social structure, mentioned earlier, started from the fact that under the conditions of scientific—technological progress, changes take place in the important dimension of the social structure "physical and mental work". Consequently, studies on social structure must also consider those structures which are situated in the working process itself. Heavy physical work, intellectual level of work, required qualification in the working process, possibilities and mechanisms of social communication in the working process — all these are problems that have considerable importance both for the characterisation of the social aspects of automation and for the analysis of social structure. Now, it is obvious that for the analysis of such problems the questionnaire method is completely inappropriate. Using it, one can merely learn whether the respondent *perceives* his work to be physically hard or intellectually interesting — but not if it really *is* such. As indentical work contents are very differently assessed by different people, it is quite normal that the same work is regarded by one group of respondents as easy, by another group, however, as difficult. The judgements, modified by individual value systems, do not adequately reflect reality.

Starting from these ideas, in both studies, a workplace analysis together with the application of a traditional questionnaire was undertaken. The researchers themselves and not the respondents judged the relevant aspects of the working conditions by means of a standardised instrument.

Provided that the evaluation criteria have been defined exactly and homogeneously for all countries, i.e. provided that for all countries "physically difficult" and "physically easy" work, "intellectually demanding" and "monotonous" work, etc. has been defined in an identical way and that the research teams adhered to it, the application of such an instrument yields data which are more easily comparable: modifications and shifts in meaning by individuals are excluded; they do not reflect opinions but facts. I call this type "hard data", and on the basis of the experiences of the two mentioned projects, I think the following rule can be defended: The more the empirical data included in the comparison correspond to the type of "hard data", the more reliable and unambiguous their comparability is. While the interpretation of workers' opinions on the possibility of participation is subject to indefinite contents and depends to a certain extent on the point of view of the researcher, this cannot be the case in the interpretation e. g. of the result that the intellectual level of the work of machine setters is higher than that of machine operators. The objectivity of data, their direct correspondence to real circumstances prove to be important conditions of their comparability. It seems to me, that this experience deserves attention also in other research projects (such as studies on problems of micro electronics and on way of life in towns).

However, this method is not completely without problems either. So in the mentioned research on social structure a strange effect appeared. By means of the outlined research instrument, essential aspects of the work contents were to be evaluated. A nine-level scale with defined extremes "1" and "9" was used to assess the level of the investigated work place. Significantly in one country and as a tendency in two others, an effect emerged which could be called a "shift to the right": in applying the scale in these countries, the researchers and the experts consulted tended to a higher evaluation of all circumstances, i.e. their assessments were more often situated on the right part of the scale.

Up to now, we do not know the reasons for this effect. More important are, however, its consequences, which are related to a general problem of comparative research. The shift to the right in the application of the scale appeared in these countries with regard to *all* social groups which were analysed in the study *in the same way* and *to the same extent*. As a result, it is e.g. impossible to conclude that the work of the unskilled workers in Country A, in which this methodical effect appeared, is physically harder than the work of the unskilled worker in Country B, where this effect did not appear. What is possible, however, is to assess e.g. the distance with regard to the difficulty of physical work (or with regard to the intellectual level of work, the required qualification, etc.) between the groups of the unskilled and highly qualified workers in Country A and to compare it to the distance between the same groups in Country B. Shifts in the application of the scale solely inflict statements on absolute data, but not statements on *structures*.

This can be generalised; let us turn to another example in the same study. Essential aspects of social structure are connected with the distribution of social wealth, personal income and material living conditions derived from it. Now it is methodically rather unproblematic to find out the income of the worker in Poland, Hungary, the German Democratic Republic, Czechoslovakia, etc. But in order to *compare* them, knowledge about absolute income is not sufficient: it would be necessary to do most detailed research on wage—purchasing power relations, on price structures and shopping baskets, expense structures, etc. Without classifying the empirical fact "income" into these general reference systems, comparisons about *levels* of consumptive living conditions would be inadmissable. There is, however, no problem in comparing — without referring to the *overriding* points of reference — the investigated groups *within* the various

42

countries. Without being able at all to draw conclusions on the consumption level of the Bulgarian worker as compared to e.g. the Hungarian one, it can clearly be said, whether the differences in the consumption level between workers and the intelligentsia in Country A are greater or smaller than in the Countries B, C, D.

The situation is similar in other fields — e.g. in comparisons of education. The different character of educational systems renders it almost impossible to compare the absolute *levels* of education of groups of persons between different countries; it is extremely difficult to establish, whether the Polish skilled worker is higher, equally or less qualified than the Hungarian skilled worker. What can safely be said is: The differences in the level of qualification between different groups have in Country A this extent, the differences between the same groups amount in Country B to that extent.

In a generalised way: the comparison of *structures* is more appropriate than the comparison of isolated phenomena in terms of their respective quantitative *levels*. In particular when single circumstances are separated from their national context and when they are compared in that way quantitatively with each other, a false and misleading interpretation is rather probable. Firstly because the real importance of a phenomenon can only be grasped within the national context, and secondly because of methodical reasons. Whether a social group can be regarded as having a high standard of living or not, does not depend on its relation to other countries but on its relation to other social groups of the same country: so the intellectual of a developing country may appear as being poor in comparison to the intellectual of a highly developed industrial country — but if in the reference system of *his* country he is regarded as being rich, this is what counts for his social position. Among 98% illiterates the one able to read and write appears as intellectual; even if in *absolute* terms he has only elementary school education of a culturally high developed country. *His* social situation results from the social structure of *his* country and not from that of another world. This, too, is one aspect of the problem, namely, to always take into consideration the relevant national context in international comparisons.

The methodical reason is to be found in the "way of working" of research instruments: as the above example demonstrates even standardised instruments are not free of shifts in meaning according to national circumstances. It is as if two non-calibrated thermometers were used: it is not possible to compare the temperatures measured by them. What can clearly be compared are the *measuring lines* of the two instruments and the indicated distances, differences and structures. We should realise that in international comparative investigations in social sciences we always work with non-calibrated measurement instruments.

4. FIELD WORK AND SAMPLE STRUCTURES. THE PROBLEM OF THE FALSE ECONOMY

I do not know of any international comparative investigation, the working conditions of which have not been characterised by limited means. Time, labour and financial means can only be disposed of within certain, mostly rather narrow limits. The closest reaction to this is to keep the necessary expenditures as low as possible. However self-evident this practical starting point may be, at the same time it is very dangerous. As a rule — and in the Automation project in an exemplary way — thriftiness starts with the field work:

43

because of the limited means, one tries to manage with the smallest possible samples. This form of thriftiness, however, can become a fatal boomerang.

Now, to be sure, I am no adherent of "large-scale research" at any price; the size of samples is not a sufficient condition for scientific solidity. My concern is rather different.

It is well known to everybody doing sociological research that if one equates the total work necessary for an investigation (from the preliminary conceptional work up to the final evaluation) with one hundred, the amount necessary for field work is even in the case of rather large projects scarcely more than 5%; in the case of the Automation project it was quite below this percentage. The consequences resulting from shortcomings in the field-work phase, however, must be calculated as being much greater: in the extreme case they can endanger the whole project. This was certainly not the case in the Automation research; but it should nevertheless be mentioned that several countries no longer participated in the second (and strictly speaking more important) stage of evaluation, namely the comparative analysis following the elaboration of national reports. The reason was that they seriously doubted the comparability of data as a consequence of non-comparable procedures and principles governing the selection of the samples. The problems touched upon here are situated on several levels. The first concerns the size of the sample. If this is below a certain minimum (of about 800 to 1000), then sub-groups will become too small, and statistically sound statements become more and more problematic. Now, if – as in the case of this investigation – the whole record of mathematical–statistical evaluation procedures is used, an *impression* of exactness is created, that does absolutely not correspond to reality; factor analyses comprising factors based on scarcely a handful of people feign more exactness than they really represent. The whole undertaking then resembles a pyramid standing on its summit, the point being the primary empirical material, the bottom (now on top) being the mathematical–statistical apparatus. Strictly speaking, it is not quite worth doing complicated and expensive computerisation and data processing in order to calculate correlations, cluster and factor analyses for samples, many of which scarcely comprise more than 200 respondents.

The second problem concerns the selection principles in sampling. Certainly nationally representative samples are the *ideal* for international comparative studies but at the same time it is highly probable that this ideal can only seldom be reached. But from this it must not follow that we now have to restrict ourselves to *any* arbitrary mechanism of sample formation according to the national judgement. Case studies e.g. are also comparable if they are drafted according to uniform, exactly defined and strictly observed principles of sample selection. I take the liberty for a critical remark that in this respect the national "freedom" within the Automation study was too wide. The selection of firms, departments and respondents was guided by too flexible rules; the countries had too much liberty for idiosyncratic interpretations.

In other words: if an investigation is to be comparable in a methodically strict sense, then not only the research instruments but also the principles of field work must be defined exactly and in detail *and* must be strictly followed. Apparent thrifts legitimated by "work alleviation" in this field must always be paid for much more dearly.

What to Take into Account when Comparing? The Problem of Context

by Edmund Mokrzycki

The problem I would like to discuss here can be stated simply in the question "what are comparative studies?" The most straightforward answer is that a study is called comparative if it is concerned with the systematic comparison of social phenomena in two or more societies, countries, cultures, etc. This sort of dictionary-like definition, helpful as it is, is of little use if we want to understand how this sort of study is related to other types of social studies, why is it considered to be a specific type of intellectual activity, and what makes us think that comparative social research is in a way a new trend in the social sciences. There must be something unique about comparing various countries, societies and cultures, that makes us single it out as a separate type of research. It is not its importance, though it is an important type of study as has been clearly shown by Jan Berting (1979). It is rather the fact that in this type of research we find problems that are not so important in other types of research. There are, of course, technical and organisational problems related to comparative studies, but that is not what I have in mind. What I have in mind may be called *the* problem of comparative study, viz. the one that underlies all the technical and methodological problems of comparative research. I will try to explain the nature of that problem. It is necessary to do this because such an explanation not only provides a clue to understanding comparative study as a specific type of intellectual activity, but it also helps to make some suggestions as to how a comparative study should be done or, rather, how it should not be done.

1. A SHORT CASE STUDY OF A COMPARATIVE STUDY

Let me start from a short examination of a comparative study that can serve as a negative example, though I think that it is a good study, compared to what usually goes under that name. Furthermore, the study I have in mind is certainly an inventive effort in social research in the sense that the research team did not and could not follow any established research practice.

The study I want to examine is the well-known international study on the role values in local politics. It was sponsored by the International Social Science Council and covered four countries: the United States, Poland, Yugoslavia and India. The research team consisted of sociologists and political scientists from all four countries. The research design was jointly prepared by the whole team and fieldwork was done mainly by national sub-teams. The whole research process — from the research design to final report — was a good example of international academic cooperation. This is an important fact in that the research team as a whole had a sound and competent understanding of social and political problems in each of the four countries. It would seem that all the preconditions of a proper cross-national study were met and there were many reasons to expect that the work would be a reliable and important contribution to comparative politics. And yet, the product of the study is a misinterpretation of socio-political reality, at least as far as Poland is concerned.

The purpose of the study was "to examine, on a strictly comparative basis, the impact of leaders' values on social change and development at the community level" (Jacob et al. 1971, p. xxi). Obviously, the study was based on the idea that at the community level, leaders' public activity is, at least to some important extent, determined by their own values and that these leaders are agents of development. This idea followed from the assumption that "what happens at the base of political pyramid has much to do with the tempo of social change, and may determine whether development occurs at all" and that "public vitality may spring as much, if not more, from the qualities of those who lead firsthand, as from the leadership of the few at the centre and the top" (Jacob et al. 1971, p. 4).

With such a theoretical framework in mind the research team decided to compare local leadership (that is, the leadership at the level of "communities"), or, as they agreed to call it, local governments, in the United States, Poland, Yugoslavia, and India. "Information was collected from a sample of at least thirty local units in each country on what local government was doing to promote the development of the community, and what the local population was doing through voluntary activities to support community interests or respond to general national development plans" (Jacob et al. 1971, p. 5). As in every empirical research, the theoretical starting point adopted by the research team determined the course of the research process and contributed, as much as anything else, to what was later presented as empirical evidence.

The first operational problem that the research team had to solve was to find in each country comparable "local units", that is, local communities with comparable "local governments". This problem was solved in the following way: "In order to select local governments that would not only be appropriate for the questions of this research but also would be as similar as possible and would thus constitute a universe of local units, criteria based on the political system were chosen. These were both structural and functional: structural in the sense that they would be located in approximately the same place in the political system hierarchy; functional in that they had the *power to make essentially the same type of decisions in all four countries.* This resulted in some probability of a similar pattern in the mobilisation of social resources and initiative. The units selected on the basis of these criteria were cities in the United States, poviats in Poland, communes in Yugoslavia and blocks in India" (Jacob et al. 1971, pp. 366–7, italics added).

In other words, it was decided that the Polish poviat is equivalent to the American city, the Yugoslav commune and the Indian block in the sense that it has local government which has "the power to make essentially the same type of decisions" as the governments in the other communities.

The next question was who belongs to "the local government" in each country and how the researchers selected the local leaders for the study. It was decided that in each country the group of local leaders would include "elected officials, appointed officials, and organisational leaders, especially those in the local political party organizations" (Jacob et al. 1971, p. 374), and that in each local unit the thirty most important leaders would be interviewed since "this number begins to approach the area where the assump-

46

tions required for calculating means based on normal distribution are approximated" (Jacob et al. 1971, p. 381). As far as Poland is concerned the group of the thirty most important local leaders was composed of:

1. Members of the Presidium of the People's Council;
2. Presidents of Committees of the People's Council;
3. Secretaries of the Poviat Committees of the Polish United Workers' Party;
4. Presidents of the Poviat Committees of the United Peasants' Party and the Democratic Party (apparently this group was chosen as the result of the observation that "the Polish party system is characterized by three parties, the Polish United Workers Party, the United Peasant Party, and the Democratic Party" (Jacob et al. 1971, p. 187);
5. Heads of the Major Departments of the People's Council;
6. Other persons holding "key positions".

Thus, theoretical considerations and methodological predilections have led to what most Poles, *poviat* officials included, would consider to be a surprising discovery, namely, that there are many important decision makers at the level of the *poviat* and that their combined role can be described as that of local government. The Polish political system is different from, say, the American political system. This is a platitude which turns into an important, indeed basic, proposition if one engages in the comparative study of political phenomena, since every political phenomenon acquires its meaning in the context of a political system. Elections in the Polish political system are not simply different from elections in the American political system — they are entirely different   political phenomena. If we use the term "local leader" with reference to Poland — you can do this, though in the context of Polish politics it sounds strange — and the United States, we use one term for two completely different social roles, that is to say, we work in fact with one term and two concepts. Party in the Polish political system is what Lenin called the party of a new type, and the secretary of the local Committee of the Polish United Workers' Party is in no sense a counterpart of a party official in an American city. What in English translation is called the Democratic Party is again another type of organisation which in Polish is called *stronnictwo* (wing) rather than *partia* (party) and which has no equivalent whatsoever in the American political system. Finally, it makes no sense to speak of local government in the Polish system, or for that matter, in any centralised system. In fact, the very idea of the study under consideration ignores the theory of centralisation.

The above-mentioned study is an example of what happens when a theoretical framework developed in one social (or cultural, or political) context is used as a starting point for the design of a comparative study, that is, a study which by definition — as we will see — has to cross contextual boundaries.

The theoretical framework used by Philip Jacob and his international team, sophisticated as it is, reflects the Western political system: the concepts of local leader, local government, elected body, party organisation, political process, political leadership, citizen participation, etc., as used in this study, are relevant for analysis of Western countries. When applied to a political system as different as ours is, it results in seeking and examining non-existing phenomena.

2. WHAT DO WE DO WHEN WE MAKE A COMPARATIVE STUDY?

If an American sociologist wants to study the role of lobbies in federal politics, he does not have to ask preliminary questions such as what is a lobby and whether it really exists in American society. He would have to ask these questions, however, if he wished to do some sort of comparative studies of lobbies in various countries, that is to say, he would first have to establish whether lobbies — as he understands them — really exist in those countries and this can be done only by a thorough examination of the political systems of those countries.

This is a trivial example of an important problem. Social phenomena are systemic phenomena: they are related to various social systems and acquire their meaning within these systems, be it a political system, a nation, a culture, a historical period. This generally accepted fact is often disregarded in research practice as if it were only of theoretical importance. We know that a political organisation is what it is in the given political system. We stress this fact in theoretical discussions and accept its methodological consequences. And yet, when it comes to doing comparative research on, say, political parties, we tend to behave as if the fact, that various political organisations located in various political systems are identified by the same term, "party", and *appear* to have similar structural and functional characteristics, were more important than these theoretical considerations. Of course, it is not by pure chance that various political organisations in various political systems (related to various historical periods, political and cultural traditions, etc.) are called "party"; they must have much in common. But what do two or more "parties" actually have in common? To what extent are they the same type of political phenomena? — these are open questions to be considered on a case by case basis.

This brings us close to what I call *the* problem of comparative research. It is a theoretical, rather than a methodological, problem (though it has important meghodological consequences) and it can be traced to the doctrines of historicism, cultural relativism, etc. The problem is as follows: since social phenomena are system-bound, they have to be studied in the context of the relevant system. This means that the cross-systemic study is hampered by difficulties not encountered in the "typical", that is, intra-systemic social research. It is precisely this that makes us single out comparative study as a separate type of research. It is neither the comparing *per se* that makes the comparative study what it is, nor is it comparison across nations, countries, etc.; it is comparisons that impose the specific problem due to the system-boundness of social phenomena.

Obviously, the system-boundness of social phenomena as a problem is a matter of degree. Theoretically speaking, it is always present, even in the most trivial type of research limited to simple phenomena within one community. In most research situations, however, we can (and we do) practically disregard it. In other research situations it is so important that the precautions of "comparative approach" are necessary.

There is no clear rule, nor can there be, as to which research situation does and which does not require the comparative approach. It is usually assumed that the intra-national comparison does not generate any special problems of the sort we are discussing, while cross-national and cross-cultural comparison does. This assumption does not stand the test, however, and must be taken as no more than a heuristic rule of thumb. A cross-national study on political decision-making in Hungary and Poland would hardly be affected by the context-boundness, perhaps less than a cross-regional study of political decision-making in the United States. On the other hand, cultural or historical complexity of a single country can make the context-boundness of social phenomena as serious a problem as those faced in the most difficult cross-national studies. In short, we can say this: the question whether context-boundness in the given research situation is a serious matter could be in itself a substantial problem to be solved by a preliminary investigation.

We can now define comparative study as that in which the contextual factor is so important that some specific methodological difficulties emerge. They are precisely these specific methodological difficulties that make us single out comparative study as a separate type of research. What is called the "comparative approach" is in fact a general research strategy developed as a response to the problem of context-boundness and designed to solve that problem. In other words, it is a methodological strategy based on substantive (rather than purely methodological) premises and it has to be evaluated against these premises, that is to say, its value depends on the extent to which it solves what has been earlier defined as the problem of comparative research.

3. HOW IS COMPARATIVE RESEARCH POSSIBLE?

Before we answer this question let us first ask whether comparative study is possible at all. To many people this may sound like a silly question because — the argument would go — we *do* comparative studies, and what is being done obviously can be done. Such an argument would, however, miss the point. The real issue is this: since the meaning of social phenomena is bound up with the social system, then is it possible to transcend this relation in the research process? This issue cannot be resolved by pointing to current research practice unless one can demonstrate that the research practice actually does solve the problem. As I have tried to demonstrate in the first part of my paper, there are studies which faced the problem under discussion but which failed to solve it and though they were "comparative studies" in a sense, they did not prove that comparative study is possible, i.e., that there exists a solution to the problem. If at all, they rather suggested the opposite conclusion. To a certain extent this is true of comparative research in general. As I tried to demonstrate elsewhere (Mokrzycki 1979), comparative social research, as it is practised today, is based on just such a system of methodological assumptions which results in by-passing the problem of context-boundness rather than solving it. Our question is then, in the present situation, quite legitimate and requires *theoretical* examination.

Is comparative study possible at all? In answer to this, one can say the following: there is no sufficient theoretical evidence to believe that it is not possible, though there are well-grounded arguments, implied by such doctrines as historicism and cultural relativism, in favour of extreme prudence in this respect. While these arguments cannot be presented here without drastic simplification, we can indicate some suggestions, based on these arguments as well as on what has been said in the first two sections as to what prudence in this case practically entails.

First of all, it means that any attempt at comparative study should be a result of, rather than a first step towards, a thorough examination and profound understanding of the systems involved. This stipulation in fact can be deduced from one of the most elementary methodological requirements which states that the research design has to be based on an adequate theory (be it an explicit theoretical system or an unexplicated set of assumptions) and that the research process should be conceived as an activity regulated by theoretical considerations. In the "normal" research situation this requirement is usually not perceived as a problem since the researcher does ground his activity, whether he is aware of it or not, on some theoretical ideas which, even if not completely adequate and sophisticated, are seldom utterly wrong (if only because the researcher being a member of a society has a good deal of common sense understanding of that society). What happens all too often in the area of comparative study, indeed it seems to be the rule, is that the research design, sophisticated as it might be, is based on, and derived from, a theoretical framework that squares well with one system but is hardly relevant, or utterly irrelevant, with respect to the other. This is clearly the case with the study on local government examined above. The research design, indeed the very idea of local government as a unit of analysis, reflects theoretical thinking related to the American (or perhaps Western) political system. It proved to be quite inadequate for tackling local decision-making processes in Poland. Had the Polish political system been analysed before the plan of the study was born, the research design could have been quite different or, more likely, the very idea of such a comparative study would have been dropped as ill-conceived.

The stipulation that the plan of a comparative study should be based on some preliminary investigation of the systems involved must be strongly emphasised as must the stipulation that this thorough examination of systems involved be carried out *prior to* the research design being worked out in any detail. What is probably most important is that such an examination can well discourage one from engaging in the particular project in the first place. As to the central question whether comparative research is possible at all, it seems to be quite clear that in many cases it is not possible or, rather, that it does not make sense since it would result in comparing different types of phenomena on the assumption that they are of one type, and thus produce purely intellectual artifacts.

Of course, such an approach makes comparative research an extremely difficult task, much more difficult than intra-systemic studies. In fact, such an approach amounts to comparative analysis of two or more social *systems* rather than some phenomena within those systems. To be more specific, social phenomena would have to be studied, as it were, within the context of their own system and compared only indirectly as a consequence of comparing whole systems.

Such a comparison of whole systems does not come into conflict with the idea of the systemic nature of social phenomena, nor with the arguments implied in, say, the doctrine of historicism. In this sense we arrive here at an answer to both the questions whether comparative study is possible as well as how it is possible. This does not provide us with any practically useful suggestions as to how to do a comparative study, except that it seems to rule out the application of standard methodology of social research, and particularly survey methodology, and, by implication, puts emphasis on *interpretative* analysis.

REFERENCES

Berting, J. (1979) "What is the Use of International Comparative Research?" In: Jan Berting et al. (eds.), *Problems in International Comparative Research in the Social Sciences,* Oxford: Pergamon Press.

Jacob, Ph. et al. (1971) *Values and the Active Community: A Cross-National Study of the Influence of Local Leadership,* New York: The Free Press.

Mokrzycki, E. (1979) On the Adequacy of Comparative Methodology, In: J. Berting et al. (eds) *Problems of International Comparative Research in the Social Sciences,* Oxford, Pergamon Press.

Part Two

SELECTED METHODOLOGICAL
ISSUES IN
COMPARATIVE RESEARCH

In the foregoing part the theory and strategy to be applied in cross-national research were discussed. This section concentrates on two related issues: problems of a quantitative and qualitative nature in international research. In fact it is another point of view on the same problems discussed up to now, and some minor overlaps cannot be avoided in a systematic treatment of these subjects.

Both papers are structured according to the various stages in the research process. *Jules Peschar* describes the "state of the art" in quantitative aspects in empirical research and presents an overview of the presently available experience in this domain. Problems of research design and country selection are discussed as well as issues in instrument and measurement, data collection, analysis and interpretation. Of course, the question often arises that specific decisions on research design and analysis require a conceptual or theoretical basis.

Manfred Nießen also relates to the various steps in empirical research when discussing qualitative problems. He deals with problems of functional equivalence as the focal point of qualitative reasoning in comparative research and investigates very concretely the influence on decisions during the research process. This is followed by brief comments on the use of country reports and qualitative methods to secure the necessary information basis. A short discussion on the impact of organisation of comparative research on the treatment of functional equivalence closes this part on selected methodological issues, and already bridges over to the problems discussed in Part Three.

Quantitative Aspects in Cross-National Comparative Research: Problems and Issues

by Jules Peschar

1. INTRODUCTION

1.1. State of the Art

At the 1972 ISSC/Vienna Centre Round Table on Cross-National Comparative Survey Research in Budapest, much attention was paid to the subject of this paper: the quantitative aspects of cross-national research. As has already been mentioned in the other chapters of this book as well, the Budapest Conference evaluated five multinational studies in various stages of completion: The International Time-Budget Study (Szalai et al. 1972); Juvenile Delinquency and Development (Malewska and Peyre 1976); Images of the World in the Year 2000 (Ornauer et al. 1976); The Cross-National Programme in Political and Social Change (Verba and Nie 1973; Verba, Nie and Kim 1978) and the International Studies on Values in Politics (The Jacobs 1971).

In the full report of the conference (Szalai and Petrella 1977) the contributions of Teune and Allerbeck focus on methods of analysis and interpretation in particular, while Glazer discusses general problems in the research process of cross-national research. These papers describe, to a certain extent, the state of the art in cross-national methodology at the beginning of the seventies.

It might therefore be worthwhile to investigate the progress having been made since. A number of other cross-national projects have been started, elaborated, completed or published, that might have taken advantage of experiences from the above-mentioned projects. Inkeles and Smith (1974) published their 6-nation study on modernity; the

International Association for the Evaluation of Educational Achievement (IEA) published 9 volumes on an enormous project involving 21 countries; Form (1976) reported on his study of Autoworkers in four countries; a number of comparative studies on social stratification and mobility have been undertaken (an overview in Mayer 1979 or Peschar 1978a); the International Research Group on Industrial Democracy in Europe will publish results in 1980 (IDE 1980) and the first of four volumes of the 15-nation study on Automation and Industrial Workers, coordinated by the Vienna Centre, has appeared (Forslin et al. 1979).

Moreover, the attention to methodological and technical problems in cross-national comparative research has also not diminished, compared with the many publications on this subject in the preceding decade. Since 1970 and the Budapest Conference, a number of methodological treatises in various fields have been published, that enable us to evaluate cross-national projects according to certain standards. Political scientists will mainly focus on Holt and Turner (1970); sociologists on Vallier (1971), Armer and Grimshaw (1973) or Smelser (1976); whereas psychologists may prefer to consult Brislin, Lonner and Thorndike (1973) or proceedings of conferences of the International Association for Cross-Cultural Psychology (for example Poortinga 1977).

With regard to the documentation of cross-national research methodology it was foreseen that the bibliography compiled by Almasy, Balandier and Delatte (1976) − that covers the period 1967−1973, and was specially prepared for the Budapest Conference − would be regularly updated and published. Unfortunately this plan has not been accomplished yet, although Elder (1976) has reviewed a number of recent studies with regard to their methodology. For some specialised fields more recent overviews are available. Comparative social mobility and race relations were the topic for a conference in the Netherlands (a full report in Berting, Geyer and Jurkovich 1979), the field of comparative education research has been evaluated by Nießen and Peschar (1980).[1]

1.2. The Purpose of this Paper

In this paper a rather loose and pragmatic definition of the term "quantitative" will be used. Quantitative aspects are to be found in a selection of topics that relate to the empirical research process. It is not meant to be exclusive and it should not be competitive with a qualitative approach. In my view both qualitative and quantitative approaches are different stages in the research process that rather complement than exclude each other (for a similar view see the chapter by Nießen on qualitative aspects.)

The following topics that relate to quantitative approaches will be discussed in this paper. In the first place problems of *research design and country selection* will be mentioned, as they constitute the basis for cross-national comparative research from quantitative data. *Instrument and measurement* problems will then be presented, as far as they are specific for this type of research. Special problems in *fieldwork and data collection* in an international setting are frequently reported, as well as in cooperation abroad. A discussion of these various problems is followed by special topics in *analysis and interpretation* of cross-national data.

[1] It must be remarked that some recent overviews with the word "comparative" in the title (for instance organisation, health) do not deal with cross-national comparisons (see Lammers 1978, Mechanic 1975).

These areas are undoubtedly not an exhaustive list of problems in quantitative cross-national research. Most of the research projects we will discuss, however, will have their special characteristics in one or the other topic. Furthermore, also cross-national empirical research encounters the same problems as we have in within-country research. As Frey (1970, p. 184) points out: it is not a matter of kind but a matter of degree that within- and cross-country research differ. We will therefore mainly touch on problems that relate to a quantitative approach if they create important problems of cross-national comparative research, and may refer for "normal" research problems to the many handbooks.

2. PROBLEMS OF DESIGN AND COUNTRY SELECTION

2.1. On Designs

a. Cross-sectional designs

Most cross-national projects that are presently reported or in progress, are based on large-scale cross-sectional survey information. The focus of comparative research has therefore almost exclusively been on problems in this type of research (Rokkan 1968, 1970; Scheuch 1968; Szalai and Petrella 1977; Almasy, Balandier and Delatte 1976; Jennings and Farah 1977; Rokkan, Viet, Verba and Almasy 1969).

Frey (1970, pp. 175—187) elaborates a number of arguments why the large-sclale survey approach in cross-cultural (-national) projects should be of high value. If I understand him correctly, the main argument is the great variation of phenomena that can be included and the high degree of information that can be achieved. Another argument seems to be that already many projects in this line have been carried out; therefore it must be a useful approach. Before we comment on this view, a number of projects applying cross-sectional designs may be referred to.

The five projects reviewed at the Budapest Conference were all of a cross-sectional nature (see Introduction). A number of current projects of the Vienna Centre also apply the same design (see the Vienna Centre Newsletters). In political science it is widely applied, ranging from the Verba and Nie study on participation and political equality (Verba, Nie and Kim 1978) to the secondary analysis of cross-sectionally obtained public opinion polls. Secondary analyisis, however, poses its own problems, that will be discussed later.

Explicitly designed cross-sectional research also includes the IEA studies on educational achievement. Studies on the achievements in six different subjects for 3 populations (10 year old, 14 year old and at the end of secondary schooling) in 21 countries were carried out in 1970 and 1971 (a "readers digest" in Walker 1976; an overview in Nießen and Peschar 1980). In addition to these surveys that collected information from students, teachers and schools for cross-national comparison, a separate study on achievement and structural characteristics was undertaken. The average achievement scores per country were correlated with national available statistics. This mixed use of primary and secondary sources, however, was not very successful, as the authors themselves admit it (Passow, Noah, Eckstein and Mallea 1976). Not only the quality of collected data was disappointing, but also the possibilities for analyses from such a model were very limited, as they were not guided by a theoretical framework.

Maybe this is the main criticism that one can put forward to the blind favour for cross-sectional designs. The choice of design is dependent on the theoretical questions one wants to be answered. Of course it may happen that method and design will allow certain theoretical questions to be investigated; but an almost automatic choice for large-scale cross-sectional surveys does not seem a very good strategy in general. If one is interested in an appropriate *description,* well-designed samples are a necessary tool to make appropriate estimates on a national level. However, many researchers imply the search for *causal relationships and explanations.* Information from different moments should be available in order to test an anticipated causal structure, derived from a theoretical framework. In status-attainment and mobility research, this topic has been discussed intensively (Duncan, Featherman and Duncan 1972; Jencks 1972; Sewell and Hauser 1975) and has led to a preference for longitudinal designs. Also in comparative educational research it has been recognised that instead of the usual paradigm of large representative samples, an alternative strategy of smaller-scale observational and developmental studies could have been more beneficial (Husén 1979, p. 383).

Of course these remarks apply to national as well as cross-national social research. Why, then, has the cross-sectional design almost exclusively been applied in this type of comparative research? I think the following explanations can be given.

A cross-sectional design is simply the easiest way to cooperate in an international framework. It is a highly standardised design with well-known sampling procedures. The formulation of the research goal — usually a complicated process in international cooperation — does not have to be extremely specified: also when one has no theory or hypotheses, the survey can always serve descriptive purposes.

Furthermore, decisions on the many possibilities for analysing the data can be postponed (and *are* postponed) until after data collection and keypunching. Potential conflicts that may arise when discussing theory and analysis, therefore, do not disturb the cooperation with colleague-researchers from other countries. Of course this heavily delays the final analysis and publication, as one can observe with a number of important projects (see for instance Verba, Nie and Kim 1978, preface; Szalai 1972; Forslin, Sarapata and Whitehill 1979). This part of the research process can of course be influenced by proper coordination and planning, although good organisation cannot compensate for bad strategy and research design.

Finally, it may be remarked that the above-described strategies lead to enormous data files for many countries. It is generally acknowledged that data from international cross-sectional research are extremely underanalysed (Szalai 1972, pp. 28–29; Allerbeck 1977, p. 374; Inkeles 1979). The question is: will they ever be overanalysed and will they then be recent and informative enough after so many years to make the enterprise worthwhile?

b. Longitudinal designs

It has been mentioned already that for testing of causal relationships (if this is one of the purposes of a project) one needs information measured at several moments. In principle follow-up studies, panel studies and experimental methods are appropriate designs. For the first two types one can hardly find applications in cross-national research.

One of the very large international longitudinal projects is the project Metropolitan, originally conceived as a Scandinavian comparative study on social stratification and mobility. But the project could only be launched in Denmark and Sweden, since both Finland and Norway had to withdraw for various reasons (practical and political respectively). Samples. of more than 10,000 children were drawn in 1966 for both the capitals and followed up with respect to school and occupational career. One can imagine the amount of work connected with this enterprise. Still no final reports are available, a number of smaller findings were reported, however (Jansson 1974). It is not suggested that this approach is *the* appropriate strategy versus a cross-sectional design. The design fits into the need for longitudinal data required for the theoretical purposes of the study. But the practical decision for such a large sample highly paralyses effective progress in the project.[2]

In the field of higher education the FORM project (on socialisation processes with university graduates) has been planned as a longitudinal one (Framhein 1980). Four waves of information collection are planned from 1977/8 until 1983/4 in five countries (Austria, Federal Republic of Germany, the Netherlands, Poland and Yugoslavia). Project coordination by the Vienna Centre should ascertain that the time-schedule can be maintained. It is clear that such a design demands much from the participant-researchers in cooperation.

In this respect it is well known that few longitudinal studies survived; resources are hard to get and maintain. Another strategy can also be found in the tracing of relevant longitudinal studies and we can establish their comparability *ex post*. For instance in the field of educational career and achievement, in the sixties various longitudinal studies have been carried out that would enable intelligent comparisons. In Sweden a national sample of 13 year olds in 1966 (Härnqvist and Svensson 1973) could be compared with a Dutch national sample of 12 year olds in 1965 (Collaris and Kropman 1978). Similar samples are available in France (Girard and Clerck 1964) and Switzerland (Girod 1971) from about the same time, and suitable for comparison.

Björn (1979) also applied a longitudinal design in his research on the influence of labour parties on the redistribution of income in five capitalist democracies from 1920 until 1970. The analysis of such data on a macro level and standardisation of already collected data afterwards (if possible) brings us to problems of secondary analysis, that will be discussed later on.

c. Cohort studies

Another form of time-design is the cohort study. This dynamic design allows for inter- and intra-comparisons as well as changes over time in the different countries. The design, however, has — as far as I know — only been applied in one study on the socialisation of youth in France, Federal Republic of Germany and Great Britain (Jugendwerk der Deutschen Shell 1977).

Three cohorts of 12, 17 and 22 year olds, with a total sample size of about 1000 per country were questioned in 1976. Unfortunately this was only one part of the design, the other part to complete it (the second measurement some years later) has not been accomplished. However, if we consider operationalisation, comparability and preliminary analysis, it might be better to forget all about this research. For a size of the lowest social strata of 5% in Germany, 19% in France and 33% in Great Britain does not strengthen

---

[2] There is also no need for such a large sample. Statistically, as one can easily compute on the basis of every statistics handbook, samples of roughly 1000 persons would be enough.

the belief in the quality of the study (see also Nießen and Peschar 1980, pp. 35–37). The design as such, however, is perfectly suitable for comparative research on social processes and change.

d. Experimental and semi-experimental approaches

Experimental designs are in the tradition of cross-cultural psychology. Brislin, Lonner and Thorndike (1973, pp. 82–108) devote ample attention to the subject. But also in sociology and anthropology experimental settings have been applied. Bovenkerk, Kilborne, Raveau and Smith (1979) conducted field experiments on discrimination against non-white citizens in Great Britain, France and the Netherlands. They not only focussed on verbal stimuli in various settings, but also on actual behaviour: renting a house and finding a job on the labour market.

Also Elder refers to experiments, and stresses that in experimental designs one can control all but a few variables which can be altered systematically (Elder 1976, p. 219). Of course this holds true for *designed* laboratory and field experiments. Not always, however, is it possible to handle the basic condition of an experiment, i.e. the random assignment of subjects to experimental and control conditions. But, also semi-experimental methods are available allowing control of relevant background variables. Matching procedures to obtain equivalent groups with similar characteristics are then in order.

Inkeles and Smith, for instance, applied such procedures in their research on modernity in six developing countries: Argentine, Chile, East-Pakistan, India, Israel and Nigeria. In each of these countries four different samples were approached, and matched according to relevant variables such as sex, age, education, culture, residence, type of work, and rural versus urban origin (Inkeles and Smith 1974, pp. 36–49). The strength of the design was not fully elaborated and multivariate analyses were run afterwards to accomplish full control of relevant variables.

In the field of organisation research Maurice, Sorge and Warner (1980) report on comparative research in manufacturing units in France, the Federal Republic of Germany and Great Britain. They matched units on size, technology, location and dependence, in order to focus better on their dependent variables. Also the fifteen-nation Vienna Centre study on "Automation and Industrial Workers" could be seen as a semi-experimental study, matching on one type of production, namely the automobile transferline (Bergmann 1979, p. 12). A detailed judgement of the applied procedures must be postponed until more specific information on the research design is available.[3]

In the field of education, a number of semi-experiments with matched groups have been conducted in the Netherlands and Sweden. Higher and lower social class children were matched on sex, age and IQ at the end of the primary school in both countries for two longitudinal data sets. The further educational career and attainment could then be compared in order to trace changes in educational inequality within as well as between the two countries (Peschar 1978b). In this project a mixture of primary and secondary information was applied.

The above-mentioned examples underline Frey's recommendation (1970, p. 196) that it is worthwhile to undertake comparative studies with matched groups on a smaller

[3]Until now only Volume 1 Part 1 (Forslin, Sarapata and Whitehill 1979) has appeared. It includes a history of the project, several national reports and the various questionnaires. Details about the selection of firms, sampling procedures and response rates are not included, but will undoubtedly be reported in the volumes to come, as will the cross-national comparisons.

scale rather than the usual large cross-sectional surveys. Computer programmes to facilitate time-consuming matching have been developed and are available (Haan 1975). Furthermore, the application of (semi-)experimental designs forces the researcher to make decisions in the early stages of the research process, also with regard to the procedures of equivalence, coding and analysis. As we suggested, these stages are normally postponed until after completion of the fieldwork and thus cause delays. It hardly needs to be emphasised that (matched) experiments are not appropriate for descriptive purposes, but rather for the testing of hypotheses and theories.

e. Secondary analysis

We have already touched various times on comparative research on the basis of existing data. In such secondary analyses a comparison is made *ex post*, while many times the original data were not collected explicitly for comparative purposes. The establishment of large data archives – such as those in Michigan, Amsterdam, Cologne, Essex – invite comparative analyses. Moreover, advanced systems are available to search for similar variables in the many available computer files, thus providing the researcher with "complete" data sets for his comparative research. Elder (1976, pp. 219 ff) warns of the danger one may encounter in such analyses with respect to the noncomparability of classifications. Also Colton (1979) discusses the differences in concepts and measurement in official and international education statistics, that are easily forgotten when one has already obtained the data. Hazelrigg and Garnier note that "even under the best existing conditions, the kinds of data with which one must work in undertaking comparative secondary analyses leaves much to be desired" (Hazelrigg and Garnier 1976, p. 500; for similar remarks see also Treiman 1977b, pp. 1045 ff, and Friedrichs 1978, pp. 8 ff).

Many examples exist of research using secondary analysis for comparative questions. In the field of educational and occupational status attainment, and social mobility, comparisons were made for instance between the U.S.A. and Great Britain (Treiman and Terrell 1975; Kerckhoff 1974, 1977); U.S.A. and France (Garnier and Hout 1976; Seeman 1976); U.S.A. and Poland (Meyer, Tuma and Zagorski 1979); Poland and Hungary (Andorka and Zagorski 1978); Finland and Poland (Pohoski, Pöntinen and Zagorski 1978); Netherlands and Sweden (Peschar 1978b).[4] Projects in the same domain, but comparing many countries at the same time include those by Hazelrigg and Garnier (1976), Weiss (1980) and in the political science domain for instance Jackmann (1975). Essentially the remarks made above on comparability and equivalence of concepts hold for all these studies: some of them account in detail how comparable the data sets and concepts can be considered, thus dealing with the problem of "credibility" (Verba 1971).

Two other approaches on the basis of available data may be mentioned finally. First, one may find replications of research carried out in another country. Many times the idea was not to compare, but to apply a model or theory in just another society. Examples can be seen in the replications of Jenck's Inequality model in Sweden (Fägerlind 1975), Great Britain (Psacharopoulos 1977), the Federal Republic of Germany (Müller and Mayer 1976) and Holland (Dronkers and De Jong 1979).[5] One has to be

---

[4] A review of these studies, with emphasis on the educational component is presented in Nießen and Peschar (1980, pp. 18–33).

[5] We are not trying to be complete here: a more comprehensive overview is found in Mayer (1979).

very careful to treat such replications as comparisons, since regularly other models, variables and methods have been applied.

Secondly, the application of advanced techniques for network analysis on existing information may be mentioned. Although strictly speaking the data (year books of companies, directories etc.) have originally served no social science purpose, one may consider the problem of data acquisition similar to those referred to above: the data were not designed to be comparable, therefore this work is to be done *ex post*. A recent cross-national project was started under the auspices of the European Consortium for Political Research and focusses on the industrial, economic and financial networks of West European countries.

2.2. On Country Selection

Decisions on the inclusion of certain countries in comparative research can be made on various grounds (see also the chapter by Galtung in this volume). One finds many variations, ranging from highly selective or random sampling to haphazard or accidental choice. Frey refers to four different strategies. The first is that of administrative convenience; the second is to maximise similarity; the third to maximise diversity among all dimensions, and finally one might select countries on the basis of a "factorial matrix" including relevant dimensions (Frey 1970, pp. 199 ff). As Elder rightly remarks the latter strategy theoretically might be most appropriate; in practice, however, the researcher is severely limited by access and availability of equally good data from all the countries (Elder 1976, p. 218).

The last three criteria by Frey are closely related to the theoretical goals of research: the first criterion, however, seems to be most applied. Inkeles and Smith selected their six developing countries mainly because of the presence of a competent researcher or research institute (Inkeles and Smith 1974, pp. 50–57). Countries involved in the IEA research did so voluntarily; the members of IEA are research institutes in the various countries that could afford the very expensive surveys (Postletwaithe 1974). The involvement of countries in the Cross-National Programme in Political and Social Change is described in detail by Verba, Nie and Kim (1978, preface): some countries withdrew while others joined during various stages of the project, apparently without a clear rationale.

Still another dimension for country selection can be found in Vienna Centre projects. The "charter" of the Centre underlines scientific cooperation between East and West Europe. Therefore countries of both socio-political systems will have to be included in research projects (Schaff 1979, p. 6, and Framhein and Mills 1979, pp. 127 ff).

Even when no clear dimension is developed according to which countries are ranked, theoretical arguments may lead to the inclusion of certain countries and the exclusion of certain others (although this is hardly ever done). Form's study on autoworkers in four countries essentially was a replication, but anticipated maximising diversity (Form 1976, preface). The Dutch–Swedish educational comparison could be presented as to maximise similarity of the two societies in many respects, but with differing educational systems (Peschar 1978b).

Nevertheless, the above-described selection mechanisms make it difficult to come from purely descriptive studies to explanatory ones, including relevant country characteristics as independent variables (see also Wiatr 1977, p. 361). With an absence of underlying theoretical concepts,[6] most of the country-difference studies must fail (see for instance Passow et al. 1976, pp. 292 ff).

3. PROBLEMS OF INSTRUMENTS AND MEASUREMENT

A central problem in comparative research is that of equivalence of indicators for the concepts to be measured. We find a wide variety of opinion and practice in cross-national research. Since the topic of comparability in this book is treated more extensively in the chapter by Loetsch, I will confine myself here to some specific questions.

In many studies one tries to establish equivalence by translating the items and questionnaires literally into another language (for instance in the IEA six subject surveys: see Walker 1976). To secure that the translations are appropriate, several techniques have been devised to exclude "noise" and imprecision. Independent check-translations, back-translations according to certain schemes and the "use" of bilinguals to establish equivalent meanings have been discussed by Frey (1970, pp. 275–279) and Brislin, Lonner and Thorndike (1973, pp. 32–58).[7]

However, a literal translation of items and questionnaires does not guarantee the equivalence of instruments (see for instance Oppenheim and Torney 1974, p. 28). Therefore, *functional equivalence* is a much more important objective in comparative research. Lengthy discussions have been published (among others Przeworski and Teune 1970; Frey 1970; Verba 1971; Armer 1973; Elder 1976; Verba, Nie and Kim 1978), but the issue has been neglected in other books (Peaker 1975; Smelser 1976; Szalai and Petrella 1977; Berting, Geyer and Jurkovich 1979).

Functional equivalence refers to a situation where the same concept or variable is indexed by various or differing numbers of indicators in different countries. What is crime in one society might not be crime in another. Social class might have to be measured in one society by indicators of wealth and prestige, in another by mobility, or in a third by religion. In all these situations one acquires relevant measures for the concept to be measured, functionally equivalent for the purpose although they are not identical. It is clear that for this differential validity — for every society a separate measure — there is no standard solution (Verba 1971, pp. 314–315; Armer 1973, pp. 71 ff; Elder 1976, p. 223). It is, however, the task of the researcher to demonstrate and to argue that he did his best to achieve this functional equivalence.

A prerequisite for valid measures is reliability. Therefore, multiple measures of the same dimension are preferable to single measures. Scales can be constructed that psychometrically can be treated according to unidimensionality, cumulativity, reliability, etc. Reliability of scales, however, is seldom reported in cross-national research. Good exceptions are the IEA six subject surveys, where such statistics on all the relevant constructs are reported (Peaker 1975 and all the relevant subject reports mentioned there). The pro-

[6]When countries are ranked, it is mostly according either to modernity criteria, or to economic development criteria. But these criteria are not necessarily the most interesting ones for *sociological* explanations. See for instance the various volumes of Comparative Social Research (formerly Comparative Studies in Sociology) for applications.

[7]For other aspects of translation and language problems see Hymes (1970) and Nagi (1977).

ject on Industrial Democracy in Europe reports reliability for the twelve included countries (IDE 1980, Appendix B). The well-known modernity scales by Inkeles and Smith are also known to have a relatively high reliability, depending on the variant and the country (Inkeles and Smith 1974, p. 89, Table 6–1).

Of course high reliability is not sufficient for the validity of a certain scale, especially not for the construct validity we discussed above as functional equivalence. How does one achieve a high validity for an instrument and establish equivalence as well? Validity of a certain measure must be ascertained for every country/nation included in the research. The most applied strategy is to search for similar factor structures in large sets of items or to look for high correlations with nation-specific items.

A good example of this approach is reported by Verba, Nie and Kim (1978, pp. 36 ff). For their six countries they wanted to develop relevant measures for political participation. Questionnaire items — both country-specific and general — were factor analysed for every country. This produced four theoretically interpretable dimensions, that were rather similar in all the countries. An identical factor structure in fact underlines the cross-national equivalence of the measure, though the items per country vary (Verba, Nie and Kim 1978, p. 40 and Appendix A). It is therefore not surprising that these researchers attach less value to the literal translations of their questionnaires in order to establish equivalence, but emphasise that comparisons can only be relative and not absolute.

It seems to me that this cannot be a general rule for comparative research. Only if the operationalisations for a certain concept differ too much between the countries, must one focus on relative measures. This is obviously the case with political participation. But if one finds that the core of all items is identical for the respective countries and still produces relevant scales, then one has the opportunity to apply either relative or absolute instruments.

We referred already to the various attempts to establish standard scales for modernity. With different versions of the scales, comparisons were made on processes of modernisation within developing countries (relative) as well as between countries (absolute) (Inkeles and Smith 1974; Smith and Inkeles 1975; Inkeles 1978).[8]

In the field of social stratification especially Treiman has tried hard to construct a Standard International Occupational Prestige Scale that correlates rather highly with existing prestige scales in various countries (Treiman 1975, 1977a, 1977b). The scale has been applied to comparisons between the United States and Great Britain (Treiman and Terrell 1975) and Poland and Finland (Pohoski, Pöntinen and Zagorski 1978), as well as in various secondary analyses (e.g. Weiss 1979). Other standard instruments for cross-national research are described by Elder (1976, pp. 221–222), Frey (1970, pp. 260–274) and Brislin, Lonner and Thorndike (1973, pp. 109–254). They include Cantrill's self-anchoring scale, Osgood's semantic differential as well as the use of projective techniques.

An important assumption in the use of standard scales is that they are invariant in time within-country, and therefore can reflect cross-national differences. This point is usually neglected and hardly investigated. Summarising the various points of view, it appears that functional equivalence might relate to rather different research situations.

---

[8]The validity of such scales was questioned by Armer and Schnaiberg (1973) who tried to demonstrate that they measured merely alienation, anomia or middle-class values instead of modernity.

First it is clear that equivalence can only be established with regard to a concept one wants to operationalise. The differential validity — for various countries — depends much on the theoretical goals one wants to reach. If one is interested in comparing processes within the countries, then identical items are not necessary to achieve functional equivalence. In fact one can include as many country-specific items as one wants, even to improve the validity of a scale for a certain country. This country-specificity is simply impossible if one wishes to compare absolute levels ("national differences") of for instance achievement, participation, prestige or modernity. Then one must have a standard scale that is invariant for a specific country. Of course, this is only possible at the cost of a loss of within-country validity: the more when the cultures/countries are divergent in various aspects.[9]

Paradoxically, such differences are, at the same time, object of investigations. As Mayer (1979, p. 49) remarks, it is still an open question which important structural differences between countries are abstracted from, or partialled out, with the use of standard measures.

4. PROBLEMS OF FIELDWORK AND DATA-COLLECTION

As Elder notices, the most elaborate and detailed instruments are of little use, if one is not able to obtain cooperation with respondents in the field (Elder 1976, p. 223). It seems to me that such problems in quantitative cross-national research have not attracted much attention. In anthropology — with its more qualitative-like methods — the position of the researcher or participant observer has always been one of the basic issues and is frequently reported on (see among others Schatzmann and Strauss 1973).

Apparently in large-scale quantitative research the investigators rather like to report about the statistical comparability, than about the interview strategies and situations. These, however, are important stages in a research process that is designed to obtain comparative data. I want to discuss three major issues in this area: the problem of getting access to the field and the interviewees; the questionnaire and interview effects; and the training of the interview staff.

4.1. Getting Access to the Field and the Respondents

Multinational comparative research multiplies problems of financing, sponsorship and access to the field in a much more progressive way than technical and methodological problems. Nevertheless there have been few systematic evaluations in this respect.

Frey (1970, p. 202–229) devotes much attention towards these problems in general and focusses on the organisational structure in particular. We shall not deal here with problems of centralised versus decentralised organisations. The chapters in Part Three of this book by Husén, Lesage and Mills will highlight specific advantages of one

---

[9]This is also referred to in the controversy between Burawoy (1977) and Treiman (1977b). Another example may be found in the rather risky comparison of (absolute) country differences on such relative judgements as job or quality-of-life satisfactions. See for instance Inglehart (1978, pp. 181 ff).

type versus another.[10] It appears, however, that organisational structure has the following consequences for the research process, especially in the fieldwork stage.

a. The sponsorship of the project is important for its image. Everybody will agree that a good sponsor is a great benefit to get the necessary *permissions,* but a good sponsor on an international level might not be the appropriate one on the national or local level. In Safari-type research "International Headquarters" and the international sponsors are important and they can maintain the standards for the international design somewhat independently of the participating countries. The problem is to find national representatives who have enough influence to support the project locally. In cooperative-type projects one is exclusively dependent on national sponsors and authorities. A higher chance of financial and topic control might be observed, in order to get the appropriate support for the research. Form, for example, extensively lists the problems of negotiating access in the automobile factories in the four countries. The question of sponsorship was extremely important to get cooperation of both management and trade unions (Form 1976, pp. 277–299). Such problems are not specific for a European situation, but also occur in the developing countries, as Inkeles and Smith report (1974, pp. 50–64).

b. The willingness of *respondents* to cooperate with a study may depend largely on the sponsorship. In certain countries sponsorship by a university or scientific organisation may be an advantage, in others a disadvantage. In some countries government sponsorship may raise the response rate considerably, while in other countries people might be reluctant to get involved in an interview, afraid of being questioned for other purposes than the stated comparative project.

A basic issue in comparative research is whether sponsorship and subsequent (non)response influence comparability. On the basis of available empirical evidence it is, however, difficult to establish a strategy in this respect. Apparently much depends also on the field: The IEA research was done in the schools and no clear differences in response rate are reported. Inkeles organised the 4-hour interviews on modernity mostly in the factory, with a very small non-response of less than 1% (Inkeles and Smith 1974, p. 30). Such examples suggest no specific bias, but response rates from the Time Budget Study for example do. These rates varied from 90–100% for the East European countries to 60 – ca. 90% for the West European samples (Converse 1972, p. 67). In such a way a carefully designed comparable sampling structure might produce systematically biased findings. The magnitude of such a bias is hard to estimate, as in most non-response analysis.

4.2. The Content and Effects of the Interview

Two forms of bias may occur in cross-national research projects during the interviewing stages.

a. The *structure or wording* of the questionnaire is such that it favours specific patterns of answers in a certain direction. Labels as courtesy bias, response-set etc. apply

---

[10] Here again no systematic research is available. Recently an evaluative study of the organisation and decision of two Vienna Centre studies was proposed. The "Automation" project and the so-called "Hierarchy" study are examples of a cooperative versus replication model of cooperation. For details see Peschar and Wintersberger (1980).

for these problems and can be solved easily (see Elder 1976, p. 224). However, great cross-national differences may exist in the experience as such with questionnaires or special data collecting techniques. In reports about 4-hour interviews, in developing countries, people complain about "hard thinking" (Inkeles and Smith 1974, pp. 50—64). With regard to the IEA-six-subject surveys it has been remarked that the low average achievement scores of the four developing countries participating might be caused by the lack of experience with standardised test situations (Inkeles 1979). Although this problem has emerged more often in cross-cultural psychology, there is little empirical research available on systematic effects and strategies to cope with it (Brislin, Lonner and Thorndike 1973, pp. 68 ff; Poortinga 1977).

b. The most important systematic bias may be caused by *social-desirable* answers: trying to give a good impression with an answer. If the research goal is known to the interviewee this distortion may possibly occur. Social desirability may also have another connotation. When it is known that government authorities sponsor a project, one might expect to get more answers in line with government policy or statements. The same holds for research under the auspices of political parties or employer federations, as election and public opinion polls show. Especially in comparative research this type of bias may easily come in, when research is carried out in different social systems. It is apparently this version of social desirability that Messing refers to in his study on job satisfaction in the German Democratic Republic and the Federal Republic of Germany (Messing 1978, pp. 28—30). With regard to this possible source of bias empirical research is hardly undertaken (see for instance Schweizer 1978). We can expect it to be an important factor, however, in cross-national comparisons.

4.3. The Training of the Interview Staff

It goes beyond doubt that training of the interview staff is not only a major organisational problem but also one of competence. In countries with different amount of experience in both respects, it is of primary importance to train the interview staff to the same level of performance. IEA organised special conferences to train staff for their tasks in the six-subject-project, to be sure that the standardised approach was understood and interpreted properly (see Husén 1979). To be sure that the interviewers of another project do their best and do carry out interviews, in some countries they were threatened rather forcefully (Inkeles and Smith 1974, p. 58). As such, this may be influenced by local customs or experience, nevertheless, it might produce different information from the interviewees.

This is of course quite different when the interviewers are members of official bodies, or employed by government institutions. The main task in training the interview staff is to accomplish as little drift as possible from the agreed plan of research. Therefore a detailed account of fieldwork procedures is necessary in order to trace systematic bias that would invalidate the cross-national comparisons.

5. PROBLEMS OF ANALYSIS AND INTERPRETATION

5.1. The Infrastructure for Analysis

Analysis and interpretation are the final stages of a research project. It is obvious that the final quality depends as much on the efforts put into the former stages as on the ingenuity of the data analysis. From various multi-national projects it is also clear that these final stages take a lot of time, many times not foreseen in the schedules. The Time Budget data, for example, were collected in 1965/1966, were not analysed before 1968 and were reported in 1972. The initial stages of the project, however, went very fast: the project was proposed to the Vienna Centre in 1964 (Szalai 1972, pp. 16, 65 ff). The same holds for the seven-nation comparison reported by Verba, Nie and Kim (1978); data collection from 1966/67–1970/71 and subsequent analysis until the final report was finished in 1978. These two examples are by no means specific illustrations, although projects also exist where the data analysis was extremely smoothened by a very strict organisation. The IEA six-subject-data were collected in 1970 and 1971, the first reports already appeared in 1973, the other ones in 1975/76 (see Husén 1979, and Peaker 1975).

Two factors may be relevant for the long period usually necessary for the final stages of multinational projects. *Firstly,* as was mentioned before, one tends to move decisions on later stages in a project ahead ("We will see later"). Therefore preparation of data processing and analysis is not optimal and tends to start *after* the data are collected. Furthermore, it is clear that at that moment discussions on technical matters will be emphasised, losing sight of the theoretical and analytical strategy. Stone (1972) describes in detail which problems had to be overcome in this respect in the Time Budget Study.

Secondly, indeed there are many technical problems to be solved. Keypunching, cleaning of data, making files, exchanging tapes, etc. are all stages that can cause technical problems. Phillipps describes how it was done in the rather centralised IEA structure with two data processing centres in New York and Stockholm. The whole data collection was highly standardised and the data could mainly be machine-read, thus saving time and errors (Phillipps 1975, pp. 221–230).

This brings in another aspect of international cooperation, also mentioned at the 1972 Budapest conference: the inequality of access to technical facilities such as data processing centres and computers. It was remarked that cooperatively undertaken studies tend to develop into Safari-type studies if computing facilities are distributed unevenly (Allerbeck 1977, pp. 398 ff). Since then, the availability of computers has been increased enormously, and also statistical software has become available on a wider basis. Standard packages such as OSIRIS and SPSS are widely known and available on many computing systems. This offers at the same time an increase in standardisation. With every computation many options are available and these options may vary per computer package. Standardisation of options in the use of standard packages offers, therefore, many advantages and facilitates the choice of options as well.

Still another problem in this respect is the availability of "computer money" to run the calculations. As wide diversity exists in this respect (in some countries one has to pay cash, others from "allocated" money, while in again others it is not accounted at all), it is not easy to present general solutions to this mere financial problem. But the problem should be recognised in advance, and implemented in the research strategy of analysis.

Then, also seminars or workshops on data analysis can be organised to equal up the experiences of the multi-national group of researchers (see for instance Verba, Nie and Kim 1978, preface; Jennings and Farah 1977).

5.2. Strategies and Methods of Analysis

Most strategies and methods of analysis are not specific for cross-national comparative research. Frey (1979, pp. 279 ff) lists various steps to be taken after data collection: (1) gross marginals, (2) controlled marginals, (3) index and scale construction, (4) specific cross-tabulations to test hypotheses, (5) empirical cluster search and (6) analysis and reanalysis. Brislin, Lonner and Thorndike (1973, pp. 255–308) focus mainly on factor analysis and other multivariate techniques to be applied in cross-cultural designs. However, the choice of method and statistical techniques one wants to apply depends largely on the theoretical goals (see for instance Gostkowski 1978, pp. 97 ff). In this respect one may generally follow the steps suggested by Frey, up to Step 3. Index and scale construction involve many different activities. When instruments have been applied that were already validated in other research, this step consists "simply" of adding the variables with the appropriate weights into scales or indexes. When, however, new scales are to be developed, this firstly takes a lot of time (in order to validate them for all the participating countries) and secondly, makes it impossible to test hypotheses. The research can at best be descriptive. Step 4 may be the idealtypic situation; in practice, however, there are only a few projects where explicit hypotheses were tested or rejected.

The Verba, Nie and Kim research may be illustrative: the dependent variable "political participation" was constructed during the stages of analysis by means of factor analysis. Although the choice of items to be analysed, was – of course – guided by theoretical considerations, no clear predictions were written down with respect to the scales. The reported findings may therefore be seen as preliminary, waiting to be tested in a strict sense.

Another example may be mentioned. The IEA six-subject-studies employed a common strategy of data analyses according to the recommendations of a Statistical Committee. The main analytical procedure was stepwise regression analysis for both between-school and between-students analysis.[11] Therefore the enormous amount of variables had to be reduced and many composites were constructed. Variables were eliminated that showed only a very small relationship with the criterion after partialising out the influence of important input (= background) variables. The remaining variables were ordered into blocks (Peaker 1975, Chapter 3; a very clear description and examples are given by Thorndike 1973, pp. 64–70). Finally, the regression analysis was carried out with the stepwise inclusion of the various blocks of variables, according to the anticipated causal position in the model. Within each block also stepwise variables were entered in the equation, according to their contribution in the explained variance.[12] Such an analytical procedure is very suitable for explanatory purposes if one wants to know which

[11] No between-country analyses were run or reported in this way.

[12] It thus becomes clear that the contents of the various blocks for the six surveys might be very different, since their composition is based on an empirical selection of variables. Moreover, in the stepwise regression it is impossible to compare portions of contributed explained variance per variable, since these are dependent on the order in which the variables are entered in the regression.

71

variables contribute in the explained variance. It is, however, noteworthy that in the selection process also important variables that did not contribute anything were removed as well as the ones that might be theoretically relevant or those which had spurious relationships with the investigated criterion. The application of such techniques favours a non-theoretical state of mind and produces in an almost automatic way descriptive findings (see also Coleman 1975, pp. 338 ff). It seems to me that the statistical significance is made more important than the theoretical relevance of variables.

This is not a condemnation of the important work of IEA. It only shows that unless clear hypotheses are formulated and procedures of analyses are chosen accordingly *before* data collection, the results will be mainly exploratory and descriptive. Apart from this good theoretical reason to focus on certain processes and test them, there is another argument to decide on analysis strategy before it has to begin. If we view the current pile of data collected in multi-national research, one simply *has* to specify what one wants to know, otherwise one is drowned in the enormous amount of variables and variations. As Husén said about his long IEA experiences: one might also risk that "those who assisted us in planning data processing and statistical analysis were steering us, not we them" (Husén 1979, p. 383).

It might be clear by now that these problems of cross-national analysis are the very same as in "normal" quantitative research. The problems are multiplied and reinforced. Two specific issues, however, may be mentioned as they occur frequently in comparative research.

First the issue of standardised versus non-standardised variables. We already referred to this when discussing functional equivalence (Section 3). If one does not employ an absolute (literally identical) comparable instrument, the use of a standardised measure can be the only solution. Verba, Nie and Kim's measure on political participation *can* only be a measure that is nation-specific and therefore they *have* to apply standardised scales. Furthermore their dependent variables are not the *level* of political activity but the *relationship* of political activity to social class. Their focus, in other words, is on the differences per nation in such relationships which make the preference for standardised variables understandable (Verba, Nie and Kim 1978, pp. 40–42). Similar approaches have been applied in status attainment and mobility research (for instance Kerckhoff 1978).

In the IEA studies, however, much emphasis was put on the comparison of the absolute achievement scores. Questions such as: Why the average achievement is higher in this country than in the other, have been studied by Passow et al. (1976). This, of course, puts a heavy load on the construction of the instruments. As there is no general for-or-against, it must be remarked that standardisation has one rather big disadvantage. Standardised scores may largely depend on the variance, which may vary considerably per country. Once one has applied standardisation of variables, no pooled analyses can be undertaken anymore, in for instance factor or cluster analysis.

Secondly, also in fields of cross-national research other than education multivariate techniques on the basis of regression analysis have been applied. Status attainment and stratification research have developed considerably since the Blau and Duncan's treatment of path analysis. The amount of replications or comparative analyses is uncountable. For cross-national comparisons mostly the amount of explained variance was the main criterion applied. But this amount of variance is heavily dependent on the model, so one should be careful if different models are applied.

Furthermore, regression and path analysis assume a number of statistical conditons:

72

linear relationships, additivity, interval measures, uncorrelated residuals, homoscedasticity, low multicollinearity, reliable and valid measures. Although most of the conditions are specific for either the data or the model applied, it is especially the condition of linear relationships between variables that is interesting for cross-national research.

As is demonstrated in many stratification studies (see for instance Mayer 1979) the processes in different societies are rather alike. It can be argued, however, that the ways in which outcomes of processes are reflected may vary considerably. Thus, especially the non-linear relationships and interactions between variables are extremely important and should be investigated. This is clearly demonstrated in the cited Participation Study where non-linear relationships and interactions are of the first order (Verba, Nie and Kim 1978, for instance pp. 85, 150 ff) and in Form's Autoworkers Study (Form 1976, pp. 218 ff; see also Spenner 1975).

Various statistical techniques have been developed to deal with non-linear relationships and interactions. Most computer packages have options to test on linearity. Dummy-variables, multiplicative or additive terms can also be included in the equations, if one expects specific interactions. This is done even more conveniently with Goodman's model for log-linear analysis, especially designed for detecting interactions of higher order (see also Treiman 1977b, pp. 1047 ff). Furthermore, Munck (1979) has applied LISREL models with latent variables on the IEA-data.

Apart from the elaboration of structural models, the LISREL-procedure also proved to be of value for the assessment of equivalent measures of achievement in various countries (i.e. functional equivalence) and the development of scales for cross-national comparisons.

All these techniques are avaliable and have been employed occasionally in cross-national research. The enormous amount of available cross-national data waiting for further analysis, however, has clearly prevented the application of such or more advanced models for the time being.

5.3. Interpretation

The same data may lead to different interpretations. This seems to be especially true for cross-national comparative research (see for instance the discussion between Galtung and Sicinsky, in Ornauer et al. 1976, pp. 45–170) and much has to do with a detailed analysis of available data. The interpretation of findings of most of the comparative projects has simply concentrated on country differences of the descriptive type.

Two points may be mentioned that are particularly important in the interpretation of findings.

a. The choice of the research design imposes certain restrictions with regard to the populations involved in the research. We do not discuss the problem of comparable samples, since it is a standard technical matter. When applying experiments, matched groups, selection of cities of a certain size, factories etc., other aspects of generalisation come in. Then it is not a matter of statistical representativity anymore, but a matter of "qualitative reasoning" and argumentation what one may learn about the comparative findings. Then again the role of theory and the choice of strategic comparisons are vital. Here we touch on problems of comparing nations and comparability, discussed in the respective chapters by Galtung and Loetsch.

b. Most cross-national comparative projects are based on information collected at the individual level. Nevertheless, one aims to draw conclusions at a system (school, factory) or national (country) level. Therefore data have to be aggregated up to the appropriate structural level. There is a massive body of literature dealing with the various kinds of fallacies in multilevel analysis to which we may refer (Hannan 1971, Falter 1978).

6. CONCLUSIONS

In the foregoing sections we have discussed various quantitative aspects of cross-national research. It has not been my purpose to give an exhaustive treatment of all research problems, especially not since many of such problems also occur in within-national research. Therefore, shortcomings in cross-national research are also present in "normal" research practice.

Should we therefore no longer be critical with regard to the applied designs, instruments and techniques? We feel that especially in cross-national cooperation the contrary should be the case. First, many more people (researchers and respondents) are linked to such an enterprise, and one should be cautious not to waste energy and time. Secondly, such an endeavour has either theoretical or political and practical consequences and therefore one should be sure that relevant issues are investigated in an appropriate way.

From our overview it became clear that the quantitative "technical" research problems are closely related to the theoretical issues of the study. Although this is not the specific subject of this chapter (see the chapter by Berting), the theoretical decisions should be taken before one can decide on aspects of design, instruments and techniques. In practice, however, such technical decisions seem to be taken on their own: We may recall the discussion on country sampling that appears to be mainly guided by the principle of convenience or political accessibility.

The preference for cross-sectional designs is also hardly related to theoretical questions, but to a principle of feasibility and easy agreement, avoiding or postponing the theoretical issues. It must be admitted that these questions might not easily be solved in a comparison of many countries. But this approach is turning the world upside down: the theoretical question should precede and then the country selection follows; and not the other way round. Furthermore if it is that difficult, then one should rather concentrate on modest questions and should not be too ambitious. Another point resulting from our review seems to be that, in general, the technical problems of quantitative research are solved. The appropriate designs, instruments, sampling techniques and procedures of analysis have been developed and are available. It is merely a problem of application and of making the appropriate choices.

If we were to sketch the average cross-national study, then it would be a project where many countries are involved in a cross-sectional design with mainly newly developed instruments, interviewing large representative (random?) samples to get a massive amount of data that can be analysed with advanced statistical techniques. This is hardly done, because there are too many data, too little time and too many unreflected questions. The massive enterprise therefore will not answer any theoretical question but end up in detailed descriptions of the many variables that have been measured without any special relationship.

Admittedly, this is a black and white picture, but I am afraid that it is not a caricature of what actually happens. One could also imagine another strategy that might pay off in a better way: the available tools do provide better opportunities. Also if one maintains that cross-national theory is not developed far enough, or that such a goal is too ambitious, one can still select critical and strategic comparisons. Przeworski and Teune (1970) discuss, for instance, the most-different or most-similar designs. Then, cross-sectional approaches do not have to be the only choices. If one concentrates on differences in growth rates, a time-design is appropriate. If one is interested in developmental processes, longitudinal designs can be applied.

This implies that more time should be spent in the first — exploratory — stages of a cross-national project, and that qualitative knowledge has to be collected and evaluated before the collaborative quantitative enterprise starts. It will then probably also become clear that on the basis of such detailed knowledge, it is not useful anymore to include so many countries in the design as is many times done. Focussed and more intensive comparisons between a few selected countries might be a better strategy to avoid the usual large-scale surface research. It may be expected that participants in such an international comparison will not be so disappointed that they can only agree with Form (1976, p. xviii): "I did enjoy most of the enterprise, but I'm glad that it is over".[13]

---

[13] This is the end of a long citation dealing with the comparative research enterprise: Since it deals with a number of relevant issues, we include the whole citation as well (without agreeing with everything stated). "But I do have some unsolicited advice for people who want to do a study something like mine. Moderate-sized comparative studies should be avoided. One can learn much from a single case or from comparing two cases; four cases are just enough to give the researcher some idea of the range of variation in the phenomena under study, but not enough to produce firm trends. It is not wise to postpone important decisions to the field-work stage. Extensive and detailed research decisions should be written down prior to taking to the field, and changed only after careful deliberation. In the field, the researcher will be tempted to take the advice of local sociologists, assuming that they know their local culture. This often turns out not to be the case especially when they are not specialists in the area under study. There is a mystique about comparative research which probably arises because a certain amount of sloppiness in inevitable. Comparative research is only a special form of replicative study where one must resolve the dilemma of maintaining a design for the sake of methodological consistency or changing it because of unanticipated events and thereby lose comparability of findings. I tended to opt for consistency, but am now not sure that I made the correct decisions. I did enjoy most of the enterprise, but I'm glad that it is over" (Form 1976, preface, pp. xvii–xviii).

REFERENCES

Allerbeck, K. (1977) Analysis and Inference in Cross-National Survey Research. In: A. Szalai and R. Petrella (eds.) *Cross-National Comparative Survey Research: Theory and Practice;* 373–402. Oxford: Pergamon Press.

Almasy, E., A. Balandier and J. Delatte (1976) *Comparative Survey Analysis. An Annotated Bibliography 1967–1973.* Beverly Hills and London: Sage.

Andorka, R. and K. Zagorski (1978) Structural Factors of Social Mobility in Hungary and Poland. Paper presented at the Research Committee on Social Stratification, ISA-Congress, Uppsala.

Armer, M. (1973) Methodological Problems and Possibilities in Comparative Research. In: M. Armer and A. D. Grimshaw (eds.) *Comparative Social Research. Methodological Problems and Strategies;* 49–79. New York: Wiley.

Armer, M. and A. D. Grimshaw (eds.) (1973) *Comparative Social Research. Methodological Problems and Strategies.* New York: Wiley.

Armer, M. and A. Schnaiberg (1973) Measuring Individual Modernity. In: M. Armer and A. D. Grimshaw (eds.) *Comparative Social Research. Methodological Problems and Strategies;* 274–281. New York: Wiley.

Bergmann, H. (1979) The Project History and Scope. In: J. Forslin, A. Sarapata and A. M. Whitehill (eds.) *Automation and Industrial Workers,* Vol. 1, Part 1; 8–16. Oxford: Pergamon Press.

Berting, J., F. Geyer and R. Jurkovich (eds.) (1979) *Problems in International Comparative Research in the Social Sciences.* Oxford: Pergamon Press.

Björn, L. (1979) Labor Parties, Economic Growth and the Redistribution of Income in Five Capitalist Democracies. In: *Comparative Social Research* 2; 93–128.

Bovenkerk, F., B. Kilborne, F. Raveau and D. Smith (1979) Comparative Aspects of Research on Discrimination Against Non-White Citizens in Great Britain, France and the Netherlands. In: J. Berting, F. Geyer and R. Jurkovich (eds.) *Problems in International Comparative Research in the Social Sciences;* 105–122. Oxford: Pergamon Press.

Brislin, R. W., W. J. Lonner and R. M. Thorndike (1973) *Cross-Cultural Methods.* New York: Wiley.

Burawoy, M. (1977) Social Structure, Homogenization and "the Process of Status Attainment in the United States and Great Britain". In: *American Journal of Sociology,* 82, 1031–1042.

Coleman, J. S. (1975) Methods and Results in the IEA Studies of Effects of School and Learning. In: *Review of Educational Research,* 45; 355–386.

Collaris, J. W. M. and J. A. Kropman (1978) *Van Jaar tot Jaar. Tweede Fase.* Nijmegen: Instituut voor Toegepaste Sociologie.

Colton, S. (1979) Chaotic Uniformity in European Higher Education Statistics. In: *European Journal of Education,* 14: 379–389.

Converse, Ph. E. (1972) The Implementation of Survey Design. In: A. Szalai (ed.) *The Use of Time. Daily Activities of Urban and Suburban Populations in Twelve Countries;* 43–68. The Hague and Paris: Mouton.

Dronkers, J. and U. de Jong (1979) Jencks and Fägerlind in a Dutch way. In: *Social Science Information,* 18; 761–781.

Duncan, O. D., D. L. Featherman and B. Duncan (1972) *Socio-economic Background and Achievement.* New York: Seminar Press.

Elder, J. W. (1976) Comparative Cross-National Methodology. In: *Annual Review of Sociology,* 2; 209–230.

Fägerlind, I. (1975) *Formal Education and Adult Earnings. A Longitudinal Study on the Economic Benefits of Education.* Stockholm: Almqvist and Wiksell.

Falter, J. W. (1978) Some Theoretical and Methodological Problems of Multilevel Analysis Reconsidered. In: *Social Science Information,* 17; 841–869.

Form, W. H. (1976) *Blue Collar Stratification: Autoworkers in Four Countries.* Princeton: Princeton University Press.

Forslin, J., A. Sarapata and A. M. Whitehill (eds.) (1979) *Automation and Industrial Workers. A Fifteen Nation Study.* Vol. 1, Part 1. Oxford: Pergamon Press.

Framhein, G. (ed.) (1980) Report of a Special Seminar on "University Students – Their Training and Conception of Life". To appear in: E. van Trotsenburg (ed.) *Higher Education – A Field of Study. Proceedings of the 3rd International Congress of EARDHE,* Vol. 3. Frankfurt: Lang.

Framhein, G. and S. C. Mills (1979) Infrastructure – the Third Element in International Comparative Research In: J. Berting, F. Geyer and R. Jurkovich (eds.) *Problems in International Comparative Research in the Social Sciences;* 123–135. Oxford: Pergamon Press.

Frey, F. W. (1970) Cross-Cultural Survey Research in Political Science. In: R. T. Holt and J. E. Turner (eds.) *The Methodology of Comparative Research;* 173–294. New York: Free Press.

Friedrichs, J. (ed.) (1978) *Stadtentwicklungen in kapitalistischen und sozialistischen Ländern.* Hamburg: Rowohlt.

Garnier, M. and M. Hout (1976) Inequality of Educational Opportunity in France and the United States. In: *Social Science Research,* 5; 225–246.

Girard, A. and P. Clerck (1964) Nouvelles données sur l'orientation scolaire ou moment de l'entrée en 6ème. In: *Population,* 19; 829–872.

Girod, R. (1971) *Mobilité Sociale.* Genève: Droz.

Glazer, W. (1977) The Process of Cross-National Survey Research. In: A. Szalai and R. Petrella (eds.) *Cross-National Comparative Survey Research: Theory and Practice;* 403–436. Oxford: Pergamon Press.

Gostkowski, Z. (1978) *Analyses of Educational Attainment and its Distribution in Selected Countries. A Study in Methodology of Measurement.* Warsawa: The Polish Academy of Sciences.

Haan, J. (1975) Het Computerprogramma MATCHEN. Bulletin no. 5 Vakgroep Methoden en Technieken, Sociologisch Instituut, State University of Groningen.

Hannan, M. T. (1971) *Aggregation and Disaggregation in Sociology.* Lexington, Mass.: Lexington Books.

Härnqvist, K. and A. Svensson (1973) The Individual Statistics Project. A Swedish Data Bank for Educational Studies, in: *Sociological Microjournal* 7; 33–42.

Hazelrigg, L. E. and M. A. Garnier (1976) Occupational Mobility in Industrial Societies. A Comparative Analysis of Different Access to Occupational Ranks in Seventeen Countries. In: *American Sociological Review,* 41; 498–510.

Holt, R. T. and J. E. Turner (eds.) (1970) *The Methodology of Comparative Research.* New York: Free Press.

Husén, T. (1979) An International Research Venture in Retrospect: The IEA-Surveys, In: *Comparative Education Review,* 23; 371–385.

Hymes, D. (1970) Linguistic Aspects of Comparative Political Research. In: R. T. Holt and J. E. Turner (eds.) *The Methodology of Comparative Research;* 295–342. New York: Free Press.

IDE – International Research Group (1977) Industrial Democracy in Europe (IDE): An International Comparative Study. In: *Social Science Information,* 15; 177–203.

IDE – International Research Group (1980) *Industrial Democracy in Europe.* London: Oxford University Press.

Inglehart, R. (1978) Value Priorities, Life Satisfaction and Political Dissatisfaction among Western Publics. In: *Comparative Studies in Sociology,* 1; 173–202.

Inkeles, A. (1978) National Differences in Individual Modernity. In: *Comparative Studies in Sociology,* 1; 47–72.

Inkeles, A. (1979) National Differences in Scholastic Performance, In: *Comparative Education Review,* 23; 386–407.

Inkeles, A. and D. H. Smith (1974) *Becoming Modern. Individual Change in Six Developing Countries.* Cambridge, Mass.: Harvard University Press.

Jackmann, R. W. (1975) *Politics and Social Equality. A Comparative Analysis.* New York: Wiley.

Jacob, Ph. and B. (1971) *Values and the Active Community. A Cross-National Study of the Influences of Local Leadership.* New York: Free Press.

Jansson, C. G. (1974) Projekt Metropolitan. In: Longitudinell Problematik II; 36–50. Report from a symposium at the Psychological Institute, 22–23. April, Stockholm University.

Jencks, C. (1972) *Inequality.* New York: Basic Books.

Jennings, M. K. and B. G. Farah (1977) Continuities in Comparative Research Strategies: The Mannheim Data Confrontation Seminar. In: *Social Science Information,* 16; 231–249.

Jugendwerk der Deutschen Shell (Hrsg.) (1977) *Jugend in Europa. Eine vergleichende Analyse zwischen der Bundesrepublik Deutschland, Frankreich und Gross-Brittannien.* 3 Bände. Bd. I Vorstudie. Bd. II Tabelenteil, Bd. III Kommentar.

Kerckhoff, A. C. (1974) Stratification Processes and Outcomes in England and the U. S. In: *American Sociological Review,* 39; 789–801.

Kerckhoff, A. C. (1977) The Realism of Educational Aspirations in England and the U. S. In: *American Sociological Review,* 42; 563–570.

Kerckhoff, A. C. (1978) Methodological Problems and Prospects in Comparative Status Attainment Research in England and the U. S. Paper presented at the Res. Comm. on Social Stratification, ISA Congress, Uppsala.

Lammers, C. J. (1978) The Comparative Sociology of Organisations. In: *Annual Review of Sociology,* 4; 485–510.

Malewska, H. and V. Peyre (1976) *Juvenile Delinquency and Development: A Cross-National Survey.* Sage Research Papers in the Social Sciences. Beverly Hills and London: Sage Publications.

Maurice, M., A. Sorge and M. Warner (1980) Societal Differences in Organising Manufacturing Units: A Comparison of France, West Germany and Great Britain. In: *Organisation Studies,* 1; 59–86.

Mayer, K. U. (1979) Class Formation and Social Reproduction. In: J. Berting, F. Geyer and R. Jurkovich (eds.) *Problems in International Comparative Research in the Social Sciences;* 37–56. Oxford: Pergamon Press.

Mechanic, D. (1975) The Comparative Study of Health Care. Delivery Systems. In: *Annual Review of Sociology,* 1; 43–65.

Meyer, J. W., N. B. Tuma and K. Zagorski (1979) Education and Occupational Mobility: A Comparison of Polish and American Men. In: *American Journal of Sociology,* 84; 978–986.

Messing, M. (1978) *Arbeitszufriedenheit im Systemvergleich. Eine emprische Untersuchung an Bau- und Montagearbeitern in beiden Teilen Deutschlands.* Stuttgart: Kohlhammer.

Müller, W. and K. U. Mayer (1976) *Chancengleichheit durch Bildung?* Stuttgart: Ernst Klepp Verlag.

Munck, I. (1979) *Model Building in Comparative Education: Applications of the LISREL Method to Cross-National Survey Data.* Stockholm: Almqvist and Wiksell.

Nagi, M. H. (1977) Language Variables in Cross-Cultural Research. In: *International Social Science Journal,* XXIX; 167–177.

Nießen, M. and J. Peschar (1980) Comparative Research on Education 1975–1980. A Review and Appraisal. Paper presented at the Conference on the Origins and Operation of Educational Systems. ISA. Res. Com. on Sociology of Education. Paris. To appear in: M. Nießen and J. Peschar (eds.) (1981) *Comparative Research on Education,* Budapest: Akadémiai Kiadó.

Oppenheim, A. N. and J. Torney (1974) *The Measurement of Children's Civic Attitudes in Different Nations.* IEA Monograph Studies no. 2. Stockholm. Almqvist and Wiksell; and New York: John Wiley and Sons.

Ornauer, H., H. Wiberg, J. Sicinski and J. Galtung (eds.) (1976) *Images of the World in the Year 2000.* The Hague and Paris: Mouton.

Passow, A. H., H. J. Noah, M. A. Eckstein and J. R. Mallea (1976) *The National Case Study: An Empirical Comparative Study of Twenty-One Educational Systems. International Studies in Evaluation, vol. VII.* Stockholm: Almqvist and Wiksell; and New York: John Wiley and Sons.

Peaker, G. F. (1975) *An Empirical Study of Education in Twenty-One Countries: A Technical Report. International Studies in Evaluation, vol. VIII.* Stockholm: Almqvist and Wiksell; and New York: John Wiley and Sons.

Peschar, J. L. (1978a) L'Histoire se répète? Na twee generaties buitenlands stratificatie- en mobiliteitsonderzoek. In: J. L. Peschar and W. Ultee (eds.) *Sociale Stratificatie;* 26–39. Deventer: Van Loghum Slaterus.

Peschar, J. L. (1978b) Educational Opportunity within and between Holland and Sweden: The Semi-Experimental Approach. In: *Sociologische Gids,* 25, 273–296.

Peschar, J. and H. Wintersberger (1980) Progress Report on the Development of the Vienna Centre Research Programme on WORK. Working Document no. 2. Vienna, European Coordination Centre for Research and Documentation in the Social Sciences.

Phillipps, R. W. (1975) IEA Data Processing. In: G. Peaker, *An Empirical Study of Education in Twenty-One Countries: A Technical Report;* 221–230. Stockholm: Almqvist and Wiksell.

Pohoski, M., S. Pöntinen and K. Zagorski (1978) Social Mobility and Socio-Economic Achievement. In: Allardt, E. and Wesolowski, W. (eds.) *Social Structure and Change. Finland and Poland: Comparative Perspective.* Chapter V; 147—164. Warsaw: Polish Scientific Publishers.

Poortinga, Y. H. (ed.) (1977) *Basic Problems in Cross-Cultural Psychology.* Amsterdam: Swets and Zeitlinger.

Postletwaithe, T. N. (1974) Target Populations, Sampling, Instrument Construction and Analysis Procedures. In: *Comparative Education Review,* 18; 164—180.

Przeworski, A. and H. Teune (1970) *The Logic of Comparative Social Inquiry.* New York: Wiley.

Psacharopoulos, G. (1977) Family Background, Education and Achievement: A Path Model of Earning Determinants in the United Kingdom and some Alternatives. In: *British Journal of Sociology,* 28; 321—335.

Rokkan, S. (ed.) (1968) *Comparative Research Across Cultures and Nations.* Paris: Mouton.

Rokkan, S. (1970) Cross-Cultural, Cross-Societal and Cross-National Research. Chapter X in: *Main Trends of Research in the Social and Human Sciences.* Part One: Social Sciences; 645—689. The Hague and Paris: Mouton.

Rokkan, S., J. Viet, S. Verba and E. Almasy (1969) *Comparative Survey Analysis.* The Hague and Paris: Mouton.

Schaff, A. (1979) Introduction in: J. Forslin, A. Sarapata and A. M. Whitehill (eds.) *Automation and Industrial Workers. A Fifteen Nation Study.* Vol. 1, Part 1; 3—7. Oxford: Pergamon Press.

Schatzmann, L. and A. L. Strauss (1973) *Field Research: Strategies for a Natural Sociology.* Englewood Cliffs, N. J.: Prentice Hall.

Scheuch, E. K. (1968) The Cross-Cultural Use of Sample Surveys: Problems of Comparability. In: S. Rokkan (ed.). *Comparative Research Across Cultures and Nations;* 176—209. The Hague and Paris: Mouton.

Schweizer, T. (1978) Data Quality and Data Quality Control in Cross-Cultural Studies. In: *Behavior Science Research,* 13; 125—150.

Seeman, M. (1976) Some Real and Imaginary Consequences of Social Mobility: A French-American Comparison. In: *American Journal of Sociology,* 82; 757—782.

Sewell, W. H. and R. M. Hauser (1975) *Education, Occupation and Earnings.* New York: Academic Press.

Smelser, N. J. (1976) *Comparative Methods in the Social Sciences.* Englewood Cliffs, N. J.: Prentice-Hall.

Smith, D. H. and A. Inkeles (1975) Individual Modernizing Experiences and Psycho-Social Modernity: Validation of the OM Scales in Six Developing Countries. In: *International Journal of Comparative Sociology,* 16; 155—173.

Spenner, K. I. (1975) The Internal Stratification of the Working Class: A Re-Analysis. In: *American Sociological Review,* 25; 237—244.

Stone, Ph. J. (1972) The Analysis of Time-Budget Data. In: A. Szalai (ed.) *The Use of Time. Daily Activities of Urban and Suburban Populations in Twelve Countries;* 89—111. The Hague and Paris: Mouton.

Szalai, A. (ed.) (1972) *The Use of Time. Daily Activities of Urban and Suburban Populations in Twelve Countries.* The Hague and Paris: Mouton.

Szalai, A. and R. Petrella (eds.) (1977) *Cross-National Comparative Survey Research: Theory and Practice.* Oxford: Pergamon Press.

Teune, H. (1977) Analysis and Interpretation in Cross-National Survey Research. In: A. Szalai and R. Petrella (eds.). *Cross-National Comparative Survey Research: Theory and Practice;* 95–128. Oxford: Pergamon Press.

Thorndike, R. L. (1973) *Reading Comprehension Education in Fifteen Countries: An Empirical Study. International Studies in Evaluation. Vol. III.* Stockholm: Almqvist and Wiksell; and New York: John Wiley and Sons.

Tomassen, R. F. (1978) Introduction: Comparative Sociology. The State of the Art. In: *Comparative Studies in Sociology,* 1; 1–15.

Treiman, D. J. (1975) Problems of Concept and Measurement in the Comparative Study of Occupational Mobility. In: *Social Science Research,* 4; 183–230.

Treiman, D. J. (1977a) *Occupational Prestige in Comparative Perspective.* New York: Academic Press.

Treiman, D. J. (1977b) Toward Methods for a Quantitative Comparative Sociology: A Reply to Burawoy. In: *American Journal of Sociology,* 82; 1042–1056.

Treiman, D. J. and K. Terrell (1975) The Process of Status Attainment in the United States and Great Britain. In: *American Journal of Sociology,* 81; 563–583.

Vallier, I. (ed.) (1971) *Comparative Methods in Sociology: Essays on Trends and Applications.* Berkeley and Los Angeles: University of California Press.

Verba, S. (1971) Cross-National Survey Research: The Problem of Credibility. In: I. Vallier (ed.) *Comparative Methods in Sociology: Essays on Trends and Applications;* 309–356. Berkely and Los Angeles: University of California Press.

Verba, S. and N. H. Nie (1973) *Participation in America.* New York: Harper.

Verba, S., N. H. Nie and J. Kim (1978) *Participation and Political Equality: a Seven Nation Comparison.* Cambridge: Cambridge University Press.

Walker, D. A. (1976) *The IEA Six Subject Survey: An Empirical Study of Education in Twenty-One Countries. International Studies in Evaluation, Vol. IX.* Stockholm: Almqvist and Wiksell; and New York: John Wiley and Sons.

Weiss, P. (1979) Twenty Years After "Social Mobility in Industrial Society". Paper presented at the Research Committee on Social Stratification. ISA, Berlin (GDR) November.

Weiss, P. (1980) A Model of Ties between Education and Social Mobility in some Industrialized Countries. Paper presented at the Research Committee on Social Stratification. ISA, Austin (Texas), February.

Wiatr, J. (1977) The Role of Theory in the Process of Cross-National Survey Research. In: A. Szalai and R. Petrella (eds.) *Cross-National Comparative Survey Research: Theory and Practice.* 347–372. Oxford: Pergamon Press.

Qualitative Aspects in Cross-National Comparative Research and the Problem of Functional Equivalence

by Manfred Nießen

1. INTRODUCTION

When dealing with qualitative aspects in comparative research one is faced with a contradictory situation: On the one hand there is a frequent demand to include qualitative procedures in comparative research, interestingly enough very often at the end of quantitative studies (cf. Passow et al. 1976, p. 290; Kelly 1978, p. 117; Husen 1979, pp. 384 ff; Mayer 1979, p. 51; Köbben 1979; Schweitzer 1979). On the other hand one hardly finds reports on qualitative comparative studies or on how qualitative aspects in comparative studies were dealt with. What is so very often requested does not seem to be realised appropriately.

The treatment of qualitative aspects in comparative research can thus only to a limited extent refer to "practical" research in the sense of presenting elaborated approaches how to proceed. There is hardly anything to be found. Therefore, we first address the question: Why are qualitative aspects so often — programmatically — referred to? Following this, the next step to clarify the topic is indicated by the question: What is the methodological core of the problem of qualitative aspects in comparative research? After briefly elaborating these two general aspects the paper will then turn to concrete examples in order to demonstrate the necessity of an explicit approach to the methodological problem. Since the realisation of requests for qualitative approaches is largely missing, the examples have to concentrate on "negative" cases, i.e. those where turning explicitly to qualitative aspects seems to be imperative but is not done. Finally, some more general considerations will follow on the role of qualitative methods (and of national background reports) as well as on the impact of organisational patterns on the research strategy as far as our problem is concerned.

83

2. WHY TO STRESS QUALITATIVE ASPECTS —
THE BACKGROUND OF THE PROBLEM

It is commonplace to begin texts on comparative methodology by stating that all scholarly thinking is comparative and that comparative studies are faced with the same methodological problems as those not predominantly designed as comparative ones; it is said that just the focal points of reasoning or the aspects on which emphasis is laid might be different. This perspective is emphasised for instance in such different texts on problems of comparative research as Przeworski—Teune (1970) on the one hand and Smelser (1976) on the other. The latter plainly asserts: ". . . the methodological problems facing 'comparativists' are the same as those facing all social-scientific investigators" (ibid., p. 3).

However, if "comparativists" are not faced with any special problem one should question the necessity of books such as, for instance, those just mentioned. Instead of general methodological considerations which one would expect following the notion that all studies are comparative in some way or another, they present and elaborate on specific problems of comparisons. This discrepancy between the programmatical starting point of the texts and the specific aspects on which they concentrate leads, therefore, to the assumption that two different meanings of "comparative" are involved. The one is that every assertion needs a point of reference and is "comparative" with regard to this point of reference. With this meaning in mind, all scholarly thinking is undoubtedly comparative.

The second meaning refers to the investigation of phenomena being situated in different contexts, where the fact of being part of different contexts is of special interest to the investigation and deliberately chosen. With this meaning in mind the emphasis on specific aspects of comparative research turns out to be comprehensible. Apparently, comparative cross-national, cross-cultural and related studies in social sciences deal with problems so complex and manifold — different levels of analysis and complexity, problems of language, of common reference, cooperation, etc. — that authors mostly forget that "everything is comparative" and concentrate on the specificity of their problems. This reflects the fact that comparative (cross-national, cross—cultural) research is faced with problems which by their special shape, combination and additional facets result not only in an increased complexity but in specific methodological requirements (as has already been stressed by Scheuch 1968, p. 179; cf. also Verba et al. 1978, p. 34). Brislin et al. (1973, p. 12) refer to the core of these methodological problems of comparative research when saying that the "*meaning* of every aspect of any investigation is important, and it is especially important for cross-cultural work since the researcher does not know the *meaning* that people of other cultures attach to our research process".

The specific feature of comparative research which requires methodological considerations of its own lies hence in the fact that its objects are situated in different contexts and that the fact of being situated in exactly those contexts is of special interest to the research. Mokrzycki's definition of comparative research as "those comparisons that are faced with the specific problems due to the system-boundness of social phenomena" (Mokrzycki 1979, p. 95; also see his chapter in this volume) is therefore adopted. Context-boundness being the "raison d'être of comparative research" (ibid., p. 96) makes up its distinctive character and is responsible for the fact that qualitative aspects are a salient feature in it.

From this Mokrzycki draws two conclusions. The first is that it is inappropriate to adopt a philosophy of science being devised for a different realm (natural sciences) in an unqualified way for social sciences and in particular for comparative social sciences — mainly because it does not take the context-boundness into account. Rather, a thorough methodological reflection of the research actually done in this field would be necessary to come to an "indigenous" methodology. Second, because of their context-boundness, phenomena and events should not be compared directly. "Traditional" comparative research is said to conceive comparability as an attribute of phenomena whereas Mokrzycki relates it to systems. These should be the object of comparisons, and phenomena only as part of them (cf. Mokrzycki 1979, p. 102).

With these conclusions a demand for an alternative approach is presented. However, when taking seriously the demand for an "indigenous" methodological reflection of the research actually done, it turns out that in this research comparability is not always conceived as an attribute of phenomena and events only, and that it does not completely disregard their contextual embedding. Verba, for example, attributes the "credibility" of comparisons to the way the context-boundness of phenomena is handled. "The problem of comparability of measures taken from two different social systems derives from the fact that the measures are embedded in different structural and cultural contexts.... . Under the circumstances the best way to increase comparability is to maintain the contextual grounding of the measures when making comparisons" (Verba 1971, p. 314; see also e.g. Inkeles 1972, p. 21). So even in the research which adheres in its programmatical statements to the philosophy of science adopted from other fields, it has proven necessary to treat elements as those of specific contexts. The demands for qualitative approaches referred to in the beginning are characteristic of that. Whether, however, the formulated insights resulted in sufficient and adequate measures is a different question with regard to which Mokrzycki's criticism is undoubtedly justified. But it is the quest for methodological reflection of the work actually done in the field of comparative social sciences — Mokrzycki's first conclusion — which shows that in the field the problem of context-boundness has already emerged and that attempts to solve it had to be made. Notwithstanding the respective philosophy of science adopted, these attempts should be made use of. With regard to Mokrzycki's second conclusion this means a shift in emphasis from an alternative approach to the elaboration of possibilities and necessities inherent in existing research.

We thus take existing comparative research as a starting point for the further elaboration of qualitative aspects. One then has to be aware that in the literature context-boundness is closely related to the problem of establishing equivalence when studying the same problem in different settings. Moreover functional equivalence can be regarded as the methodological core of the problem to cope with the context-boundness of phenomena.

3. FUNCTIONAL EQUIVALENCE — THE CORE OF THE PROBLEM

In 1968 Scheuch graded as "major progress" in comparative research the "willingness . . . to aim at equivalence in meaning". This essential step should however be followed "by the understanding that equivalence of meaning is only a special case of the general property of 'functional equivalence of indicator meaning'" (Scheuch 1968, p. 184).

Yet, three years later Verba still complained that "there is more reference in the literature to the importance of functional equivalence than there are clear definitions of what exactly a functional equivalent is or how you know one when you see it" (Verba 1971, pp. 314 ff). However, the wish to "know a functional equivalent when you see it" might be misleading and not quite adequate to the very concept of functional equivalence, especially when regarding Scheuch's demand for equivalence of *indicator* meaning. Accordingly, Verba himself in a later text refers to functional equivalence by stating that "the same variable may be indexed by a variety of items, and different items may be the most appropriate indicators in different settings" (Verba et al. 1978, p. 36). This means that in order to ascertain whether an item is functionally equivalent to another one, one has to regard both their functions as an indicator for *one* more general dimension (be it a concept, hypothesis or another theoretical notion). It is therefore inadequate to strive for "knowing a functional equivalent when you see it" as *there is no one single functional equivalent.* The property of functional equivalence can only be ascribed to items (by definition more than one) when the relations between these items and one single more general dimension prove to be equivalent. Therefore, phenomena are not equivalent as such but only "in those respects that are relevant to the problem at hand" (Verba et al. 1978, p. 36).

This, then, is the point to be made. "Functional equivalence" is a concept describing *relationships.* On the basis of this concept comparability cannot be conceived as an attribute of elements but as an *attribute of the elements' relationships to a more general point of reference.*[1] When ascertaining whether functional equivalence can be assumed or not, the context is as important as the elements themselves. For the elements' qualification to indicate a more general dimension in an equivalent way depends on their meaning and status in their respective contexts. Therefore, by way of equivalence considerations the contexts or what Mokrzycki called the systems are included in any sound comparison.

A parallel discussion can be found in the fields of cross-cultural anthropology (see for instance Goodenough 1970, pp. 112 ff) and psychology (see, for instance, Brislin et al. 1973, pp. 24 ff). It centres around the distinction between "emic" (internal and context-bound) and "etic" (generalised and not context-bound) categories which is derived from linguistics. It is not questioned that comparison requires the use of "etic" concepts, i.e. those applicable to all the cases compared. However, much attention is given to the necessity to relate them to the "emic" concepts, i.e. those which are characteristic and specific for the various contexts and which are used in them. Berry (1969, p. 125) breaks down this process into three steps: comparative research must begin with tentatively predefined categories and concepts which are applied in a tentative way as an "imposed etic" to the units to be compared. They are

---

[1] Frey (1970, pp. 188 ff) is concerned that the "truly cross-cultural quality of the most abstract conceptualisation trickles away in the parochial subordinate conceptualisation that actually defines the research" so that "the particular measures employed in relation to a seemingly cross-cultural concept reintroduce specific cultural limitations". This is apparently based on a conception of comparability as an attribute of elements (or concepts). The "parochialism" of subordinate concepts or of measures is not a threat to comparability provided that their qualification to represent a "cross-cultural concept" is given.

subsequently to be modified to become "an adequate description from within" the units so that they turn to "emic" concepts. Based on these "emic" concepts new categories are to be built up which are again valid for all the compared units ("derived etics").

The emic–etic discussion stresses more the procedural aspects of relating context-bound elements to more general dimensions than do many of the remarks concerning functional equivalence (which are often merely concerned with the question of definition). The emic–etic distinction may thus help to clarify that functional equivalence requires two processes: *theorising and qualitative reasoning.* Theoretical considerations are indispensable in order to formulate relevant general dimensions and criteria of pertinence to them. This is commonly accepted (see e.g. Wiatr 1977, p. 367 and Berting in this volume). [2] They have to be supplemented by qualitative reasoning which is necessary for knowing, identifying and interpreting the context-bound elements. Both together are the basis for relating the specific phenomena and the general dimension, for interpreting the context-bound events in the light of theoretical notions, and for modifying the general concepts in the light of context-specific phenomena. To strive for functional equivalence includes all of this.

Therefore, both aspects, i.e. the character of the concept as one describing relationships and the necessity of theorising as well as of qualitative reasoning for ascertaining whether given indicators are in their relationship to a more general dimension functionally equivalent, render obsolete a distinction between "appropriateness" and "equivalence" as has been proposed by Armer (1973, p. 53). Appropriateness of concepts and methods in the different contexts of investigation is an essential aspect of functional equivalence. (Without being appropriate it is senseless to speak of anything as being functionally equivalent to something else — except that this is inappropriate as well.) The assessment of appropriateness is closely connected to qualitative reasoning. Without this aspect, equivalence considerations are confined to an abstract and strictly theoretical level not referring to the diverse contexts in which the research takes place. "Functional equivalence", thus, is the more general concept which by means of theorising and qualitative reasoning encompasses and relates the different aspects and which is therefore more relevant to the problem under discussion.

That the assessment of equivalence rests to a great extent on qualitative judgement has already been explicitly acknowledged by Scheuch (1968, p. 180). Implicitly this is taken for granted by all those authors who stress "intimacy" with the country (or culture) to be studied as a necessary prerequisite, as well as in those statements which point out that "personal observations, anecdotal evidence, descriptions of logical relationships, and other contextual information may give added credibility" to findings in comparative research (Brislin et al. 1973, pp. 147 ff). However, it does not seem appropriate to leave the role of qualitative reasoning implicit or to conceive it as "faith or subjective

[2] There is, however, also the possibility that the application of general concepts for all units compared may lead to a trivialisation. For, as for instance Mokrzycki (1979, p. 100) points out, the higher one goes on the level of generality in order to achieve applicability for all units, the less specific information for each single unit is retained. The strategy to strive for functional equivalence clearly means to introduce general concepts. They are, however, to be related to context-bound phenomena which means that the general concepts have to be (re)formulated in a way that enables the meaningful interpretation of context-bound elements as indicators. Functional equivalence, thus, requires not a mere shift in generality but the establishment of meaningful relationships between levels of generality.

judgement" (Frey 1970, p. 243). For even with this view Frey has to admit that one has to rely "increasingly" on it when probing back into the "empirical support" for demonstrations of equivalence (ibid.), i.e. when one tries to identify and interpret the relevant phenomena in the units under study and when one relates them to the respective more general dimension. Qualitative reasoning thus being indispensable in the process of establishing functional equivalence must neither be neglected and excluded from consideration nor be regarded and executed as impressionistic or exclusively subjective. Both attitudes keep it out of the realm of "scientific" consideration and thus away from any control. Rather, the decisive role which it plays demands its inclusion in the domain of scientific discourse. The qualitative aspects involved in any judgement on functional equivalence must therefore be documented, open to criticism and systematised (criteria which may define "qualitative reasoning").[3]

It may well be the case − as stated by Mokrzycki (1979) − that the neglect of qualitative and context-bound aspects is a salient feature in a great part of social research and that it is due to the prevailing general philosophy of science. Already in 1952 Siegfried Kracauer complained that "within the framework of quantitative analysis, qualitative exegesis is condemned to play a black-sheep role. Recognised mainly as a means to arrive at suitable quantifications, its use in analysis proper is regarded as shameful and may in fact be pursued with guilty haste and lack of discipline" (Kracauer 1952, p. 637). Not only since then have there been pleas for alternatives and a new beginning in the philosophy of social sciences, unfortunately with too little influence on the mainstream of social research. However, in the case of comparative social sciences the necessity to take into account qualitative reasoning has emerged in the process of research itself, notwithstanding the philosophy of science adopted by the researchers. To subdue qualitative reasoning to the standards of public criticism and systematisation in order to avoid a "lack of discipline" is thus a widening of traditional methodology, not as an alternative but as an explication of problems implicit in actual research.[4]

[3]Somers (1971) attempts to restructure an extensive qualitative comparative and historical analysis in order to trace it back to a set of systematised categories. Some illustrative examples can be found of the usefulness of documentation and systematisation in qualitative reasoning. In general, however, the attempt to demonstrate this falls short because of the rigid application of an "Expanded Survey Research Model" to a different domain and approach.

[4]This extension of traditional methodology is in line with the one proposed by Hoeben (1978). In a discussion of Critical Rationalism, Symbolic Interactionism and Ethnomethodology, he concludes that the standards of Critical Rationalism, which aim at refutability, have to be maintained. However, its methodology has to be supplemented in order to allow a scientifically controlled way to come from context-bound, "emic" phenomena to general "etic" statements. With regard to comparative research Berting (1979) also proposes a more comprehensive methodological approach.

An enlarged methodological model has of course its implication for the adopted philosophy of science. It is not the purpose of this paper to discuss these questions. However, when looking for adequate approaches I would refer to A. Schütz. His methodology and philosophy of science are a lead to overcome thinking in fruitless dichotomies dominating too often the debate on "qualitative" and "quantitative". On the one hand, Schütz's starting point is M. Weber's notion that the object of social sciences has a specific character insofar as it is meaningfully prestructured by the actors in the social world. The constructs of social science are to be founded upon the actors' constructs and this has to be reflected in methodology. On the other hand, there is no doubt for Schütz that social science has to proceed according to its scientific standards. Formulation of a problem, observation, interpretation and explanation are to follow procedural rules of social science which are designed according to a scientific − not an everyday − "system of relevances". Undoubtedly, the joint observance of both aspects is not entirely clarified in Schütz's writings. However, this is a promising approach for combining "interpretive" and "explanatory" purposes in the philosophy of social sciences.

4. FUNCTIONAL EQUIVALENCE IN VARIOUS PARTS OF THE RESEARCH PROCESS: EXAMPLES

The question of whether functional equivalence can be sufficiently reached or not is crucial for the success of any comparative investigation. In a recent review of comparative mobility research — a field where cross-national comparisons play an important role — shortcomings in equivalence are held responsible for the fact that despite all efforts no conclusive evidence is available on differences in mobility rates between countries (cf. Mayer 1979, pp. 44 ff). This indicates the complexity and difficulty of the problem to be surmounted.

Equivalence considerations are connected with all parts of the research process. Its classification into "object of research", "research instruments", "sample", and "fieldwork" is certainly incomplete (cf e.g. Frey 1970, p. 243). Furthermore, problems of equivalence which come up in the various parts cannot be isolated from each other. However, the classification and the analytical separation enable us to turn to a more concrete level and to discuss examples which are in the various research phases characteristic of the general methodological problem.

4.1. The Object of Research

The object of research represents one pole of the relationship "context-bound phenomena — more general dimension". It has to be defined in theoretical terms valid for all compared units. But from the foregoing discussion it should be clear that it is not unchangeable once it has been formulated. Rather it has to be defined or redefined in a way which allows equivalent relationships with the respective specific indicators. To establish equivalence means that the research object must be meaningful in terms of the compared units. If this cannot be reached the research object itself has to be modified and redefined. In these cases the conclusion to compare systems (cf. Mokrzycki 1979) can be the ultimate step of redefinition of the research object (and for this case Mokrzycki presents in his chapter in this volume an illustrative example). This depends, however, on the case in question and is not a necessary general conclusion.

In Inkeles (1979) a further example can be found which illustrates the necessity to consider the research object in view of its meaningfulness and of its aptness to be assessed in a functionally equivalent way in different countries. Inkeles reviews the IEA "National Case Study" (Passow et al. 1976)[5] This study investigated the relationships between attributes of the national school systems and the national social-cultural-economic systems on the one hand and school achievement as measured in IEA's Six-Subject-Study on the other. The National Case Study included all in all 19 countries. However, the analysis did not reveal systematic relationships between system characteristics and school achievement with one exception: countries classified as less developed ranked systematically lower in achievement scores that those classified as developed. Inkeles concentrates on this result and tries to find an explanation for it. The hypothesis he finally adopts attributes the difference in school achievement between the two groups of countries to the factor "social deprivation" of children in less developed countries, to a "general lack

---

[5] Just because IEA is such an outstanding and impressive undertaking in the international comparative field, it attracts attention so that examples are drawn from its studies to demonstrate general problems.

of enrichment of their environment" (Inkeles 1979, p. 407). This factor is indicated for example by "books per household" and "time spent with watching television". This explanation, which could not be independently tested by Inkeles, being confined to the IEA material, uses a concept common in Western socialisation research. There is, however, no consideration whatsoever of whether it is possible and meaningful to apply it to less developed countries. The indicators cited above are obviously not independent of certain social and cultural contexts. Yet, this is not a problem of choosing adequate indicators, but of the general concept "social deprivation", i. e., the research object itself. In its theoretical foundations this concept is bound to exactly those social und cultural contexts, because it was developed and is used in relation to the outcomes of socialisation and learning in Western societies. The circumstances, styles and requirements of the process of socialisation, learning and teaching which prevail in these societies had to shape the concept to become theoretically useful.

When investigating different societies, it is necessary to rethink the concept and – if necessary – to adjust it to those circumstances, styles and requirements prevailing in these new contexts. A different concept of "social deprivation" – provided it proves meaningful for the countries investigated – would in turn raise the question of whether it can still, theoretically meaningfully be related to the original criterion of school achievement. For it is in research in Western countries that this relationship proved relevant. In order to retain its relevance also a modification of the concept "school achievement" might be the necessary consequence (as partly indicated by Inkeles) of questioning the former one. In any case, the problem is to find general concepts which are applicable to all the compared units and are meaningful in their context. If this is not possible, the shift to comparing systems may ultimately be necessary.

Only further probing into the questions raised in regard to the cited example can demonstrate the adequacy of the original or of different solutions. By now it should however have become clear that the emphasis in striving for functional equivalence can move from the indicators to the more general concept to which they are related.

4.2. Research Instruments

By far most cross-national comparative investigations use questionnaires as a means of collecting information. Although it is not denied that – depending on the problem under study – other procedures are often more adequate (cf. Köbben 1979, p. 4), only a few examples of other instruments can be found in comparative research (e.g. Bovenkerk et al., 1979). This may – among other reasons – have been due to the assumption that equivalence problems are easier to surmount when using questionnaires rather than other methods (this seems, for example, to be expressed by Mayer 1979, p. 50).

The outstanding aspect when dealing with comparability of questionnaires is their translation from the language in which they were originally developed into the languages of the other countries involved. Various procedures have been discussed and are used with back-translation being the most prominent. Even rules for writing translatable English have been formulated which, however, lead to a reduced form of English (cf. Brislin et al., 1973, pp. 34 ff).

In order to avoid that "translation problems will always be plausible rival hypotheses for any obtained results" (empirical) evidence is required to support the assumption that

90

the different language versions are functionally equivalent with regard to the research object (ibid., p. 32). Brislin et al., who deal extensively with translation problems, list five techniques to demonstrate equivalence (ibid., p. 58): "(1) comparisons of meaning between the original and back-translated forms; (2) comparisons of meaning, by bilinguals other than the translator, between the original and translated form; (3) answering questions written about the content of the original version; the questions should be answered correctly by people who have read only the target version; (4) comparing performance to instructions written in the original and in the target language; (5) administering both versions of a text or questionnaire to a sample of bilinguals."

Whith the exception of the first one, these techniques do not rely on back-translations but most of them try to incorporate evidence from behaviour elicited by the questionnaires. This is in accordance with criticisms of translation procedures (forcefully launched by Scheuch 1968) which concentrate on literal translation. Hymes (1970, p. 324) stresses that equivalence entails three levels: message form, conceptual context and communicative context. Although the overt message form is by far the most unimportant in view of functional equivalence "back-translation tends to focus attention" on this "most superficial aspect of the work" (ibid., p. 327). However, and this is the danger inherent in it, back-translation as a control technique can "instil a false sense of security in the investigator by demonstrating a spurious lexical equivalence" (Deutscher, 1968, p. 322).

Two examples may be illustrative. In his comprehensive overview of IEA's Six-Subject-Study, Walker reports, referring to the study of "English as a Foreign Language", that the original English items, scales and tests were first translated into the other languages, necessary for the questionnaires, and subsequently back-translated in order to check the quality of the translated versions. From this evidence they were judged as "accurate and literally appropriate" (Walker 1976, p. 41). However: "Some of the National Centres considered that the nature and amount of the divergence between the native language and English were so important that the tests would have to concentrate on them, but this would have necessitated the use of different tests for each participating country, and international comparisons would have been impossible" (ibid., p. 42). Yet, functional equivalence as a relationship between indicators (here tests) on the one hand and more general concepts and hypotheses on the other is just to provide the possibility of comparisons in case that the indicators have to diverge. If the point stressed by the National Centres was in fact vital for understanding the process of learning English as a foreign language, then a feature especially meaningful and important to be included in international comparison has been excluded for the sake of retaining surface-level identity of instruments. Different tests do not prevent international comparison as long as they can be and are related in an equivalent way to a common concept of learning the foreign language. On the contrary, they might have been necessary to render the comparisons meaningful in terms of all of the participating countries.

Again, these are questions raised from outside. It is necessary to go into much more detail in order to judge which solution of the problem is appropriate. The respective IEA Committee chose what is called "a neutral strategy of assessing the degree of mastery of the English language" (ibid., p. 42). If this, however, means not to take into account features which are considered as essential for the situation in a given country, the question cannot be avoided, whether this strategy leads to trivialisation (as supposed by Mokrzycki 1979; see Footnote 2).

91

Another example can be found in the Vienna Centre's Automation project. According to the first volume of its publications (Forslin et al. 1979) comparability was sought by literal identity of the questionnaires. In cases where questions were apparently not appropriate in a given country it seems that one did not look for an equivalent solution. Instead, the strategy for part of the investigation seems to have been either to skip the question or, where one could reach agreement to include it, to put it "in standard form" and to leave it to the respondents to "determine themselves what is applicable and inapplicable to the given situation" (Ussenin–Notchevnik 1979, p.27). This means that the respondents had to decide whether to answer a question – because it seemed applicable – or not. And for those questions they answered, it was the respondents who had to define in what way they thought them to be appropriate (or else inappropriate). As there has apparently been no control and registration of these decisions, this of course leaves the researcher (and the reader) no chance to verify the reported results and the evidence on equivalence.

The situation is more favourable for the researcher where he himself and not the respondents has to assess the meaning of questions in the national context. Seemingly in those parts of this investigation where the respondents were supposed to answer *all* questions, the strategy of literal identity led to the inclusion of: "Do any of your supervisors or the administrative staff invite you to their homes?" This question was accepted "even though it was known that it had different shades of meaning according to general country practice about inviting acquaintances – of what social level – to one's home" (Bergmann 1979, p. 16). Striving for functional equivalence of the questionnaires would have required formulation of the questions in such a way that their respective "shades of meaning" would fit into the intent of the research. If this is not done, the comparative analysis of this question demands controlled knowledge of the different country practices so that a *retrospective* "control of the factors that affect equivalence" (Hymes 1970, p. 323) be possible.

This knowledge must of course be documented and open to scientific criticisms so that the reader has access to the basis of the conclusions. This requirement is just a special case of the general necessity to document and systematise the reasoning which leads the steps to gain functional equivalence, in order to make this reasoning intelligible and controllable. This can, for example, to a certain extent be found in the study on "Participation and Political Equality" by Verba, Nie and Kim (1978). Insisting on functional equivalence, they refuse literal identity of the questionnaires, the more so as divergent interests of national teams had to be respected and the fieldwork was spread over several years. However, the reasons for differences in the questionnaires and for assuming functional equivalence are but sketched throughout the book.

4.3. Sample

The characteristic of samples relevant with regard to equivalence has been named by Scheuch (1968) "scope of a sample". It refers to the qualification of a sample "to permit the intended inferences" (ibid., p. 195). The scope of a sample can thus only be defined with reference to the question to be investigated. In contrast to the statistical considerations necessary to determine a sample's representativeness, it is theoretical considerations which guide decisions on its scope.

It is out of the question that comparative research has to reckon with essential differences in the structure and composition of the included units. The conclusion to be drawn from this fact is here the same as has already been discussed: "Rather than insisting on identical procedures, one should postulate that, if significant aspects of the universes to be studied differ, the designs should differ accordingly" (Scheuch 1968, p. 190). Hence, the task to strive for equivalent scopes of samples is one of relating, by theoretical considerations and by qualitative reasoning, the various national solutions to the problem under investigation. Attempts to come to samples equivalent in scope are thus a matter of theoretical relevance of attributes displayed by the various units and of qualitative reasoning in identifying and estimating the role of these attributes within the units (and of the interplay between theoretical and qualitative reasoning which can only be separated analytically). The controversy between Treiman (1976) and Burawoy (1976) demonstrates the necessity to consider explicitly the definition of the various samples, and it shows at the same time the potential of disagreement if different criteria are used (cf. also Mayer 1979, pp. 49 ff).

Another example illustrating the difficulties to come to samples equivalent in their scope can be found in Garnier and Hout's (1976) comparison of the educational attainment process in France and in the United States (cf. also Nießen—Peschar 1980). In contrast to many other authors they present and discuss the reasons why they accept differing samples in the two countries as being equivalent with regard to their research object. On the background of Turner's typology of sponsored vs. contest mobility Garnier and Hout classify the American educational system as a contest, the French as a sponsored one. This is mainly related to the point of curricular selection. In the U. S. "the principal point of selection" is assigned to the twelfth grade where entrance to higher education or to the labour force is decided. Up to this point there are, according to Garnier and Hout, no considerable selectivity effects and no differentiation (1976, p. 228). The French system in contrast is described among other things as highly differentiated, having well-defined boundaries between curricular tracks and an early selection point, namely at the end of primary school around age 11 (ibid., p. 229). It is there that the crucial decisions on the further educational career are taken.

Garnier and Hout decide to compare with longitudinal data the subsequent educational career and attainment of French students first investigated in fifth grade with American students first investigated in twelfth grade, the argument being: "cross-national comparisons must be made at a point of functional equivalence, i.e. at a point where the processes under study are at comparable points in their internal development, not arbitrary points defined by characteristics which are treated differently in the societies to be compared. To the French, it would appear wasteful to give everyone university preparation when only a few can go. To Americans, it would appear unjust to close the door to college on an 11 year old (. . .). The relevant comparison is at the common decision point. For French students the question 'how much education?' is answered at age 11; for most American students it is answered at age 17 or 18" (ibid., p. 231).

The explicit discussion — seldom to be found in comparative studies — is valuable and indispensable if the scientific public is to follow and check the argumentation. Without being able to do justice in this case, several questions can be asked: starting the investigation with American (actually only Wisconsin) twelfth graders and with French fifth graders means to compare the attainment process of around the top 70—80% of the American age group with almost 100% of the French one. What effects does this have on the relationship between social origin and educational attainment, with "leaving age" and "years completed" as indicators of attainment? (For example, all Americans having left school prior to graduating from high school are not included.) What relevance for the argumentation on equivalence has the fact that the underlying theoretical model by Turner has hardly been empirically confirmed (cf. Nießen–Peschar 1980, pp. 42 ff)? Are there no relevant differences to account for in the processes by which factors of social origin influence 11-year-old children and 17-year-old youth?

These – and related – questions concern the equivalence of the scope of the samples and they are different from those concerning their representativeness (which are no less important regarding the generalising conclusion of "greater inequality of educational opportunity in France compared to that in the Unites States" (Garnier–Hout, p. 243; cf. Nießen–Peschar 1980, p. 46). They reveal also that problems of equivalence in the various domains (sample, research instrument, research object etc.) mostly cannot be separated from one another. For it is the preoccupation with "academic" attainment which leads the argumentation in favour of grade twelve as the American point of comparison. Specific vocational education, formal on-job training etc. is not found in the U. S. in the way it is common in certain European countries. Garnier–Hout point to it as part of the French system, where it starts – for those entering it – prior to age 17. However, it is only the question of entering higher education – probably adequate for the U. S. – which is considered as relevant for educational attainment and which is used to decide on equivalence of sample scope. In contrast to this, Hamilton and Wright (1975) argue that the non-existence of specific vocational training in the U. S. and its existence in a European country are essential for a comparison. Whether this holds also for the problem investigated by Garnier and Hout deserves special attention; but if so, it should have influenced the argumentation on samples. However, how to take into account the specific features of the national educational systems when the comparison of educational attainment is a question of conceptualising the research object in an equivalent way, but it apparently has implications for the equivalence of the samples (and measures), too.

4.4. Fieldwork

The way a researcher acts to collect information and the way he interacts with people from whom he wants to elicit it may have an important impact on the result of his effort. This is well known and treated in the realm of non-comparative research under headings such as "the social psychology of experiments" or the "sociology of empirical social research". The additional feature in comparative research is that the impact of the research procedure on the results and the interplay between context-bound communication and behaviour patterns and the research procedure may be different in different investigated units. Brislin et al. criticise, for instance, a number of comparative psychological conformity studies which use Asch's experiments: "The great fault in these studies is that no measurement was made of what the experimental situation means from culture to culture... . The Asch situation may be a cue for arousing social approval needs in culture A, rugged individualism in culture B (. . .) and disgust with human experimentation in culture C" (Brislin et al. 1973, p. 100).

The different possibilities listed make it clear that the assessment and knowledge of the meaning which the situation has to the respondents is necessary for the appraisal of the validity of the results. Thus, here again the point is whether the aim of the study is pursued in an equivalent way by the researcher's behaviour and by the way he wants people to behave. Closer connected to the widespread interview approach is Hymes' rigorous demand to take into account the rules governing the "interrogative behaviour" in the respective contexts. It is a matter of discovering "just who can ask whom, in what way, by what means, when and where, about political attitudes and activities, and with what intents and what likely effects" (Hymes 1970, p. 384). The relation to the attitudes and activities in question stresses the criterion with regard to which equivalence has to be discussed, namely the object of the respective investigation. (The specification for their "political" character is due to the fact that the paper was written for an audience of political scientists.)

An attempt to reflect the complex processes of getting access to the field in comparative research can be found in Form's report on "Field Problems in Comparative Research: the Politics of Distrust" (1976). He tries to systematise these processes according to the specificities of the various countries and to interpret their implications on the research. Whereas in the domain of equivalence of sample scope, strictly theoretical considerations seem to prevail, the lack of confirmed knowledge on the questions posed by Hymes seems to stress the necessity of qualitative reasoning when dealing with fieldwork questions. Form's report illustrates the merits of systematic and documented interpretation.

Where this is neglected consequences are brought about which may be exemplified by turning once again to Inkeles' IEA review (1979). Before proposing the above-mentioned explanation for the systematic achievement differences between developed and less developed countries, Inkeles discusses three other possible hypotheses. One of them assumes as an explanatory factor a lack of familiarity with the testing procedure in the less developed countries. According to Inkeles none of these three hypotheses can alone sufficiently explain the difference so that he turns to the fourth one. However, the assumption that lack of familiarity with the testing procedure has an important influence is rejected mainly with the argument that the National Centres of IEA gave their consent to the test. However, as far as can be seen (from, for instance, Walker 1976, Passow et al. 1976, Carroll 1975), there is no systematically gathered information from the parties directly concerned — students and teachers — on possible test effects and on how they perceive the procedure. Thus, the basis for rejecting the strangeness of the testing procedure as an influential factor and for accepting the equivalence-assumption is not very strong. The consent given by National Centres to administer instruments in their countries may depend on various other considerations and not primarily on the adequacy of fieldwork procedures. It is not a matter of reintroducing the factor "fieldwork procedure" as the sole explanation. But there is no material provided to enquire into its eventual contribution as part of an explanation.

Another aspect to be considered are the units in design. Scheuch (1968, p. 188) for instance, warns: "That all units matter, and that individuals are the relevant units for the purpose of the study — this is by no means self-evident; in many societies and for many purposes this assumption is quite wrong". Nevertheless, attempts to define these "units" according to the "interrogative behaviour" (Hymes) in the respective countries are not often to be found in comparative research. For example in a report on fieldwork problems in developing countries, Inkeles (1972) also mentions that interviews had to be done in the huts of the individual respondents with the family and relatives inside or on the market with a crowd gathered around. "Nevertheless, more than 90 percent of the interviews in all countries were judged by the interviewees to have been conducted either in 'absolute privacy' or under conditions in which there may have been onlookers, but who did not interfere" (ibid., p. 61). However, it might have been advisable first to clarify what "absolute privacy" in the various societies means and, second, to consider an adjustment of the interrogative strategy to the local rules (where interference of onlookers may or may not be the normal course).[6] This might have raised the question of different units being equivalent.

5. PROBLEMS OF THE INFORMATION BASE FOR DECISIONS ON EQUIVALENCE AND THE ROLE OF QUALITATIVE METHODS

The basic dilemma encountered in the attempts to secure equivalence is that one already has to have extensive knowledge of the countries and societies involved, prior to dealing with the equivalence problem. It is a common topic in texts, divergent in almost any other respect, that comparisons have to be "well informed" (King et al. 1974, p. 26), have to presuppose "some knowledge of the instances to be compared" (Zelditch 1971, p. 288) and that "the investigator must be familiar with the cultural context before construct-ing instruments" (Deutscher 1968, p. 337). In particular the latter, "familiarity" and "intimacy" with the societies under study, is the most often repeated requirement. It demonstrates that whether methodical steps are taken or not, the task not to miss the specific features of each of the societies compared is felt to be an essential problem (see also Mokrzycki in this volume).

Furthermore, this knowledge is regarded as the basis for establishing equivalent relations between the context-bound phenomena and the more general concepts and theoretical assumptions. This is not something outside the scientific realm but is part of the foundation of comparative conclusions. It is, therefore, not reasonable to leave it outside the domain of methodological consideration and methodical care as is usually the case. To refer to "intimacy" with the societies or cultures comparatively studied too often simply means to rely on tacit routine procedures. This, however, may be one of the sources for the often lamented lack of "rigorous standards of comparison" (Mayer 1979, p. 45) and for the lack of cumulative comparative knowledge (cf. Nießen–Peschar 1980). For: "Too many of the presumably routine decisions which must be made prove on experience not to have been routine, and the resultant misunderstandings have severe consequences when one comes to analyse the data" (Inkeles 1972, pp. 20 ff). So the criteria for qualitative reasoning – and "familiarity" undoubtedly refers to it – have once again to be stressed: explicitness and systematisation.

One approach to provide the scientific public with the required information is by including qualitative national background studies in the publications. They are to give information on the "context of each country" which are relevant for the investigation (King et al. 1974, p. 20). Provided that they fulfil this expectation, they could render it possible to grasp context-bound aspects in the research. This presupposes, however, that the qualitative national case studies are designed and carried out in close connection with what is required by the theoretical problems of the project and by the comparative research.

[6]The topic of the appropriate unit of investigation is extensively discussed in "non-comparative" methodology. See, for instance, Blumer 1969, Kreutz 1972 and Nießen 1977.

But unfortunately they are often isolated from the subsequent comparative study and give a general account on patterns of the respective countries. They are too often not guided by and designed according to theoretical perspectives from the overall investigation. So sometimes even the topics dealt with differ from country to country (cf., for instance, King et al. 1974 and the Jugendwerk of Shell study 1977). Background studies carried out and presented in such a way have to remain arbitrary and at most of incidental use for informing the researcher and the reader on equivalence matters (and of course also for the interpretation of empirical results). This is because the link is missing between them and the comparative investigations, a link which can only be provided by theoretical perspectives. [The descriptive comparison of urban development in Friedrichs (1978) is an example for the use of case studies which are structured according to a common and explicit framework.]

The quest for theoretical orientation of national background studies calls our attention back to the basis of what is — perhaps "intimately" — known and how far this can reach. From Section 4 above it became evident that the necessary background knowledge can mostly not be supposed to be available from the beginning. The aspects to be taken into account are very specific to the respective research — to its objects, instruments, samples and fieldwork procedures. The examples discussed already include so many divergent features that hardly any single person can be familiar whith them in more than one country. This means that the information has to be collected on purpose. Furthermore, much of what is considered as well-known routine knowledge may need verification, especially when it is to be explicitly and systematically included in the argumentation. Therefore, *qualitative research methods* may be necessary to get access, in a controlled way, to the necessary information on context-specific aspects. In hindsight, Torsten Husén, for many years chairman of IEA, identifies as one of the lessons to be learned from the project history that "historical, cultural and economic circumstances which affect formal educational systems ... ought to be taken into account in conducting empirical studies of differences between national systems" (Husén 1979, p. 383), circumstances which also require qualitative methods to reveal them. At the time when IEA's research design was developed, however, the adopted paradigm practically excluded qualitative methods to study the specific features of the compared countries or societies.

One task of qualitative research methods is thus to enquire into the "circumstances" of the phenomena in question, i.e. the context-bound aspects they are connected with and which they have to be linked with for each country in the research. If this task can be conceived as an auxiliary (but necessary) one to both qualitative and quantitative comparisons, there is a second and self-contained role of qualitative research. It is not directed towards within-country investigation of the contextual embedding of phenomena but it concerns the use of qualitative methods for the comparison itself. There are many problems worth comparative scientific investigation for which, for example, the prevailing survey approach is not the best solution or even "simply out of question" (Köbben 1979, p. 5).

Following Köbben's plea to choose the research methods so that they fit best to the problem under study, qualitative techniques may prove in certain cases to be the most appropriate ones. In order to be fruitful for the carrying out of the study this decision has to be taken at its beginning. Up to now the positive appraisal of qualitative methods is mostly to be found in hindsight, when looking back at the purely quantitative study. To give two examples: Anderson (1976, p. 271) in a comment on the IEA enterprise, doubts

97

whether the surveys could reach some of the "important parts of the overall configuration" which influences school achievement. To identify among other things the "lore" of teachers, i.e. their common sense assumptions and "tricks of the trade", qualitative techniques are advised. In another study based on IEA's survey data and dealing with sex differences in school science achievement Kelly (1978) succeeds in demonstrating that girls consistently achieve less then boys. With regard to the main aim of her study, however, she was "unsuccessful in specifying the causes of girls' under-achievement in science" (ibid., p. 117). In resuming her report she proposes for this purpose — at least "in the short term" — qualitative techniques (ibid., p. 117).

More generally, Masemann recommends qualitative methods for the comparative "examination of the process by which structural variables ... are related to educational performance and other outcomes" (1976, p. 374; for further examples see, for instance, Köbben 1979). This suggestion is not confined to the educational field. Just as Masemann is startled at the "stunningly similar results of quantitative studies in various countries" (ibid., p. 376), Mayer (1979, p. 51) is puzzled with an analogous "invariance" in mobility research. This arouses his interest in the mechanisms which bring about the similar mobility patterns, an interest which "would quite likely require to abandon a 'pure' quantitative stance in order to tap the level of institutional practices".

The link which is established by Mayer as well as by Masemann between quantitative results on the one hand and comparisons based on qualitative techniques on the other, illustrates that the above-mentioned two tasks of qualitative methods are by no means strictly separated. The two authors recommend qualitative methods in self-contained studies in order to get further insights into the meaning of quantiative findings. But whatever interplays there may be, the important role qualitative methods have to play in comparative research forbids either to disregard them or to treat them as impressionistic and not to proceed in a systematic and documented way.

6. THE IMPACT OF ORGANISATIONAL PATTERNS

The late Stein Rokkan (1970), one of the promoters of international comparative research in the social sciences, has formulated a typology for classifying cross-national research according to its level of internationalisation. Reducing drastically the degree of differentiation of Rokkan's typology we may distinguish two poles: on the one hand a more or less *centralised* organisation of the research. Conception, data collection in the various countries, analysis and interpretation are done or supervised and controlled by one institution or research team. This organisational pattern has often been renounced as "Safari-type" or "imperialistic" research. It is contrasted on the other hand by a highly *decentralised* model where part of the study's conception, the data collection, and to varying degrees the analysis and interpretation are done by independent but closely cooperating national research teams. This is the Vienna Centre "type" of internationalised projects (with variations in its concrete forms).

The decentralised type of cross-national research has become the preferred and perhaps the only feasible one — because of various reasons: there is not only political resistance to giving "imperialistic" research access to the field; there are "moral problems" in centralised projects to exclude participants at the periphery from decisions (Frey 1970, p. 217); and there is the commitment of the international scientific community to make possible "indigenous social science" in all countries (cf. Kumar 1978) for which decentralised projects are felt to be more helpful. They thus correspond to what Berrien (1970) called the "super-ego" for cross-national research.[7] In addition to these reasons also the argument of scientific benefit is strongly emphasised. Verba for instance favours the decentralised type of organisation with equal national participation, because in such projects one can do "systematic comparisons across nations (which involves simplification and abstraction from the specific setting of any particular nation) and at the same time not do injustice to the significant special features of each of the nations being considered (which involves sensitivity to complex contextual factors within each nation)" (Verba 1977, p. 172). Here the possibility to overcome the equivalence problem is regarded as a main advantage of the decentralised project type (see also Frey 1970, pp. 244 ff).

However, somewhat in contrast to these expectations, it seems that the problems of functional equivalence, comparability and of including the context-bound events in the comparison are more explicitly treated in the more centralised projects (cf. for instance Form 1976; Inkeles 1972; to a certain degree Verba et al. 1978; the emic-etic discussion on cross-cultural psychological investigations which are almost exclusively "centralised"). One of the reasons may be that in such projects foreigners are bound either to do the research or to steer and supervise it in foreign countries. They know the local rules, common sense assumptions and lore only to a very limited extent. They have to rely on the assistance of persons or institutions from these countries but remain responsible themselves for every decision in the research process. One could hypothesise that this situation brings about an awareness of context—specificities and of the difficulties to grasp them in comparisons.

The organisation of decentralised – Vienna Centre type – projects on the other hand seems to favour tendencies to leave problems of equivalence implicit. In Vienna Centre projects for instance independent national teams have agreed to cooperate in one study. The national teams remain in every respect responsible for carrying out the investigation in their own country. The bonds between the different teams and their parallel progress are to be ensured by the Vienna Centre's constant coordination and by regular meetings. It is here that the outlines of design, instruments, data collection and analysis as well as interpretation are decided upon. Now, the cooperation of independent national teams with – more or less – equal rights may enforce the tacit background assumption that each national team will possess the necessary information on relevant context-specificities. More important is the tacit background expectation that each team will take into account the context-bound aspects for its own country when designing and carrying out its investigation. This means that the national teams are expected to influence the common research design in order to make it appropriate for their national purposes. In addition, they are to provide, in their national studies, proceedings which are functionally equivalent with regard to the common international design.

The point is that the performance of tacit background assumptions is mostly not reported. So one learns, for example, from the final publication of a project with 10 participating countries that the standard version of the questionnaire was prepared in English (by persons whose native language was apparently not English), that it was translated into the different languages by the respective national teams and that there was

---

[7]For an informative discussion of problems which are based on the mentioned and on other reasons see Portes 1973. The relevance of the outlined case is certainly not confined to U. S. sociology.

no systematic and general control of the various translations (cf. Ornauer et al. 1976, p. 596). It is, therefore, difficult to see what has been done with regard to functional equivalence. But if anything has been done, it is difficult to verify the plausibility of measures which have been taken but not reported.

The procedure just described is not completely unusual. What, however, is unusual and deserves merit is that it is openly reported. The problem of language and of adequate understanding, for instance, is common to all projects where researchers from many countries participate. The fact that the working language is for many or all of them not their native one primarily affects the degree to which they are able to participate in discussions and decision-making (cf. Nießen 1980). Second and more important, it also affects the development of research instruments for the various countries and all other steps in the research process (as the above example demonstrates). But too often measures to secure comparability and equivalence in this situation are hardly mentioned. This is in itself an indicator that the research relied on the assumption that the national teams will provide for them (and maybe one mainly has to trust in them).

So one may suppose that in highly centralised projects the difficult circumstances force the researchers to pay attention to problems of comparability and equivalence, whereas the style of international cooperation and the delegation of responsibility to national teams may in decentralised projects enhance the *tendency to neglect explicit considerations* of these problems. But this confrontation of two organisational types aims by no means at disregarding decentralised "international" research. It merely reflects conjectures on factual tendencies, not on necessary relationships. The actual solutions for functional equivalence found in one or the other of the organisational models may be adequate or not; it depends on the respective case as can be seen from the examples discussed (for a positive example in a Vienna Centre project, confined to the analysis stage, see Sandberger–Bargel 1980). Whether the hypothesised relationships do really exist can therefore only be proved by detailed objective descriptions of research projects, by "research about research itself, in order to learn the scientific consequences" (Glaser 1977, p. 430). To understand such scientific consequences of organisational patterns is the prerequisite for a sound judgment on their value.

Yet, whatever the results of investigations about modes of project organisation should be, the Vienna Centre type of decentralised cross-national research will remain the preferred one, if only because of the above-mentioned extra-scientific reasons. Therefore, one should also strive to secure the scientific advantage of decentralised projects, which means that functional equivalence must not be based solely on tacit background assumptions but on explicit effort.

7. CONCLUSION

In the preceeding paragraphs problems related to qualitative aspects in comparative research have been discussed. Starting from considerations on the concept of "functional equivalence" the necessity of paying more attention to disciplined qualitative reasoning has been stressed and exemplified for various stages of the research process. It was followed by an outlook on the functions of qualitative methods in its narrower sense and on possible implications of organisational patterns for the way the problem of functional equivalence is approached. With regard to this problem the paper concentrated on the argumentation which is necessary to reach functionally equivalent solutions. It did not deal with possibilities at the analysis stage (existing e.g. in survey research). Such are, for example, the use of relative instead of absolute measures and the comparison of internal relationships between countries (cf. Verba et al. 1978, p. 40 and Loetsch in this volume; Sandberger—Bargel 1980; also see Przeworski and Teune's [1970, p. 117] strategy of multiple indicators). Necessary and valuable as such strategies are, they have to be preceded by measures to establish functional equivalence as have been discussed in this paper. To proceed otherwise would mean to take the insecure, namely lacking equivalence argumentation, as the basis for the more secure, namely refined analysis strategies.

REFERENCES

Anderson, C. Arnold (1976) Interpreting National Contrasts in School Achievement. Chapter 13 in Walker (1976), pp. 259—281.

Armer, Michael (1973) Methodological Problems and Possibilities in Comparative Research. In: M. Armer—A. D. Grimshaw (eds.), pp. 49—79.

Armer, Michael—Allen D. Grimshaw (eds.) (1973) *Comparative Social Research: Methodological Problems and Strategies.* New York etc: John Wiley.

Bergmann, R. H. (1979) The Project-History and Scope. In: J. Forslin et al. (eds.), pp. 8—16.

Berrien, F. K. (1970) A super-ego for cross-cultural research. In: *International Journal of Psychology* 5, 33—39

Berry, J. W. (1969) On Cross-Cultural Comparability. In: *International Journal of Psychology* 4, 119—128.

Berting, J. (1979) A Framework for the Discussion of Theoretical and Methodological Problems in the Field of International Comparative Research in the Social Sciences. In: J. Berting et al. (eds.), pp. 137—157.

Berting, J., Geyer, F. & Jurkovich, R. (eds.) (1979) *Problems in International Comparative Research in the Social Sciences.* Oxford: Pergamon Press.

Blumer, H. (1969) Public Opinion and Public Opinion Polling. In: H. Blumer: *Symbolic Interactionism. Perspective and Method.* Englewood Cliffs: Prentice Hall.

Bovenkerk, F., B. Kilborne, F. Raveau & D. Smith (1979) Comparative Aspects of Research on Discrimination Against Non-White Citizens in Great Britain, France and the Netherlands. In: J. Berting et al. (eds.), pp. 105—122.

Brislin, R. W., Lonner, W. J. & Thorndike, R. M. (1973) *Cross-Cultural Research Methods.* New York: Wiley.

Burawoy, M. (1976) Social Structure, Homogenization and "the Process of Status Attainment in the United States and Great Britain". In: *American Journal of Sociology* 82, 1031—1042.

Carroll, J. B. (1975) *The Teaching of French as a Foreign Language in Eight Countries. International Studies in Evaluation, vol. V.* Stockholm: Almqvist & Wiksell and New York: Wiley.

Deutscher, J. (1968) Asking Questions Cross-Culturally: Some Problems of Linguistic Comparability. In: H. Becker et al. (eds.): *Institutions and the Person.* Papers presented to E. C. Hughes. Chicago: Aldine pp. 318 –341.

Form, William H. (1976) Field Problems in Comparative Research: The Politics of Distrust. Appendix B in: W. H. Form: *Blue-Collar Stratification.* Autoworkers in Four Countries. pp. 277–299 Princeton: Princeton Univ. Press.

Forslin, J., A. Sarapata & A. M. Whitehill (eds.) in collaboration with F. Adler–S. Mills (1979) *Automation and Industrial Workers. A Fifteen Nation Study.* Vol. I, Part I. Oxford: Pergamon Press.

Frey, F. W. (1970) Cross-Cultural Survey Research in Political Science. In. R. T. Holt–J. E. Turner (eds.), pp. 173–294.

Friedrichs, J. (ed.) (1978) *Stadtentwicklungen in kapitalistischen und sozialistischen Ländern.* Reinbek: Rowohlt.

Garnier, M. & Hout, M. (1976) Inequality of Educational Opportunity in France and the United States. In: *Social Science Research, 5*, 225–246.

Glaser, W. A. (1977) The Process of Cross-National Survey Research. In: Szalai–Petrella (eds.), pp. 403–435.

Goodenough, Ward H. (1970) Description and Comparison in Cultural Anthropology. Chicago: Aldine.

Hamilton, R. & Wright, J. (1975) Coming of Age – A Comparison between the United States and the Federal Republic of Germany. In: *Zeitschrift für Soziologie 4,* 335–349.

Hoeben, W. (1978) Zur Integration von kritisch-rationalistischer Methodologie und interpretativen Theorien in der Soziologie. In: K. O. Hondrich & J. Matthes (eds.): *Theorienvergleich in den Sozialwissenschaften.* Darmstadt: Luchterhand.

Husén, T. (1979) An International Research Venture in Retrospect: the IEA-Surveys. In: *Comparative Education Review 23,* 371–385.

Hymes, Dell (1970) Linguistic Aspects of Comparative Political Research. In: R. T. Holt–J. E. Turner (eds.), pp. 295–342.

Inkeles, A. (1972) Fieldwork Problems in Comparative Research on Modernization. In: A. R. Desai (ed.): *Essays on Modernization of Underdeveloped Societies.* Vol. 2, pp. 20–75 New York: Humanities Press.

Inkeles, A. (1979) National Differences in Scholastic Performance. In: *Comparative Education Review 23,* 386–407.

Jugendwerk der Deutschen Shell (ed.) (1977) *Jugend in Europa. Eine vergleichende Analyse zwischen der Bundesrepublik Deutschland, Frankreich und Großbritannien.* 3 Volumes. Distributed by the Editor.

Kelly, A. (1978) *Girls and Science: An International Study of Sex Differences in School– Science Achievement.* IEA Monograph Studies no. 9. Stockholm: Almqvist & Wiksell.

King, E. J., Moor, C. H. & Munday, J. A. (1974) *Post-Compulsory Education. A New Analysis in Western Europe.* London: Sage.

Köbben, A. (1979) Cross-National Studies as Seen from the Vantage Point of Cross-Cultural Studies; Problems and Pitfalls. In: J. Berting, F. Geyer and R. Jurkovich (eds.) 1979, pp. 1–9.

Kracauer, S. (1952) The Challenge of Qualitative Content Analysis. In: *Public Opinion Quarterly* 16, pp. 631–641.

Kreutz, H. (1972) *Soziologie der empirischen Sozialforschung.* Stuttgart: Enke.

Kumar, Krishna (1978) Some Reflections on Transnational Social Science Transactions. In: *International Journal of Comparative Sociology,* XIX, pp. 219–234.

Masemann, Vandra (1976) Anthropological Approaches to Comparative Education. In: *Comparative Education Review* 20, pp. 368–380.

Mayer, K. M. (1979) Class Formation and Social Reproduction. In: J. Berting et al. (eds.), pp. 37–56.

Mokrzycki, E. (1979) On the Adequacy of Comparative Methodology. In: J. Berting et al. (eds.), pp. 93–103.

Nießen, M. (1977) *Gruppendiskussion. Interpretative Methodologie, Methodenbegründung, Anwendung.* München: Fink.

Nießen, M. (1980) *International Scientific Cooperation in Vienna Centre Projects: An Interpretation of Reported Experiences and Evaluations.* Mimeo. Vienna: Vienna Centre Working Paper.

Nießen, M. & Peschar, J. (1980) *Comparative Research on Education 1975–1980.* A Review and Appraisal. Paper presented at the Conference on The Origins and Operations of Educational Systems, Paris. Vienna: Vienna Centre.

Ornauer, H., H. Wiberg, A. Sicinsky & J. Galtung (eds.) (1976) *Images of the World in the Year 2000. A Comparative Ten Nation Study.* The Hague–Paris: Mouton.

Passow, A. H., Noah, H. J., Eckstein, M. A. & Mallea, J. R., (1976) *The National Case Study: An Empirical Comparative Study of Twenty-One Educational Systems. International Studies in Evaluation, vol. VII.* Stockholm: Almqvist & Wiksell and New York: Wiley.

Portes, Alejandro (1973) Perception of the U. S. Sociologist and Its Impact on Cross-National Research. In: M. Armer–A. D. Grimshaw (eds.), pp. 149–163.

Przeworski, A. & Teune, H. (1970) *The Logic of Comparative Social Inquiry.* New York: Wiley.

Rokkan, S. (1970) Cross-Cultural, Cross-Societal and Cross-National Research. In: Unesco (ed.): *Main Trends of Research in the Social and Human Sciences.* The Hague: Mouton.

Sandberger, J. U. & Bargel, T. (1980) Subjektive Indikatoren im internationalen Vergleich: Wertorientierungen und gesellschaftlich-politische Vorstellungen jüngerer Hochqualifizierter in fünf europäischen Ländern. In: Hoffman-Nowotny, H. J. (ed.): *Soziale Indikatoren VII.* Frankfurt: Campus.

Scheuch, E. K. (1968) The Cross-Cultural Use of Sample-Surveys: Problems of Comparability. In: S. Rokkan (ed.): *Comparative Research Across Cultures and Nations.* pp. 176–209. The Hague: Mouton.

Schweitzer, David (1979) Comparative Social Mobility: Problems of Theory, Epistemology and Quantitative Methodology. In: J. Berting et al. (eds), pp. 57–91.

Smelser, N. J. (1976) *Comparative Methods in the Social Sciences.* Englewood Cliffs N. J.: Prentice Hall.

Somers, R. H. (1971) Applications of an Expanded Survey Research Model to Comparative Institutional Studies. In: J. Vallier (ed.), 355–420.

Szalai, A. & Petrella, R. (eds.) (1977) *Cross-National Comparative Survey Research: Theory and Practice.* Oxford: Pergamon Press.

Treiman, D. J. (1976) Toward Methods for a Quantitative Comparative Sociology: a Reply to Burawoy. In: *American Journal of Sociology* 82, 1042–1056.

Ussenin, V. & Notchevnik, M. (1979) The Experience of the International Comparative Study. In: J. Forslin et al. (eds.), pp. 17–28.

Vallier, I. (ed.) (1971) *Comparative Methods in Sociology: Essays on Trends and Applications.* Berkeley & Los Angeles: University of California Press.

Verba, S. (1971) Cross-National Survey Research: The Problem of Credibility. In: I. Vallier (ed.), pp. 308–356.

Verba, Sidney (1977) The Cross-National Program in Political and Social Change: A Histroy and Some Comments. In: Szalai–Petrella (eds.), pp. 169–199.

Verba, S., Nie, N. H. & Kim, J. (1978) *Participation and Political Equality: A Seven Nation Comparison.* Cambridge: Cambridge University Press.

Walker, D. A. (1976) *The IEA Six Subject Survey: An Empirical Study of Education in Twenty-One Countries. International Studies in Evaluation, Vol. IX.* Stockholm: Almqvist & Wiksell and New York: Wiley.

Wiatr, J. (1977) The Role of Theory in the Process of Cross-National Survey Research. In: Szalai–Petrella (eds.), pp. 347–372.

Zelditch, M. (1971) Intelligible Comparisons. In: I. Vallier (ed.), pp. 267–307.

Part Three

ORGANISATION
AND COOPERATION IN
INTERNATIONAL
COMPARATIVE RESEARCH

This section contains a topic that is rarely discussed: the organisation and cooperation in international comparative research. In various relevant overviews it has been remarked that no good solutions have been found for the coordination of multinational projects. But there has certainly been an enormous amount of experience accumulated in this area.

The following three chapters describe and analyse various types of organisation, cooperation and project management.

Michel Lesage elaborates systematically on problems of cooperative research in Eastern and Western Europe. He outlines basic features of the way research is structured and institutionalised in the different systems and their impact on cooperation. Based on extensive experience and observations in the field, various problems are discussed and proposals presented of how to cope with them.

Torsten Husén reflects on his 20 years' experience in the comparison of educational achievement in more than 20 countries. A special organisation of the national research institutes participating in the project was set up (International Association for the Evaluation of Educational Achievement — IEA). The author reflects on the way the organisation works, including the question of what impact it had on solving the scientific problems.

Stephen Mills approaches the organisational problems of cooperation from quite another point of view. He discusses the structure of the European Coordination Centre for Research and Documentation in Social Sciences (Vienna Centre) established to facilitate East—West cooperation in the social sciences. Since the Vienna Centre acts as an "umbrella structure" for many different projects in various fields, no special reference is made on the project level, as is done in the two former contributions. However, the rather liberal attitude towards the organisation of projects could be an interesting topic of future study: the comparison of many different forms of project management under the same conditions of the Vienna Centre. One might then identify the influence of the diversity of intellectual styles and the resulting problems in cooperation, to which Johan Galtung also referred.

Cooperative Comparative Research between Eastern and Western Europe

by Michel Lesage

1. GENERAL ISSUES

For 20–25 years exchanges have developed between scholars of Eastern and Western Europe. Mutual visits and symposia have enabled them to get to know each other better and to try to begin working together on the same problems. In this chapter we will analyse the specific features of organisation and communication in an East–West network working on comparative research.

With this purpose in mind we will use examples taken from the experience of numerous bilateral symposia between French jurists and jurists of almost all European socialist countries[1] and from two multilateral projects on the control of public administration and public administration employment systems, which are realised under the sponsorship of the Vienna Centre. Bilateral and multilateral cooperation have many common features but, of course, multilateral cooperation is of a more complex nature. The interest in common research may be different for the different participants and the profit from it may also be very different.

A first benefit of common research may be a transfer of methodology between countries. For example, the use of quantitative methods to study certain juridical phenomena may be used in some countries and – by way of a common research – may be transferred to all other countries in a project. Sometimes even a new methodology may jointly be elaborated by researchers from East and West.

Secondly, the research may produce new information and the comparison may clarify some differences. An institution which is in the centre of a system in one country may be very well studied whereas an analogous institution in another country which is secondary in this system may only be known to a lesser extent. A comparative study will encourage the analysis of this institution having the possibility of using references in the other systems. For example, letters to the press criticising the administration are in

---

[1] With the exception of the German Democratic Republic and Albania, with whom such symposia have not been organised yet.

socialist countries considered as a very important means of control of administration and consequently are studied in these countries. But in Western countries criticism by interest groups and representative organs occupy more of the public scene and relations between the press and the administration are less observed and studied; as a consequence of this difference, the project on the control of administration decided to undertake a special study on this topic in France.

Conversely, some questions which are studied more in Western countries can be asked in socialist countries. For example, deputies who are also members of various assemblies of different levels (local, regional, national) play a special role in the political administration systems concerning the relations with administration. Data exist in Western countries, but the phenomenon is less studied in socialist countries. With reference to the Western phenomenon, it was possible to ask the same kind of questions in socialist countries.

Thirdly, some research studies may be directly connected with policy problems. For example, the jurisdictional control of administration is developing in some socialist countries. The comparisons with foreign systems made by jurists of these countries enabled them to find solutions earlier.

Fourthly, the contribution to general theory has already been mentioned several times in this book and we will not elaborate on it further. But I would like to mention another benefit of comparative studies: the contribution to the knowledge about foreign countries. This point was recently underlined by the MacBride report.[2] The bias of ethnocentrism is always present. Comparative studies are a good way of enlarging our knowledge: they allow for a better understanding of foreign countries through direct contacts and by confrontations of ideas between participants from the various countries. Concerning the knowledge of socialist countries, this approach is connected with a choice between the classical "sovietology" on the one hand, where Western people are the authors of the analysis and the people of socialist countries its objects, while on the other hand there are comparative studies where people of the two parts of Europe are at the same time subject and object of the analysis in the fields which are chosen for the study. An example of change from one approach to the other can be given by the transformation in France in 1974 of the "Revue de l'Est" into the "Revue d'Etudes Comparatives Est−Ouest", published by the French National Centre for Scientific Research (CNRS).[3]

In East−West comparative research three levels can be distinguished. The simplest one is just a description of the same institution or the same phenomenon in two countries. Many of the French/East-European juridical symposia are of this kind. Even at this first level of comparison there is already an evident benefit: better knowledge of the other country and the beginning of a comparison between the two systems.

In such a juxtaposition of different systems, a second level of comparison may be obtained with the inclusion of an internal evaluation of the relative efficiency of institutions within the system. This is, for example, the case with the control of administration project. For scientific and for political reasons (the divergence of points of view between researchers in East and West on the characteristics of the two political systems), the goal of the common research cannot be to discuss whether the administration is more or less

[2] Voix multiples, un seul monde, Paris, UNESCO 1980.

[3] Cf. for example, Les services dans les pays de l'Est et de l'Ouest, comparaison internationale sur l'organisation et l'utilisation des services dans les pays de l'Est et de l'Ouest. (Vienna Centre research project.) Revue d'études comparatives Est−Ouest, Vol. 10, 1979, No. 1−2.

controlled in the West or in the East. But it is possible to try to find out what the more efficient means of control *within* each system are and to compare the advantages and disadvantages of each technique of control.

The third level and a more difficult one to reach consists in trying to elaborate a unique and common model to study the same kind of phenomena in the two systems and to draw conclusions from the comparison. It is more difficult because many concepts in social sciences have an ideological and political connotation.

It is clear that there is a direct connection between the goal or the level of the research and the complexity of organisational problems. The more one tries to move from juxtapositions to real comparisons, the more difficult the problems of cooperation become.

The main problem concerns the communication within the international network of researchers.

Some problems are of an *objective* nature. They are connected with differences of the researchers' situation and of their knowledge. A first difficulty is one of communication between the disciplines. For example, since even within the same country sociologists and jurists do not speak the same language, do not use the same concepts or the same techniques, a fortiori the difficulties of communication between them in an international multidisciplinary network are even greater. Moreover, within one single discipline, for example, such as law, there may be differences of communication between subdisciplines. Public Administration employment systems are studied in the West by specialists of public law and in the East by specialists of labour law. They will not be immediately in agreement because they do not have the same approach to the problem.

A second difficulty is connected with problems of the knowledge of foreign countries. The risk of misunderstanding is very high because a researcher naturally tends to transpose his national framework to the study of foreign problems. He will tend to minimise the influence of the national context of the foreign countries, their history etc. That is why it may be very useful to include in an international network both specialists of disciplines and specialists of foreign countries who work as specialists in area studies. They may avoid elementary mistakes concerning the interpretation of foreign phenomena.

Thirdly, these problems are connected with another kind of objective difficulty: difficulties of language. Very often there are inequalities in the knowledge of foreign languages and in access to foreign documentation. The socialist researchers mostly speak English, German and French and are able to read the literature of these countries. Of course probably they personally do not speak languages like Norwegian, Dutch or Finnish. But on the Western part of the network: who is able to speak Polish, Hungarian, Serbo-Croatian or Czech? Furthermore, who speaks the Russian language and reads social science literature published in Russian or other East-European languages?

The difficulties of a *subjective* nature are more subtle. A first category of difficulties exists when in a group "the one thinks that the other knows". For that reason, he does not even think of giving him information because he assumes that the other already knows. Many misunderstandings are of this kind. For example, before the first encounter between a Western and an Eastern specialist on Public Administration employment systems, the Eastern specialist might already have read about Western institutions and thus know that this field is covered in Western countries by public law. In contrast, the Western field specialist may think about socialist countries in his own categories and ignore the special features of public Administration employment systems in these countries. This approach may not be clear to the Eastern specialist and it may take some time before the fundamental differences are realised by both of them.

Sometimes such misunderstandings may last for a long time if there are problems of communication of a second type: "the one knows that other does not know, but nevertheless, he will not tell him." It is an elementary psychological problem: it is not easy to confess publicly one's own weakness in front of foreigners. Could you, without hesitation, explain that your accounts are already exhausted and that you cannot buy a ticket to attend a meeting in London or Prague? Instead, you will explain that you will try to find money, probably even when you know that it will be impossible to get any new subsidies. Perhaps you can talk about it unofficially and that is why informal communications are absolutely vital for this kind of cooperation. If there is a good atmosphere of confidence, it is possible to clarify all kinds of difficulties which are not easy to expose publicly at general meetings where many representatives from different countries are present.

When an international network of representatives from various countries is established, it is at first necessary to know the national restraints of each representative very well. In addition it is necessary to elaborate and define an international strategy for working in an international network of cooperation.

2. NATIONAL RESTRAINTS

In each country of both systems there are a number of structural restraints. In the following we systematise and present them in a typological way.

2.1. Eastern Europe

The research system in Eastern Europe may be characterised by three features: institutes, programmes, rules for international cooperation.

a. Institutes

The most characteristic feature is the fact that in the socialist countries researchers are working in large institutes. These are institutes of the academy, ministries or universities but they all have a hierarchical organisation, generally with three levels: the researchers, the Head of Department, the Director (or Deputy Director) of the Institute.

The general contradiction which applies to the administration of science in the Western world also applies to socialist countries: scientific research is work *and* communication. The higher the position, the more opportunities occur for participation in numerous meetings, round tables or business meetings, but the shorter the time for research work. And in contrast, the lower the position in the hierarchy, the longer the time for research work and the fewer the opportunities for travelling.

But as the institutional context is more important in the East than in the West and the hierarchy as a rule is more rigid, the consequence for international cooperation is that having good contacts with a researcher and opportunities to meet him very often means having good relations with the Head of Department and with the Director of his institute and organising contacts at all the three levels at the same time.

112

b. Programmes

The institutes in socialist countries are working on the basis of a national programme approved by the scientific authorities (Academies of Sciences for Academic Institutes). International cooperation is always connected to these national programmes. Interest and possibilities for international cooperation are extremely variable.

Generally, if international cooperation is proposed on a subject which is already included in the national programme, cooperation is easier. But another factor may also be important: the personal authority of the Director of the institute. If the director of an institute is really interested in a particular cooperation and if he has enough personal influence at the academy, then he may be able to include new topics in the programmes of the institute.

But an essential point is that the programmes are prepared for one or several years (very often in connection with economic planification) and that it is necessary to respect time-schedules. The annual programme for the next year for example is generally prepared between July and December and it is only then that it is possible to add new items. During the year of execution of the plan itself it is almost impossible to introduce new elements.

c. Rules for international cooperation

A third particularity of Eastern European research systems concerns cooperation between institutions, for both international cooperation and national cooperation in the country itself. First, there are three different institutional systems: Academies of Sciences, Ministries, Universities. Cooperation between institutes of these three sectors is difficult because they are not in the same hierarchical organisation. There are, of course, exceptions. For example, in a particular country, it is possible that for a national programme researchers of universities or of ministry institutes are included in teams led by institutes of the Academies of Sciences.

For international cooperation, it is certainly easier to cooperate with only one national institute. But for some multidisciplinary projects it could be very useful to have researchers from different institutes. This is always very difficult, as the "natural" trend of every institution would be to choose a researcher of its own institute for international cooperation, even if a researcher of another institute is more qualified.

Even for institutes within the same sector, for example, within the Academy of Sciences, difficulties may exist. For example, cooperation between a sociological institute and a juridical institute may be easy in a country where contacts are close between the two institutes, but very difficult if the relations are poor between the two institutes or the two Directors.

2.2. Western Europe

The panorama of research organisation in Western Europe is very different and characterised by small research units and a different system of financing.

a. Research units

As the research units are small, the hierarchy generally includes two levels: a director and a collaborator, or there is even no hierarchy at all. This means that, in fact, for international cooperation contacts will directly be established with individuals and not with hierarchically organised institutions. Of course, institutions also exist particularly for the evaluation of the researchers' work and for financing, but the procedures differ from those in the East. The possibility of cooperation depends on financial possibilities.

b. Financing

The present purpose is not to describe the different financing systems of research in Western Europe. We will limit ourselves to stress some dimensions which have a direct influence on international cooperation.

The first dimension is the respective influence of internal financing and of contract or foundation financing. The first one means regular receipt of credits, but there are generally difficulties in obtaining big changes of allocations from one year to the other, in order to begin an important international cooperation. In contrast, the second one could mean for instance important funds for some years but no certitude with regard to the continuation for longer periods.

A second dimension is the sensitivity of the system with regard to international cooperation, and more precisely, to cooperation with Eastern Europe. This dimension is connected, first, with the importance dedicated by the respective country to international cultural and scientific relations. For example, France uses a more important part of the State budget than, for instance, the Netherlands and thereby gives more opportunity for international cooperation in the field of social sciences. Secondly, the financial possibilities of cooperation with Eastern Europe are connected with the general policy towards the East. The scope of scientific and cultural agreements with Eastern Europe differs from one country to another. The larger the country, the easier it is to organise missions or bilateral symposia since the governments pay the travel expenses for the implementation of the agreements.

A third dimension is the multiplicity of the ways of financing. Additional sources help to collect more resources for international cooperation, but the system can be very complex as the time-schedules are not the same for the different procedures. From this point of view, it would be a mistake to believe that the multiplicity of sources exists only in countries which have a number of foundations for financing research. This multiplicity of sources may also exist in countries where the only *original* source is the State budget. France can illustrate the case of such a complexity. In the main research institution, that is the National Centre for Scientific Research (CNRS), there are already three different procedures: research units have their annual budget, funds are allocated for special operations (so-called "actions thématiques programmées", for example for developing research on European problems) and there are also funds for international cooperation (for multilateral cooperation, round tables and conferences and bilateral cooperation including individual missions and symposia). There are bilateral agreements between the National Centre for Scientific Research and the Academies of Sciences in various socialist countries. Universities also have such procedures in order to invite foreign scholars and organise symposia. And the Ministry of Foreign Affairs' general directorate for cultural, scientific and technical relations also has parallel procedures for such purposes (invitations and symposia). The combination of different procedures is complex but not impossible and becomes more necessary at the present time as the global budget is diminishing, not only in France but also in many other countries.

***

114

These many different institutions and procedures in various countries in the East and the West necessitate that all the operations needed in realising international cooperation have to coincide with each other in time. The Vienna Centre can in many ways be of great help in achieving this end. First, as is well known, it gives information concerning eventual partners. But two other advantages are also very useful. If a research project is accepted by the Vienna Centre, it will help to integrate the project in a national plan of Eastern European Institutes. Thus it will raise the status of the research. But one should not forget that the final decision on cooperation and on the degree of cooperation will always be taken on the national level. Secondly, the Vienna Centre may also provide opportunities for meetings and facilitate effective participation of representatives from socialist countries. But here again a country's participation will depend on the country's own national interest in the project; only this interest can help (particularly in the case of socialist countries) to diminish the restraints we have mentioned.

Another restraint must be mentioned as well: it concerns the release of data. There are national rules concerning access to data. Some data cannot be consulted even within the country; some others can only be treated within the country itself and only the results, not the data themselves, can be communicated abroad. If there is a great interest in comparative research, the rules can sometimes become less rigid.

Organisers of comparative research must be very familiar with national constraints which exist in the different countries participating in an international study. This is an absolutely necessary basis for a strategy of international cooperation.

3. INTERNATIONAL STRATEGY

How to manage such a set of contradictions? The two main problems which are to be solved are problems of organising an international research team and of communication within the team.

3.1. Team Organisation

The *constitution* of the team asks for a number of very important decisions, which are fundamental for the success of the research.

The first decision is, how many countries will be included? It is clear that a project is easier to manage if there are only a few countries involved. But the extension of the number of participants will very often be necessary for political reasons and for reasons of science policy.

With regard to political reasons the question is: why exclude a country? It is difficult to decide *a priori* on the exclusion of any country and there is no reason to do so. If many Eastern countries are interested, they will naturally participate and therefore it will be necessary to find the same number of participating countries in Western Europe.

A second reason is connected with science policy: an unequal development of social science is not favourable for its general development. If in certain countries social sciences have been less developed in a certain field, it is better to invite these countries in order to give them the opportunity of progressively rejoining countries where social sciences are more developed.

A third reason is a purely scientific one: it is evident that the more countries are

115

involved, the larger the basis for comparisons will be and thereby the results will be more interesting.

A second type of decision connected with the constitution of the team concerns the disciplines involved. A multidisciplinary project will allow carrying out the research from different points of view. But on the other hand it will be more difficult to organise, because of communication problems between the disciplines, and it will increase the cost of the research. It could be very useful to include specialists of area studies in the team, who will bring their knowledge about the particularities of the country under study into the comparative research. But that will also increase the cost of the research (travel costs etc.).

When the team is constituted, the distribution of work within the team is a very important task. It is absolutely necessary to know the real interest of the participants in the research because otherwise some participation might be purely formal and would not be translated into real work. The distribution of work must be based on the knowledge about the real interest in participation if one does not want too great a discrepancy between promises and expectations on the one side and actual contributions and work fulfilment on the other.

A classical problem is how to decide whether a study on one country will be made by scholars from this country, by foreigners with the help of local researchers or by mixed teams. The latter two solutions are more expensive, but they are certainly more fruitful: more ideas will appear in discussions between researchers from different countries, considering problems with "new eyes", than from the exclusive observation by scholars from the respective country itself. Some questions are easier to ask by foreigners, and if these foreigners have enough tact and good contacts with their colleagues, the mixed team may reach new insights in some problems.

Closely connected is another classical problem, namely how to decide whether the work will only be distributed among countries – each country studying itself – or whether it will be possible to distribute the work according to topics between representatives of different countries – each participant studying a topic jointly with participants from other countries. The second solution will impose the comparison, but it will also need a clear distribution of the work. Many comparative studies are just juxtapositions of different works on the same topic in each of the countries. The organisation of such studies is relatively simple as each country is responsible for its own study. The main problem, however, is to be sure that the various countries are really studying the same subjects. Distribution of work according to subjects is more complex, because it needs cooperation from each country with a researcher responsible for a topic and in many cases only the responsible person will see his name published as the author of the part of work he has been charged with. It is therefore necessary to clarify the real responsibility of each participant and to make sure that they really agree with the distribution of work and will be able to do it in time.

In all the cases, the level of possible comparison will depend directly on the quality of communication within the team.

3.2. Communication within the Team

Two models of communication can be distinguished. Model A is essentially a model of vertical communication. The different countries communicate through general meetings or with one or two responsible persons which are at the "centre" of the project but the teams do not communicate directly between themselves.

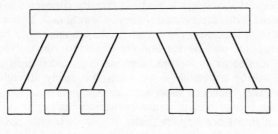

A

Model B is a model which combines vertical and horizontal communication.

It adds to the way of communication in Model A a direct communication between the research units of different countries.

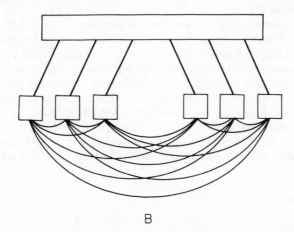

B

Model B allows for a deeper study because there are more exchanges possible between participants. Particularly at the beginning of the study, these exchanges can be very fruitful in order to understand in a better way the differences between countries and to elaborate a common framework.

Two phases in the research can be distinguished. We will call Phase 1 the formulation of the common framework for the research. In this first stage the establishment of bilateral communication between Eastern and Western researchers allows the undertaking of a first approach to the subject, to determine the scope of the study, to understand the differences between the countries, the meaning of the concepts which are used in order to translate them into the working language of the project and so determine common concepts. This work needs a lot of time but if it is well done much time is gained in Phase 2.

The second phase encompasses the collection of information. One very important difficulty is the inequality of information which results from the inequality of the intensity of participation of the different countries. In order to cope with this situation,

117

it is necessary to be able to use different scopes for comparison, depending on the information that has been effectively collected.

The development of the research study is directly connected with administrative procedures, this means with the restraints already mentioned. It is necessary to start planning a long time prior to starting the operation. As was mentioned before, the official plan in Eastern Europe as well as the budgets of institutions in Western Europe are prepared from July to December for the following year, and if decisions are not made during this time, it will be impossible − or at least extremely difficult − to organise a meeting during this year. Then one must wait for one more year. Furthermore various operations e.g. raising funds from different institutions may have different calendars. However, although it might not be very easy, it is certainly possible to have the scientific development coincide with administrative procedures! Yet what is to be done if it appears to be necessary to collect more information on a point or to have more intensive discussions on a specific problem? Wait for one year? Generally it is impossible to wait and it is necessary to work with the information that has already been collected. Therefore, the better the work in Phase 1, the shorter Phase 2 and the more intensive the exchanges in this phase can be.

All these organisational aspects are very complex and the work is generally difficult and delicate. But it is worth doing it. Sometimes there seems to be a discrepancy between the initial goals and the final results. But in order to evaluate the results of a project, all the elements have to be taken into account: the original information produced, the translated information, new concepts, as well as the conclusions. But also indirect results have to be recognised which are no less important than the direct results: the experience gained by researchers during the study and the possibility to use it in further projects, the 'opening' of local authorities for further and deeper studies, etc. All that depends on efforts made during the study, on the situation existing before its beginning and, more generally, on problems of communication and understanding between East and West.

Coordinating an International
Research Venture: The Case of IEA

by Torsten Husén

1. INTRODUCTORY REMARKS

The International Association for the Evaluation of Educational Achievement (IEA)[1] was established in 1961 as a cooperative venture between educational research institutes in a dozen countries, the directors of which had met regularly since the mid-1950s and had begun to contemplate the task of evaluating on a comparative basis national systems of education. The history of IEA is an interesting piece of recent educational research history which is worth writing up in more detail for the benefit of posterity. It illustrates not only the incipient attempts to establish a science of empirical comparative education based on cooperation between research institutions in several countries but also how closely tied to the prevailing *Zeitgeist* and its dominating paradigms a research endeavour can be. Changes in paradigms (see, e.g. Husén, 1979) have, to be sure, occurred since we embarked on our venture two decades ago, and hindsight provides us with a different perspective of many of the theoretical and methodological problems we were struggling with at the beginning.

Some of the experiences gained in launching a cross-national large-scale survey research that we embarked on two decades ago deserve to be put on record. Our difficulties, successes, and failures — administrative, economic, and methodological — need to be more closely and concretely identified for the benefit of future endeavours of this kind. The present paper is not an attempt to do this comprehensively and in detail. It is a report of my personal views on selected problems and how I *ex post facto* perceive them.

There is a second motive behind my attempt to take a retrospective look at the IEA research work, particularly the Six Subject Survey. This huge project was reported

---

[1] IEA as an organisation and its research activities are presented in *International Association for the Evaluation of Educational Achievement (I. E. A.)* (Stockholm: Institute of International Education, 106 91 Stockholm, Sweden) which also gives a directory of its membership. An *Annotated Bibliography of IEA Publications 1962–1978* (Stockholm: IEA, Institute of International Education, University of Stockholm, 1979) edited by T. Neville Postlethwaite and Arieh Lewy, lists some 300 items, both monographs and papers in scholarly journals which report IEA research.

firstly in nine volumes that appeared from 1973 through 1976.[2] In addition, a host of special studies based on further analyses of data available in the IEA Data Bank have been published in a Monograph Series under IEA auspices.[3] A venture which no doubt has been hazardous and conducted in an adventurous and pioneering spirit in all its aspects, administrative, economic and methodological, is of course begging for criticism. The mathematics survey which was conducted in 1962 through 1965 with the data collection taking place in 1964 was, ten years *post facto*, harshly criticised by a professor of mathematics education, Freudenthal (1975). His criticism was directed mainly against the mathematics tests, their content, and how they were developed. The reading survey reported by Thorndike (1973) was heavily criticised by a specialist in reading, Downing (1974–75). One of his major points is that the tests have been inadequate for the less developed countries. The most comprehensive, incisive – and informed – critical review of the Six Subject Survey, however, is the one by Inkeles (1978), who was commissioned by the U.S. National Academy of Education to take a look at the IEA research in its entirety. His review covers all the subject area reports but not the technical report by Peaker (1975), which is unfortunate, since most of the criticism deals with the methodology of the survey.

The purpose of this paper, however, is *not* to advance any rebuttals. This would not only require another format but also take me far afield. The main purpose is to deal with some problems we encountered in the coordination and administration of the IEA surveys. There is, it ought to be said, a problem of philosophical significance involved. The self-reviewing exercise I am doing here covers a period of some 20 years. Its retrospective character leads to its being conducted in a spirit of what the French refer to as *l'esprit de l'escalier:* that I indulge in second, or even third thoughts that occur to me on the staircase quite a while after having left the rooms of emotionally loaded encounters. In this case I have had ample opportunity to indulge in that spirit. A long time has elapsed since we began to conceptualise the surveys and to take methodological decisions

[2] The most comprehensive and at the same time "official" reporting of the Six Subject Survey has been available in the series "International Studies in Evaluation" published jointly by Almqvist & Wiksell International, Stockholm and John Wiley & Sons (Halsted Press), New York. The volumes are the following:

L. C. Comber and John P. Keeves, *Science Education in Nineteen Countries: An Empirical Study* (1973);

Alan C. Purves, *Literature Education in Ten Countries: An Empirical Study* (1973);

Robert L. Thorndike, *Reading Comprehension Education in Fifteen Countries* (1973);

E. Glyn Lewis and Carolyn E. Massad, *The Teaching of English as a Foreign Language in Ten Countries* (1975);

John B. Carroll, *The Teaching of French as a Foreign Language in Eight Countries* (1975);

Judith V. Torney, A. N. Oppenheim, and Russell F. Farnen, *Civic Education in Ten Countries: An Empirical Study* (1975);

A. Harry Passow, Harold J. Noah, Max A. Eckstein and John R. Mallea, *The National Case Study: An Empirical Comparative Study of Twenty-One Educational Systems* (1976);

Gilbert F. Peaker, *An Empirical Study of Education in Twenty-One Countries: A Technical Report* (1975);

David A. Walker, *The IEA Six Subject Survey: An Empirical Study of Education in Twenty-One Countries* (1975);

[3] The Monograph Series which until now comprises 12 volumes is published jointly by Almqvist & Wiksell International, Stockholm and John Wiley & Sons (Halsted Press), New York.

which had far-reaching implications. I have, indeed, been descending the staircase of a skyscraper!

My point is that what we did some 15—20 years ago in planning the surveys which then evolved should be judged with standards pertaining to the state of the art *at that time.* We were, as all researchers are, to some extent, prisoners of the prevailing paradigms of the research community with its theoretical and methodological orientation and with the corresponding difficulties of breaking out of the prison of conventions. Of course, being able to do this is a proof of creativity which, however, is easier to achieve by an individual than by a collective. Anyhow, one cannot employ standards derived from the present insights and competencies achieved in the social sciences in general and in comparative education and survey research in particular on research planned and/or conducted more than a decade ago under quite different paradigmatic auspices. For example, the IEA research was initiated before the intensive debate on the theory and methodology of large-scale survey studies took off as a result of the Coleman (1966) and Plowden (1967) surveys. When the IEA surveys were first planned, comparative education was conceptually still in its infancy. Attempts to advance theories and to develop methodological frameworks by, for instance, Noah and Eckstein (1969) had hardly begun. However, Bereday's (1964) book on methods in comparative education was available and referred to in the mathematics study. As Inkeles (1978) points out in his review of the Six Subject Survey, IEA had to conduct groundbreaking work by developing a methodology for quantitative comparative studies. At that time no cross-national surveys in education by means of representative national samples had been launched.

*

Thus, this paper is an attempt, in a personal vein, to account for some of the lessons learned in a — still — rather unique research venture. The retrospective observations are made partly for our own benefit, since IEA is presently engaged in a second round of surveying mathematics education.

2. HOW IEA EVOLVED

The bold idea of conducting an empirical study of cognitive development in children from different national systems of education was first advanced and tried out at a meeting of educational researchers from a dozen countries at the UNESCO Institute for Education in Hamburg in 1958 (Foshay 1962). One year before, the Institute had hosted an international meeting of educational psychologists, most of them psychometricians, on problems of evaluation. In Europe at that time, this was a field to which little thought had been devoted, whereas in the United States, not least through Ralph Tyler's (1950) pioneering research, it had already in the 1940s become an area in which leading educators took great interest.

At the 1957 meeting it was realised how little empirical evidence was available to substantiate many commonplace sweeping judgments about the relative merits and failings of various national systems of education. Concerns about the quality of secondary education in general and science education in particular had begun to be aired in the United States by, for example, Admiral Rickover (1959) and history professor Arthur Bestor (1953). American schools were under heavy attack and accused of lack of intellectual rigor and quality standards. Similar concerns had begun to crop up in other countries, where secondary education was in the process of becoming universal. These concerns reached an almost hysterical level in connection with the launching of Sputnik. This spectacular achievement was ascribed in the last analysis to superior science education in the Soviet Union. At the meetings of the researchers during the late 1950s it was realised that very little, if any, empirical evidence was available to substantiate judgments about science or mathematics education in a given country. We simply lacked *internationally valid standards* in terms of student competence in key subject areas. It was, after all, the level of student competency that was in the centre of concerns about standards.

Given the lack of hard evidence, why not take stock of the experiences gained in some countries from large-scale testing programmes, particularly experiences in the Anglo-Saxon countries, and the survey techniques that had begun to be employed in the fact-finding American positivist spirit? Such techniques had already made their way into authoritative handbooks of social science research. Given the state of the arts at that time in the field of cross-national social science research, already the development of instruments appeared to be, and indeed was, quite an achievement.

Most of us who met in Hamburg in the late 1950s had our background in educational psychology, including tests and measurements. William D. Wall, who chaired the early meetings, was a British psychologist who, after a period of university research in education in England and some years at the UNESCO Headquarters in Paris, had become Director of the National Foundation for Educational Research in England and Wales (NFER), an institution that provided the local Educational Authorities in England with testing programmes for the "eleven-plus" examinations. NFER had also begun to conduct national surveys. Wall was succeeded on the IEA Council by Douglas Pidgeon as a representative of the NFER. The Federal Republic of Germany was represented by Walter Schultze of the *Hochschule für internationale pädagogische Forschung* later *Deutsches Institut für internationale pädagogische Forschung,* founded in 1952 with considerable financial and intellectual input from the American Government. He had after the war been involved in developing psychological tests for selection to the *Gymnasium.* France was first represented by Gaston Mialaret of the University of Caen and later by Françoise Bacher of the *Institut national d'étude du travail et d'orientation professionelle* in Paris, which was responsible for the development of tests needed for vocational guidance and secondary school examinations in France.

Of the Americans who belonged to the "founding fathers" only C. Arnold Anderson of the Center for Comparative Education at the University of Chicago came from outside the educational research establishment. He had started as a rural sociologist and had moved into educational sociology and then comparative education. Arthur W. Foshay from Teachers College, Columbia University, had conducted most of his research in curriculum and classroom didactics. The other three Americans were leading psychometricians. Benjamin S. Bloom of the University of Chicago had been under Ralph Tyler's tutelage in Chicago and had served as University Examiner there. He had recently (Bloom, 1954) published the first volume from a project on the taxonomy of educational objectives, which was a grandiose neopositivist exercise attempting to operationalise educational objectives. His work served as a paradigm in the curricular analyses that preceded the construction of the IEA achievement tests. Robert L. Thorndike of Teachers College, Columbia University, was an outstanding psychometrician, whose handbook on educational measurement (together with Elizabeth Hagen, see Thorndike and Hagen 1955) was used all over the English-speaking world. Donald A. Super, also of Teachers College, Columbia University, had specialised in aptitude testing as related to vocational guidance and had turned out an authoritative handbook on aptitude testing (Super, 1949). He joined the team later when we were about to embark on the Six Subject Survey and wanted to develop a more elaborate theoretical model for that study.

My own background, which I have described in more detail elsewhere (Husén, in press), was in important respects similar to that of most of my colleagues on the IEA team. I had completed my graduate work in development psychology and published a monograph on the later adolescent years, when by accident I was called upon to develop a system of aptitude testing and personnel selection in the Swedish Armed Forces in the early 1940s. Since all twenty-year-old males in Sweden had to show up for a medical and psychological examination of their suitability for military service as conscripts, I gained some ten years' experience in conducting surveys of complete age cohorts. The first major project I undertook in the early 1950s, after having been appointed to the chair in educational psychology at the University of Stockholm, was the development of achievement tests given to all second, fourth, and sixth grade students in Sweden. T. Neville Postlethwaite, who in 1962 was employed by the UNESCO Institute as the coordinator of the IEA survey research, came from NFER.

As noted earlier, the UNESCO Institute for Education, shortly after its establishment in the early 1950s, began to host international meetings in the format of week-long seminars. Already the international representation was instrumental in promoting the development of a still fledgling discipline of comparative education. The core group, who conceived the idea of evaluating national systems of education on a comparative basis, met for the first time in 1955. At the third meeting of the group in 1957, evaluation problems had been put on the agenda and at the fourth meeting, in 1958, it was proposed that the Institute should sponsor a cross-national study of how schools contributed to shape cognitive development of children in different countries (Foshay 1962). The idea of conducting cross-national surveys was intriguing and was discussed at two meetings in 1959, one at the Hamburg Institute and one at Eltham Place in England. It was decided to launch a feasibility study with the purpose of finding out whether it was methodologically feasible and administratively possible to develop instruments which were cross-nationally valid and could be administered uniformly over a range of countries with different school systems. We also, of course, wanted to find out whether the data collected could be made accessible in such a way as to make data processing and subsequent statistical analyses possible at one central place.

The outcomes of the feasibility study have been reported in detail in Foshay (1962). Suffice it to mention here that data were collected in a dozen countries. The outcomes were reported at a meeting in Hamburg in 1961 when it was also decided to go ahead with a full-scale survey in mathematics. Since it was taken for granted that the participating research institutes would be able to draw representative national samples according to a uniform sampling design, such an exercise was not included in the feasibility study. Given the later experiences, this was a wrong assumption. There was no time for an elaborate, time-consuming exercise of test development. Therefore, those in the group who were experts in test development drew upon items already available, most of them from England and the United States. Thus, a 120-item test measuring competence in reading, arithmetic, science, and geography was put together. Some

123

non-verbal, "culture-free" items measuring abstract reasoning of a type that NFER was using were included in order to assess non-verbal intelligence. The National Centres participating made the data available on punchcards to Teachers College, Columbia University, where Thorndike was in charge of the processing and the statistical analyses.

The question whether it was feasible to administer a set of tests uniformly across a series of countries and to process the data at one place was answered in the affirmative. Given the shortcomings of the exploratory study, the findings from our analyses had to be taken with a grain of salt. There were some unexpected findings which had to be checked in full-scale studies. For instance, the carefully developed reading items (with translation and independent back-translation) yielded a *smaller* between-country variance than did the non-verbal "culture-free" test items!

In the feasibility study we were, for the first time, confronted with obvious cultural differences with regard to, for instance, how seriously people in various countries take an agreed timetable. This was a major headache for the coordinator. If the data processing and the ensuing statistical analyses were going to be genuinely cross-national in the sense that all countries contributed, the pace with which the machinery could operate was evidently determined by the slowest-moving member.

The reasons for the decision to choose mathematics for a full-scale survey were obvious. In the first place, it was a subject area where language was universal and where curriculum content showed a high degree of cross-national overlap. Secondly, it was a subject where the development of standardised tests appeared to be rather straightforward and simple and did not entail problems of the kind later encountered in developing tests in, for instance, civic education. We could, then, hardly foresee the controversies among mathematics educators about inclusion of content areas and the relative weight that should be assigned to them. Almost all who had not been involved in the actual test construction thought that the content was to the disadvantage of students in their own country, even in England whose contribution to the test development had been dominating, even to the extent of giving the mathematics test a bit of British bias. We were, it should honestly be admitted, somewhat careless in not drawing upon a wider range of mathematics education competence, which would, not least for diplomatic reasons, have been advisable. Such a step would probably not have made the tests employed in the first full-scale survey much different, but it would certainly have made them less controversial.

A major technical problem that surfaced right from the beginning of the full-scale survey research was that of proper sampling design and the execution of it. Very few countries had, at that time, experience with drawing nationally representative random samples of schools and student populations for educational research purposes.

3. COORDINATING THE INTERNATIONAL MACHINERY

Organisational "machinery" had to be set up for a research endeavour that over the next ten years in (pre-inflation) dollars, including both national and international costs, would amount to at least one million. The twelve cooperating research institutions therefore, in 1961, constituted themselves as the International Association for the Evaluation of Educational Achievement, referred to and known under the acronym IEA. The decision-making body on matters of overall research policy and their operational

124

implications was the IEA Council on which each institution had one representative. The Council held at least one statutory meeting per year. Between Council meetings decisions could be taken either by a Standing Committee, which met more frequently, or by the Chairman of the organisation, a post to which I was elected in 1962. The Chairman had at his disposal a full-time coordinator. During the first years the Chairman was also the Technical Director of the ongoing survey work but later, as the burden of the Six Subject Survey became too heavy, the two functions were split.

Until 1967 IEA was a loose association; then it became incorporated. Before that it could, for instance, not sign contracts on research grants. Thus, the generous grant in 1962 from the United States Office of Education cooperative research programme had to be made available to the University of Chicago, where Benjamin Bloom was the Principal Investigator. He was, of course, primarily responsible to his University and to the Office of Education and not to IEA. Since the Coordinator was placed at the UNESCO Institute in Hamburg, where most of the meetings were held, certain funds were subcontracted to that institution via its Director, who in the first place was responsible to the UNESCO Secretariat. Thus, for several years there were lines of authority and responsibility that sometimes were at cross-purposes with each other and in some instances led to conflicts and crises. The decision-making machinery that produced research designs and data processing plans and initiated expensive international meetings was not involved in the authorisation of expenses and in the accounting for them. At one point, when the Council had a conflict over decision-making with the Director of the UNESCO Institute, the mood of the Council was to walk out and place the project somewhere else. The Office of Education grant, which was administered at the University of Chicago and not at the Hamburg Institute, strengthened IEA since one of its members served as Principal Investigator and a subcontract for certain services could be set up with the Hamburg Institute.

Thus, the lesson learned from this is that the international consortium of researchers and/or research institutions conducting cross-national research of the kind we conducted *must*, right from the beginning, be incorporated in order to act with a degree of autonomy that leaves necessary leeway for professional integrity. It should, in this connection, be pointed out that some of the participating National Centres were completely private and thereby enjoyed autonomy under some kind of Governing Board, such as NFER or the Graduate School of Education at the University of Chicago, which "represented" England and the United States respectively, on the IEA Council. Other Centres were institutions within state universities that by tradition were autonomous in their choice of research projects and their conduct of them – once funds were available. But support had to be solicited from the government both in terms of funds and endorsement vis-à-vis the schools and the teachers' union. This could sometimes be quite tricky when it came to studies with important implications for national policy in education.

In the case of Sweden, where the country was "represented" by the School of Education in Stockholm, national funds for the mathematics survey were obtained from the Social Science Research Council. The cooperation of schools that had been drawn for the sample had to be secured in each individual case. Even with considerable and eloquent persuasion some schools refused to cooperate, because they regarded the completion of questionnaires too onerous. Therefore, in the second stage of the Six Subject Survey, the National Board of Education provided not only the funds needed to remunerate the teachers-coordinators responsible for the testing at the individual schools and to cover the expenses for bringing coordinators together for briefing, but also the costs for printing the tests. The Board also made participation in the study mandatory and part of the regular duty that rested on the teachers and principals.

In some countries, such as Hungary and Japan, the National Centre coordinating the study was either part of or directly reporting to the Ministry of Education. This had two implications. In the first place, once the government had decided to participate, the necessary funds were made available. Secondly, the schools were by ministerial order obliged to cooperate, even if in some cases conflicts with the teachers' union could result. This meant, however, that in these countries the executed samples were pretty much identical with the planned ones and therefore could be relied upon. Even if, as in the Six Subject Survey, a parallel sample was drawn at each level, so that there was a reserve school for each school in the first drawn set that refused to cooperate, a considerable loss of schools was suffered in at least one instance.

Another problem area in the general domain of setting up "machinery" was that of *funding*. In the case of IEA we instituted right from the beginning a policy of separation of national and international expenses. The general rule was that all expenses that were incurred at the national level, such as establishing a national coordinating staff, drawing of national samples, trying out instruments and conducting preparatory processing before dispatching data to the international data processing centre, were to be carried by funds raised within the country. Clear-cut international costs, such as setting up and maintaining a coordinating staff and a data processing centre, computer time for central data processing and statistical analyses and international meetings, had to be covered by internationally raised and earmarked funds.

Problems of authority in the management of funds for the first mathematics study were mentioned above. Here, practically all international costs were carried by one single grant. In the Six Subject Survey the international expenditures were multi-funded by grants from both private foundations, such as the Ford Foundation and the *Stiftung Volkswagenwerk*, as well as from governments, such as the United States Office of Education and the Bank of Sweden Tercentenary Fund.

There are three different kinds of funding problems that international ventures of the IEA type have to face:

There are problems of *coordination*. This applies in the first place to efforts to synchronise international and national funding. There is no point in being assured of funds in a series of countries if international financial support is lacking and vice versa. When a project is multi-funded, grant-givers may require that their contributions should cover identifiable parts of the project and be available during a particular period or phase of the project, for instance the stage when instruments are developed. Thus, in the Six Subject Survey a grant from one foundation was given under the condition that it should exclusively be used to support the development of instruments used in the evaluation of science education. Since all the subject area studies were conducted more or less simultaneously with the same staff, and all the data were processed together and by the same data processing team, etc., it was in practice impossible to comply with such conditions. If we had tried to follow the contracts literally, the cost would have been much higher due to overlap.

There are problems of *timing*. Both national and international grants are usually given under conditions spelled out in a research proposal with a structured timetable. Thus, it is expected that the money is spent for certain specified purposes during a specified period of time. If the coordination of the timing of grants fails, for instance, if inter-national grants are given later than anticipated or national centres fail to meet deadlines, the entire project is delayed. The consequences can be that in countries where funds have been allocated for certain fiscal years researchers run into difficulties. They have either to do what they can to spend the money, with the result that they are out of funds when these are needed for the delayed work, or, if they halt the field operations, they have to pay staff salaries anyhow.

There are, finally, *bureaucratic* problems that ensue from the strings attached to the funds or the regulations that have to be met. Such problems are, of course, encountered in national as well as cross-national research, but they are magnified in the latter case by cross-national variability in regulations and by differences in scientific behaviour. It is in the nature of scientific inquiry that it is impossible to predict not only its outcomes but the course of the research process itself. There is a wide margin of uncertainty when and how the venture one is engaged in is going to end. In planning industrial manufacturing, one plans for the processing of an already known or clearly envisaged end product. But in planning research one does not know, often not even in broad terms, what the end product is going to look like.

Thus, both the timetable and the budget in a research proposal are, at best, informed guess-work. The difficulties in making a number of national research institutions move in a lock-step fashion and stick to a timetable agreed upon are enormous. Those in grant-giving agencies who are monitoring the research venture attach great importance to the way the project is progressing and how the line items in the budget are followed, if not for any other reason than for the fact that they are easy things to refer to in accounting.

Sometimes government requirements are in conflict with the scholarly ethos. In one case, the Ministry of Education did not release the data because some of the data proces-sing was going to be conducted in the United States and we were told in that country there were concerns about what the CIA might do with that information! Another ministry urged us to drop the statistical analyses for this particular country because, among other things, its level of performance was embarrassing. In the case of the Federal Republic of Germany one problem was to secure participation of all the *Länder*, which in matters of education at that time were constitutionally completely autonomous. The *Ständige Konferenz der Kultusminister*, a standing consultative body of the German ministers of education, had to be approached and had to give the green light for a survey that required a nationally representative sample.

4. ACCEPTABILITY AND VALIDITY OF PARADIGMS
AND INSTRUMENTS

A highly pertinent question that could be raised, when it comes to the staging of cross-national research in the social sciences is: How do you arrive at *paradigms* that are acceptable to all the participating national centres? It really did not become an issue in the IEA research simply because the question was never sharpened from the outset.

The IEA cooperative research was initiated by a group of predominantly European and North American researchers who regularly met in the late 1950s at the UNESCO Institute in Hamburg. Practically all of us from 12 countries had our training as

127

behavioural scientists in psychology, particularly in differential psychology including tests and measurements. Several of us had gained experiences during the war in test construction and mass group testing on military personnel. The research tradition of launching large-scale surveys of school children established in the Anglo—Saxon countries, such as the ones in England and Scotland, had spread to the European continent. The survey approach was a product of the Anglo—Saxon empiricism, sampling statistics and the neopositivism that became so dominant in the social, and in particular in the behavioural sciences, in the 1940s and 1950s. Sample surveys were considered to be the only approach in attempts to get the facts about, for instance, the state of affairs in the schools, including student competence.

It therefore seemed to those of us who in 1958—9 planned the feasibility study that the survey approach in evaluating the outcomes of school teaching was the self-evident one. Such a decision about the paradigm implied a whole array of techniques, which at that time were not taught in courses in education or even psychology in most universities outside the Anglo—Saxon sphere: test construction, sampling statistics applied to education, questionnaire techniques, computer-based data processing, and analytical statistics. This also included curriculum development by means of empirical methods based on the taxonomy of educational objectives as developed by Benjamin Bloom (1954) at the University of Chicago.

Thus, the analysis of the mathematics curriculum was done according to the taxonomy scheme. The tests were designed and tried out according to the standard procedures used in England and the United States. The sampling referee was Gilbert Peaker, an Englishman trained in the tradition of R. A. Fisher. The data processing and the statistical analyses were planned by people like Robert Thorndike and Gilbert Peaker. In the feasibility study we did not meet any serious problems because of the Anglo—Saxon dominance in paradigm and ensuing methods, even if in some countries the competence needed to execute the survey according to the agreed-upon scheme was somewhat weak. In the first mathematics survey the coordinator, together with one of Bloom's graduate students, had to visit the national centres in order to give advice about the data processing. More serious problems were encountered in the Six Subject Survey when another 8 countries (among them 4 non-industrialised) joined our venture. We soon realised that IEA should take responsibility for building research competence in these countries. This led to a decision to organise international seminars on curriculum development and evaluation to which I shall come back later.

The question of the *validity* of the entire approach by means of tests and questionnaires in assessing student competence and in mapping out the pedagogic milieu in which teaching took place has, of course, repeatedly been raised, and for good reasons. In the first place: how valid in terms of their content could the instruments be for the teaching of, say, science in the so-called less developed countries? After all, the experiences of children in countries with a predominantly rural economy must be different from those of children in urban, industrialised economies. The teaching that goes on in the school can make reference to these different spheres of experiences and would tend to emphasise different topics. In testing mathematics competence among 13-year-olds in the first IEA survey that took place in industrialised countries only, children in, for instance, Sweden and the United States were somewhat handicapped because certain more abstract topics in algebra and geometry had not yet been introduced in the curricula of these

128

countries whereas the 10–11-year-olds in England and Germany who went to the grammar school and *gymnasium* already had obtained some familiarity with them.

I shall not embark here on a detailed discussion of the question of content validity. It has been dealt with in the six international reports. Suffice it to say that the cross-national validity on the whole turned out to be higher than could be anticipated for reasons hinted at above. We were able to obtain information both by curriculum experts and by the classroom teachers about the emphasis put on the different topics in each major subject area and how much opportunity students had to learn the content of the respective topics. For obvious reasons, the test in reading comprehension had more cross-national validity than the test of knowledge in civics. In my view, the main deficiency of the achievement tests was that they did not sufficiently differentiate at the low achievement level because of too few easy items and too many difficult ones. This meant that a considerable number of students from developing countries scored very close to the test "floor", and, since correction for guessing was administered, even scored below that floor.

Another handicap was that we have not been able to estimate the effect of variability in "test wisdom", or rather, the familiarity with the format of taking examinations by means of standardised, objective tests, as accurately as that of differing content validity. Quite evidently, children in some countries were more used to taking tests than children in other countries. However, children everywhere have to some extent to take essay-type examinations where they have to write short or long answers to open-ended questions. The technique of giving multiple-choice tests where answers had to be entered onto cards which could be read by scanners and then entered onto magnetic tape as well as the encouragement to guess if they did not know the answer, obviously elicited different reactions among pupils from different cultures. We have looked into the matter of how children tend to guess in different countries in a study of the responses conducted by Bruce Choppin (1974) of the National Foundation for Educational Research in England and Wales.

5. COMPETENCE BUILDING

The first major IEA research venture, the mathematics survey, involved twelve research institutions (Husén 1967). As a rule, the heads of these institutes had gone to the Hamburg meetings at the end of the 1950s and through the early 1960s. Thus, they were personally involved in the planning and the execution of both the feasibility and the first mathematics study.

When we embarked on the Six Subject Survey, there was a considerable change in this respect. The number of participating countries increased from twelve to twenty-one, among them four developing countries. Several of the institutes that at this stage joined IEA had, even if they had staff members of high competence and with experiences in other research areas, little experience in survey research. In some cases, though, they had researchers of high quality whose competence in survey studies was almost nil. In two cases, the heads of National Centres had doctorates in developmental psychology, but had no background at all in measurement and evaluation.

Thus, at this stage attention had to be given to institutional competence building. Within each National Centre one person, as a rule on full-time, was named Technical Officer and was put in charge of the day-to-day operations of the project. All the technical officers were on several occasions brought together for combined briefing and training sessions for a week or two. The directors of the participating institutes had, of course, also to consider the technical aspects of the surveys in connection with the Council meetings, when decisions were taken on the general research strategy, for instance, about sampling procedures, subject areas to be tested, the kind of tests to be used, the setting up of data processing procedures, etc.

In many cases assistance by the IEA coordinating centre beyond that given to all National Centres had to be provided. For instance, in one case the coordinator had to travel to an Asian country and assist in the actual drawing of samples. The technology used in data collection and data processing, such as using answer cards that could be read by a machine and from which data could be transferred directly to magnetic tape, was at that time new to the majority of research institutes.

During the late 1960s it became increasingly clear that IEA, being an organisation set up to promote international cooperative research in education, should also bring its competence to bear in building up research capability, in the first place in the countries that participated in IEA projects. IEA has discharged its duties in competence building by two types of international seminars and workshops. In the summer of 1968 the first workshop on research and the educational process was held outside Stockholm. John B. Carroll, Chairman of the International Committee on French as a Foreign Language, assisted by Neville Postlethwaite, served as director of this workshop which was later repeated in Germany and in France, in the latter case with proceedings in French.

The Six Subject Survey was conducted in two distinct phases: (1) planning, instrument construction, and try-out which took place 1966–69, and (2) field testing, data processing and statistical analyses which took place 1970–72. The curriculum analyses and subsequent item construction were done by one international subject matter expert committee in each subject area. We soon realised that empirical methods in curriculum development were used in very few countries. On the whole, curricula both at the national and local level tended to be developed in a rather unsystematic way. Following a recommendation made by an international group of curriculum experts convened under UNESCO auspices in Moscow 1968, IEA decided to launch an international seminar on curriculum development and evaluation in cooperation with UNESCO. The hardships of securing funds and the hectic attempts in the last minute to get additional support from some governmental and private funding agencies is a fascinating story which would have to be told in another context. In short, in the summer of 1971 a six-week international seminar was conducted in Gränna in Sweden under Benjamin Bloom's directorship. He had, prior to the seminar, visited the countries in Latin America, Africa, and Asia who had expressed preliminary interest in sending teams, mostly from the ministries of education, to such a seminar. An impressive faculty of experts from the United States and Europe was brought together, with the "Altmeister" in evaluation, Ralph Tyler, as the leading figure. Teams of 4–6 persons from some 25 countries participated. This was the first large-scale attempt to set the stage for a massive exchange of experiences in curriculum development and to create a common frame of reference for such endeavours. The experiences gained were encouraging enough so as to follow them up with regional seminars. One of these took place a few years later in Africa. Neville Postlethwaite, who served as the IEA Executive Director through 1972, later came to the International Institute for Educational Planning in Paris where he took the initiative to arrange 3–4 week so-called intensive courses in evaluation techniques, where he could draw upon the experiences gained in the previous large-scale seminars.

Last, but by no means least, we had the annual IEA Council meetings which were attended not only by the Directors of the National Centres or their representatives, but by various consultants, experts, and international committee members as well. Apart from the formal business that had to be transacted during one week, most of the time was spent on problems of administering the surveys, which meant that quite a lot of technical problems had to be discussed. This was as a rule done in a seminar setting, which considerably contributed to the competence-building in centres where prior to the IEA research no survey research had been conducted. The importance of gradually strengthening the competence by such meetings became evident in the case of one country, where the ministry decided to dismiss the institute (and the director) handling the IEA matters and to give the charge to another institute and another director. The new team was almost completely lost and had to start from scratch in spite of an extensive documentation in terms of manuals, research memoranda, and letters that had gone out from the coordinating centre.

6. SOME CONCLUDING OBSERVATIONS

This paper on the IEA survey research has been prepared with the hindsight wisdom that the French call "l'esprit de l'escalier". Some of the weaknesses of this research resulted simply from the fact that the study was the first of its kind with the flaws that unavoidably are associated with pioneering ventures. Other errors stemmed from the prevailing paradigms of research at that time: the use of an input—output model of design, extensiveness of scope, and emphasis on quantitative methods and statistical techniques with no reliance at all on qualitative observations and anthropological methods.

Important questions in the comparative study of educational systems cannot be answered by means of extensive survey techniques. There are problems which have to be tackled by intensive studies of a few classrooms in the respective countries. Why, for instance, are Japanese schools "producing" such good results in mathematics and science? Is it primarily due to superior classroom practices or to certain values and other characteristics inherent in the Japanese society? Comparative studies of competitiveness (for instance by Dore[1976] and Teichler [1976]) suggest that the answer could be found in employing the methods of social anthropology.

REFERENCES

Bereday, George Z. F. (1964) *Comparative Method of Education*. New York: Holt, Rinehart & Winston.

Bestor, Arthur E. (1953) *Educational Wastelands: A Retreat from Learning in Our Public Schools.* Urbana: University of Illinois Press.

Bloom, Benjamin S. (Ed.) (1954) *Taxonomy of Educational Objectives. Handbook I: Cognitive Domain.* New York: Longmans, Green and Co.

Choppin, Bruce H. (1974) *The Correction for Guessing on Objective Tests*. Stockholm: IEA.

Coleman, James S. et al. (1966) *Equality of Educational Opportunity.* Washington, D. C.: Government Printing Office.

Dore, Ronald (1976) *The Diploma Disease: Education, Qualification and Development.* London: Allen and Unwin.

Downing, John and Dalrymple-Alford, E. C. (1974–75) "A Methodological Critique of the 1973 IEA Survey of Reading Comprehension Education in 15 Countries", *Reading Research Quarterly,* vol. 10, 1974–75, 212–227.

Foshay, Arthur W. (Ed.) (1962) *Educational Achievement of Thirteen-Year-Olds in Twelve Countries:* Hamburg: UNESCO Institute of Education.

Freudenthal, Hans (1975) "Pupils' Achievement Internationally Compared – the IEA", *Educational Studies in Mathematics,* vol. 6, 1975, 127–186. Cf. commentary by G. F. Peaker in the same journal, vol. 7, 1976, 523–527.

Husén, Torsten (Ed.) (1967) *International Study of Achievement in Mathematics: A Comparison of Twelve Countries* I–II. Stockholm, Almqvist & Wiksell and New York: John Wiley & Sons.

Husén, Torsten et al. (1973) *Svensk skola i internationell belysning I: Naturorienterande ämnen* (Swedish School in an International Perspective. I: Science). Stockholm: Almqvist & Wiksell.

Husén, Torsten (1977) "Evaluation Reflections: Policy Implications of the IEA Findings and Some of their Repercussions on National Debates on Educational Policy", *Studies in Educational Evaluation,* vol. 3, no. 2, 1977, 129–141.

Husén, Torsten (1979) "General Theories in Education: A 25 Year Perspective", *International Review of Education,* vol. 25, 1979, 325–345.

Husén, Torsten (in press) "A Marriage to Higher Education or A Life as an Academic", *Journal Higher Education.*

Inkeles, Alex (1978) "The International Evaluation of Educational Achievement", in *Proceedings of the National Academy of Education,* 4. Washington, D. C.: National Academy of Education.

Noah, Harold J. and Eckstein, Max A. (1969) *Toward a Science of Comparative Education.* London: Collier–Macmillan.

Peaker, Gilbert F. (1975) *An Empirical Study of Education in Twenty-One Countries: A Technical Report.* Stockholm: Almqvist & Wiksell International and New York: John Wiley & Sons (Halsted Press).

Plowden Report (1967) *Children and Their Primary Schools: A Report of the Central Advisory Council for Education (England): (Plowden Report) II: Research and Surveys.* London: Her Majesty's Stationery Office, 1967.

Rickover, Hyman G. (1959) *Education and Freedom.* New York: Dutton.

Super, Donald E. (1949) *Appraising Vocational Fitness by Means of Psychological Tests.* New York: Harper and Brothers.

Teichler, Ulrich (1976) *Das Dilemma der modernen Bildungsgesellschaft.* Stuttgart: Klett.

Thorndike, Robert L. and Hagen, Elizabeth (1955) *Measurement and Evaluation in Psychology and Education.* New York: John Wiley & Sons.

Thorndike, Robert L. (1973) *Reading Comprehension Education in Fifteen Countries: An Empirical Study.* Stockholm: Almqvist & Wiksell International and New York: John Wiley & Sons (Halsted Press).

Tyler, Ralph W. (1950) *Basic Principles of Curriculum and Instruction.* Chicago: University of Chicago Press.

International Cooperation
in the Social Sciences and the Role
of the Vienna Centre

by Stephen C. Mills

1. INTRODUCTION

The purpose of science for many centuries has been both cognitive and instrumental: to enable society to know and to do.[1] In today's world of complex and often man-made problems, social science knowledge is needed to devise new strategies of human behaviour and social action. At every level a direct and progressive contribution from social science is in demand. Yet whilst the number of trained social scientists and the amount of social science knowledge are both larger than ever before, a sizeable number of social scientists are realising that many of their concepts, criteria and methods may well be based on "culturally given taxonomies of human experience".[2] And they understand, too, that these culturally defined blinkers are inappropriate to our world where increasing integration, interdependence and inter-relatedness require global or regional and not local solutions to our problems.

In the face of the need and desire for an international social science there is a large number of different organisations; UNESCO lists over a hundred. And these exist at the global, regional and subregional levels. They encompass research, exchanges of information, documentation and teaching, and are national and international professional disciplinary associations. They draw their resources from a wide variety of sources: governmental, semi-governmental, from private foundations and so on.

Two main characteristics stand out in this mass of organisations: first that the infrastructure they provide for international social science is heavily biased towards Europe and North America; and, second, that this infrastructure has been developing at a rapid rate.

One attempt to broaden social science perspectives and contribute to the formulation of problems, methods and solutions on a supra-national basis has been the work of the European Coordination Centre for Research and Documentation in Social Sciences (known as the Vienna Centre). Although now there are similar centres in Latin America

---

[1] Russell, B. (1968) *The Impact of Science on Society.* London, Unwin Books.

[2] Strodtback, F. (1964) Considerations of Meta-Methods in Cross-cultural Studies, In: *American Anthropologist,* 66.

133

and Africa, and may soon be in Asia, the Centre was one of the first such regional coordinating organisations in the realm of social science, aimed at taking social science systematically and collaboratively towards a cross-national plane.

2. THE FOUNDING OF THE VIENNA CENTRE

Setting up such a Centre was not an easy task. There were two kinds of obstacles: political and scientific. In the 50s Europe was divided by the "cold war" between East and West which made scientific contacts very difficult. The first steps leading to the creation of a Centre to facilitate contacts between researchers in the social sciences in both parts of Europe date from the end of that "cold war" period. They came even when the political situation itself was still delicate, but when there was slow progress towards a lessening of international tension as European societies seemed to be looking for a new form of coexistence. In this climate of opinion, conversations began in Paris during the 1960 UNESCO General Conference between social scientists from East and West who wanted to promote comparative research in the social sciences in spite of existing ideological differences. The International Social Science Council (ISSC) was given the task of making the necessary contacts to constitute a European organisation for such cooperation and this initial link with ISSC has been maintained throughout the Centre's actual existence. The next UNESCO General Conference in 1962 adopted a resolution authorising the Director General to facilitate the establishment of the Centre in Vienna, under the responsibility of the ISSC, and with the help of the Austrian Government. The actual agreement between UNESCO and the Austrian Government locating the Centre in Vienna as a non-governmental international organisation was signed in 1963.

UNESCO gave original life to the Centre and its valuable help and assistance have continued throughout the Centre's existence. At first the Centre received an annual subvention direct from UNESCO. This ended after ten years in line with UNESCO's rules for such organisations and the Centre became a free-standing body (although still a part of ISSC). Now the Centre benefits from UNESCO contracts for specific projects, conferences and other activities.

Whilst setting up the Centre needed political activity between East and West on a high level, there were also scientific difficulties. The situation of comparative studies in the period after the Second World War in Europe was not at all encouraging. Comparative studies were almost entirely the domain of American and not European scientists. The late Stein Rokkan described the situation as follows: "In the rest of the world (apart from the USA) you could count on two hands the number of social scientists who were actively pursuing comparative studies. The great majority of social scientists carried out their work within strictly national or even local frameworks and only rarely tried to compare their findings with those established for other countries".[3]

Many of the techniques of research were either not known in various countries or were not adapted to the carrying out of multinational studies. Early projects of the Centre had, for example, to draw up rules for packaging and sending punch cards and

---

[3]Rokkan, S. (1979) The ISSC Programme for the Advancement of Comparative Research: Frustrations and Achievements. In: *ISSC Executive Committee Document 1979/5.*

134

formulate long and detailed instructions about how to carry out the fieldwork. Similarly, funding agencies then — as today — preferred to give money for studies which related to national or local problems, and there was little career credit for participation in multi-national projects.

3. HOW THE CENTRE HAS WORKED

However, perhaps the largest problem at the beginning was an outgrowth of the European political situation, the fear that one side or other — East or West — would dominate the institution. To prevent this a Board of Directors was set up to formulate the Centre's policy and it was made up of an equal number of social scientists from Eastern and Western Europe. At the beginning there were twelve members of the Board of Directors, but now as affiliation to the Centre has increased there are twenty members, but the principle of East—West balance is still maintained. Ten members come from the East and ten from the West. The fact that the Centre was set up jointly and with this principle of balance, rather than by one side and then inviting the other, has meant that the problem of domination has been successfully overcome, unlike in some other institutions which also sought to be all-European.

The Centre was set up to cover any realm of social science and not restricted to one or other theme of social science work. Its original remit, which is still adhered to, was very broad: "The target of the Centre will be to stimulate, mainly in Europe, international comparative researchers in social sciences. This domain includes, in particular, anthropology, demography, economy, ethnology, social psychology, sociology, law and political sciences".[4] As will be seen later when the Centre's projects are reviewed, it has carried out one or more projects in most of these disciplines and has maintained a broad-based social science activity.

The original project selection criteria developed in the early months of the Centre's existence enunciate the aims of the Centre even more clearly. These criteria were:

a. that research projects should enable points of view, concepts and methods prevailing in countries with differing ideologies and social and economic structures and at different stages, to be brought closer together;

b. that projects should not be purely academic nor should they be concerned with imprecise or very general problems;

c. that projects should take into account the concrete possibilities both of the institutes called upon to collaborate and the problems on which they were concentrating.

Taking these aims into account, as well as the Centre's basic aim of facilitating East—West scientific contact, initial emphasis was given to comparative and interdisciplinary research and the following topics were proposed in its initial programme:

i. overall comparative planning – this led to a project on "Backward Areas in Industrialised Countries";

ii. the concepts underlying the giving of aid to developing countries — resulting in a project "Comparative Forms of Aid to Developing Countries";

iii. the economic and social consequences of disarmament which brought about the "Images of a Disarmed World" project.

---

[4] Statutes of the Vienna Centre: Article 3.

From the beginning it was clear that the Centre with its limited budget could not pay for the research it stimulated and that what would be required would be the national financing of parallel studies. This meant that the Centre would not be a research centre, but would coordinate the work of different research teams from East and West on the same topic. To clarify the basic division of labour entailed in the Centre one must return to the original statutes: "In order to carry out these activities it will appoint the scientific directors of the projects and choose members participating in them. In cooperation with the project directors it will ensure the coordination of the works to be carried out, in particular, by creating special working groups." Additionally, the Centre "will elaborate an adequate documentation on the selected subjects. . . [and] will ensure by all appropriate means the publication of works carried out under its patronage". Thus, the main functions of the Centre's full-time secretariat have been to coordinate the work of the different teams, implement the scientific policy of the different projects, and document and publish the works which have resulted from this. Different secretariat members have played different roles according to their skills, the role of the project directors, and the working capacities of the different teams. Some have been largely administrators and diplomats; others have been virtual scientific leaders of their projects. As with the Board of Directors, recruitment has been both from East and West although perfect balance between the two subregions has not been possible. All in all, the secretariat has been the invaluable permanent arm of the Centre.

The original project selection criteria lasted extremely well and still underpin the Centre's work. However, in 1974 it was felt necessary to outline them in more detail to make them appropriate for the second decade of the Centre's existence. This was done in a document entitled "Project 80". The phrasing of this new programme showed real confidence in the special role of the Centre. "In coordinating cross-national research the Centre must not be content simply to register the demands of European scientists. Drawing on its position and past experiences, the Centre must aim at becoming an active growth point for intellectual initiatives and innovations. To do this it must have clear priority domains." The document then went on to spell out four priority domains which were not meant to be rigid constraints but "simply a core" for the future activities of the Centre:

"a) studies which focus on the most critical forces changing the structure and characteristics of European society;

b) studies which aim at ascertaining the dynamics and direction of development of major societal institutions;

c) studies which involve an attempt to visualise the future development of society;

d) studies which contribute to the advancement of social science."

Further, it was declared that these studies should be "transnational" and "of practical relevance". A number of research topics were spelt out; amongst others the following have been taken up in subsequent activities — technological change and its effects, culture and leisure activities, the family, and school and university.

To increase the selectivity of the Centre's projects, a Programme Committee was set up in 1976. The Programme Committee — which is a subcommittee of the Centre's Board of Directors — meets twice a year to consider project and conference proposals and makes recommendations to the Board. It is to make more systematic the proposal review procedure.

4. WHAT THE CENTRE HAS DONE

What has the Vienna Centre done in its seventeen years of existence? It has developed four main lines of activity. The most traditional and still the most important is that of comparative research projects. These make up the bulk of its activity. Then, it holds topical conferences on current social science problems. Since 1977 it has been coordinating the development of a programme for all-European cooperation in social science information and documentation. And in 1980 it has organised its first training course for graduate students interested in comparative research.

So far the Centre has completed sixteen cross-national comparative research projects and published twenty-nine reports on its projects and conferences.[5] The Centre has organised twelve international round table conferences. And scientists from more than 300 institutes coming from 26 European and 13 non-European countries have participated in its activities.

Currently, the Centre is coordinating the work of international research teams engaged in 12 cross-national comparative projects. There are also three "sponsored projects": a recent innovation to enable the Centre to help projects which started outside its auspices, but which now feel they would benefit from working under the Centre's umbrella.

Table 1 gives a list of the Centre's past and present research projects.

The Centre's conferences have ranged very widely in their subject matter and have dealt with both substantive and methodological problems.

Table 2 gives a list of conferences held by the Centre.

The Centre's social science information and documentation programme is made up of four working groups on different problems: on exchange of primary and secondary materials and user studies; on registers of on-going research; on the development of compatible hardware and software; and finally on the training of users and experts in social science information and documentation. In addition, international publications from this programme are in preparation: a guide to European social science information and documentation centres, and two series of specialised bibliographies – one of Eastern literature, and one of all-European material. Like the Centre itself, this programme also publishes its own regular newsletter.

How can one categorise the different research projects of the Centre? Although disciplinary differentiation is difficult because of the variety of disciplinary definitions, a number of projects may be classed as *economic research* (AIDE I, AIDE II, PLAN/CONS, PLAN/LOC, REG and RUR III). CURB and CURB Stage II are largely economic but also have some interdisciplinary aspects.

The Are several *sociological projects,* covering various branches of sociology, such as the sociology of education (EDUC, FORM, FORM II), industrial sociology (HIER), rural sociology (RUR I), the sociology of everyday life (BT); projects IMD and IM2 are peace research projects and futurological studies; cultural change (CULT), social welfare (ELD) and the sociology of law (LEG) are also included. In addition, there are two projects on family research (CFP and DIV) and one specifically related to the realm of *jurisprudence* (SD).

[5] A list of Vienna Centre publications is presented in the Appendix of this book.

Table 1. Projects completed or in progress

	Title	Abbrevation	Number of participating countries	Duration	Directors
1.	Comparative forms of aid to developing countries	AIDE I	5	1964–1965	V. Kollontai E.A.G. Robinson
2.	The absorptive capacity for foreign aid of developing countries and problems of transference of techniques	AIDE II	8	1965–1968	E. Boserup I. Sachs
3.	Automation and industrial workers	AUTOM	15	1968–	Steering Committee
4.	Time-budgets and industrialisation	BT	12	1964–1972	A. Szalai
5.	Changes in the life patterns of families in Europe	CFP	17	1978–	K. Boh
6.	Directions and tendencies of cultural development in modern society, interaction of national cultures	CULT	12	1976–	J. Arutunjan J. Cuisenier V. Filias I. Vitányi
7.	The cost of urban growth	CURB	8	1971–1978	R. Drewett
8.	Costs of urban growth Stage II	CURB Stage II	13	1977–	Executive Committee
9.	Juvenile delinquency and economic development	DEL	4	1964–1972	H. Michard P. Wierzbicki
10.	Comparative research on national legislations with regard to fertility	DEM	16	1971–1975	M. Livi-Bacci E. Szabady
11.	Effects of divorce on families with dependent children	DIV	17	1978–	L. Cseh-Szombathy
12.	Training of students from developing countries	EDUC	4	1967–1970	O. Klineberg R.V. Kerschagel
13.	Open community care for the elderly – a multinational pilot research project	ELD	7	1976–1979	A. Amman
14.	University graduates: their training and conception of life	FORM (Pilot)	6	1967–1977	W. Markiewicz H. Peisert
15.	University graduates: their training and conception of life (panel study)	FORM II	10	1977–	W. Markiewicz H. Peisert
16.	Effects of organisational hierarchy on the reaction of organisation members	HIER	7	1970–	A. Tannenbaum T. Rozgonyi

	Title	Abbrevation	Number of participating countries	Duration	Directors
17.	Images of a disarmed world	IMD	3	1964—1965	J. Stoetzel
18.	Images of the world in the year 2000	IM2	14	1966—1972	J. Galtung
19.	Law and dispute treatment	LEG	10	1976—	D. Kalogeropoulos J. Kurcewski
20.	Criteria for choosing between market and non-market ways of satisfying population needs	PLAN/CONS	9	1968—1977	V. Cao-Pinna S. Shataline
21.	Location of new industries	PLAN/LOC	8	1968—1975	M. Penouil V. Rasković
22.	Backward areas in industrialised countries	REG	12	1964—1970	S. Groenman P. Turcan
23.	Diffusion and innovation in agriculture	RUR I	7	1965—1970	B. Galeski H. Mendras
24.	The future of rural communities in industrialised societies	RUR II	16	1970—1977	B. Galeski O. Grande H. Mendras H.H. Stahl
25.	The internationalisation of the conditions of production and exchange and the international division of labour in the food sector	RUR III	7	1977—	A. Mollard H. Wirsig
26.	The sources of law	SD	11	1976—	E. Melichar I. Szabó
27.	The economic and social problems of tourism in Europe	TOUR	13	1972—	P. Barucci R. Freitag R. Galeski B. Jansson M. Mihovilovic D. Prielozny
28.	Programme on Work	WORK	formative stage	1980—	expert group

SPONSORED PROJECTS

	Title	Abbrevation	Number of participating countries	Duration	Directors
29.	Control on public administration	ADMIN	16		G. Braibant C. Wiener J. Letowski
30.	Inter-cultural investigation of the situation of women with two jobs in rural societies	FEM	6		B. van Deenen B. Tryfan
31.	The residential areal bond	RAB	7		E. Bodzenta P. Peachey

Table 2. International Conferences

Date	Title	Place
1964	Symposium on Juvenile Delinquency and Socio-economic Development	Warsaw
1967	Conference on Backward Areas in Advanced Countries	Varenna
1972	Round Table on the International Comparative Survey Research: Theory and Practice	Budapest
1974	Simulation Exercise on Evironment and Tourism	Vienna
1975	Round Table on the Quality of Life	Budapest
1977	International Conference on Information and Documentation in Social Sciences	Moscow
1978	Conference on the Social Effects of Using Nuclear Energy	Vienna
1978	Conference on Social Science and Social Policy	Bucharest
1979	Socio-economic Problems and Potentialities of the Application of Micro-Electronics at Work	Zandvoort
1979	Symposium Vienna Centre – FLACSO (Facultad Latinoamericana de Ciencias Sociales)	Madrid
1979	The Elderly and the Care System	Warsaw
1979	PLAN/CONS Evaluative Meetings	Rome Milan
1980	International Seminar on Cross-national Research	Warsaw
1980	Conference on the Situation of the Rural Family in Europe	Warsaw

The Centre's five other research projects may be considered as *interdisciplinary* requiring close collaboration between experts from different disciplines of the social sciences or other sciences. For example, there were sociologists, economists, engineers and social psychologists participating in the research into automation (AUTOM), and there will be a similar wide spread in the nascent WORK programme. Criminologists, jurists and sociologists all collaborated in the project on juvenile delinquency (DEL). Demographers and jurists working together in the study of legislation relating to fertility (DEM), whilst economists, sociologists and government tourism experts constituted that on tourism (TOUR). Finally, the project on the future of rural communities (RUR II), although it is a follow-up to RUR I, has progressively led to various fields of research, some derived from sociology and social anthropology, others from economics.

Of the three sponsored projects one is founded on administrative science (ADMIN), one on rural sociology (FEM) and the third (RAB) on urban sociology.

5. CHALLENGES IN THE CENTRE'S WORK

Having considered the Centre's organisational structure, its project selection criteria and its past and present activities, let us now turn to consider the challenges inherent in carrying out this work.

In studying European society, the diversity which must be accounted for in each project is enormous. The cultural and historical contexts of social phenomena are extremely complex. States are differentiated between capitalist and socialist forms of socio-economic and political systems, and thus with regard to the ideologies which prevail within them. There are clear differences of economic development. And there are many different languages some of them with transnational cultural influence, others only recently intellectually and scientifically productive.

With such variety and variability there are naturally very different social science milieux and "establishments". In the socialist countries Academies of Science play a prominent role in the organisation of science in general and social science in particular. In many non-socialist countries similar functions are carried out by social science councils or their equivalent and these link closely with social science activities in the different national universities through their role as funding agencies. Other countries have little or no coordination and leave the development and funding of research to government agencies, private foundations, marketing agencies or universities themselves. In some countries there are strong national centres dealing with social science information and documentation in general or specific themes in particular, in others there is next to nothing. Curricula and training of social scientists vary and the membership and strength of the different professional associations also varies.

Even once the group of international researchers is sitting together trying to confront their different social realities and find a working agreement on what to do, many challenges still exist. There are many different conceptual, terminological and methodological approaches and problems. On one project, for example, it was necessary for a subgroup of researchers to meet together a number of times to agree on the definitions of 20 or so key terms to be used in the research and which were later operationalised in the research design. It can take a number of meetings over two years or more to refine the original project proposal into a research design for a project which is workable in a European context. There are differences between the participants in terms of resources available for the project, time horizons of funding and work schedule, and personal scientific and career goals and interests. The project has to bridge different research experience, different research practice and different research cultures.

Differences can develop when creating common research instruments for the project. Often it is necessary to have a common core of instrumentation and then allow for extra parts to explore areas additional to the common frame. This may be either because of different interests among the researchers or because there are social phenomena which exist only in some and not all countries. In the Automation project, for example, four different methods of measuring automation were used and there were some aspects of industrial life which could not be generalised across the socialist and capitalist systems but which were important to study within a given system — e.g. "socialist emulation", the brigade system and the role of the Party could not be studied in a cross-system comparison.

Fieldwork and sampling instructions have to be drawn up in considerable detail. And, inevitably, different researchers opt for different ways of analysing and interpreting the data they and others have collected. Some require only simple percentages and four way tables, others require sophisticated cluster or factor analyses. In writing up in at least one project the possibility of writing rejoinders to different chapters had to be allowed to cope with methodological and ideological differences; in another project it was necessary to have in each section of the book one author from the East and one from the West.

Another problem which has to be taken into account is that many researchers come to confront the problems of cross-national comparison for the first time. This calls on researchers to recognise differences which cannot simply be swept under the rug. And, as well, as with any other group these are the normal factors of "group dynamics" which play an important part.[6]

6. AN OVERVIEW OF THE CENTRE'S EXPERIENCE

Today the Centre is funded by Academies of Science, Social Science Councils, UNESCO Commissions, and Ministries from 21 countries. Its resources — including both convertible and non-convertible currency subventions, specifically allocated funds, and seconded staff salaries — amount to approaching 1 million US dollars per year.

The Vienna Centre has to date completed or started 28 projects and sponsored three others. These projects cover a wide range of topics and disciplines. They tend to be increasingly symmetric in their internationalisation of the research process: that is, all the national groups are participating on an equal basis with a steering committee on which all national research teams are equally represented. This contrasts with the asymmetrical type where one country prepares the programme, sends its members to collect data and then interprets it without the collaboration of indigenous researchers in the other countries concerned: namely, Safari research of the old and increasingly obsolete style.

These projects have been undertaken in line with an evolving set of selection criteria which have both scientific and political content so as to ensure wide coverage of the region and its systemic differentiation. Important and lasting selection criteria have been, for example: the likelihood of increasing cross-systemic scientific cooperation and the need to yield meaningful results of interest to national research programmes.

The sources of initiative for the projects have been both national and international. Projects have been suggested by individual scholars as well as Academies of Sciences. That so much has been accomplished despite the lack of institutionalised incentives for cross-national research, indicates that the tenacious desire of social scientists to gain the benefit of broadening their horizons can conquer many obstacles and bring together those from widely different disciplines, subjects and with different methodological propensities and preferences.

Although the Centre's projects have ranged widely, they have mainly concentrated on recognising, describing and analysing societal phenomena which have been found to be of common occurrence and significance in different countries and especially in different socio-economic systems. This has had two consequences for the nature and character of the Centre's work. First, cross-national research in the Centre's terms has been about the study and comparison of data on discrete phenomena as they exist in different countries, rather than about cross-national or cross-systemic processes. Second, whilst

[6]Framhein, G. and Mills, S. C. (1979) Infrastructure — the Third Element in International Comparative Research, In: J. Berting et al.: *Problems in International Comparative Research in the Social Sciences.* Oxford, Pergamon Press.

142

methodological and theoretical questions have been tackled, this has been in the course of finding commonly agreed ways to carry out projects oriented primarily to understanding social and scientific subject matters and problems.

The Centre's experience gathered in the 17 years since it was first set up as a regional social science centre by UNESCO is of both scientific and organisational relevance. Scientifically, it has shown the possibility of continuous and systematic cross-national research; such research and its application is an essential part of any move towards universalisation since it is particularly through this channel that more general and particularly regional concepts and criteria may be derived and validated. Also, it is through collaborative multinational research with mutual advantage and the advancement of knowledge as its aims that social scientists are able to realise the specificity of their own national situations, which are largely taken for granted until one is called upon to work with others whose experience and scientific, cultural and intellectual perspectives originate from sources different from one's own. Organisationally, the Centre has worked on a decentralised pattern with national research teams finding their own funds and working parallelly on common research programmes. This is in contrast to the other model where the coordinating and initiating institution supplies the funds for the national research and may even provide the possibility for the international group of scholars to work together in one place for some period of time to carry out the project. This second model does look attractive; but it is not possible for the Vienna Centre given its current level of resources. However, the work of the Centre has shown that even with relatively small resources it is possible to overcome apparently daunting obstacles which stand in the way of common scientific work in a region as diverse and differentiated as Europe.

Part Four

CASE STUDIES

In this part, two case studies are presented by *Chantal Kourilsky* and *Oskar Vogel* which at the seminar served as a basis for working-group discussions. Each one deals with a comparative project coordinated by the Vienna Centre and concentrates on some selected problems which are relevant to it. The problems of theory, strategy, methodology and organisation, which have been discussed in the foregoing contributions analytically separated from each other, appear together and in a compound way in every comparative project. Of course, the case studies cannot do justice to the whole figuration of these problems in the respective projects — this would certainly require a book of its own. But they can give examples of the complexity in which these problems appear in actual research, by throwing light on selected parts of the research process of these two projects.

The Sources of Law Project:
An Example of the Application of
Quantitative Methods to the Study of Legal
Normative Systems

by Chantal Kourilsky

INTRODUCTION

The research project on "Sources of Law" is concerned with the study of the dynamics of legal normative systems, both at the level of structural relations between the elements and at the level of the evolution in time. It can be situated at the cross-road of comparative legal sociology and comparative law and aims to enrich these two fields by a more detailed empirical knowledge of the functioning of legal systems that are investigated and compared.

In comparative legal sociology, as well as in comparative law, the dynamics of legal normative systems have been mainly studied from the point of view of the *content* of the legal rules and institutions, stressing to different degrees their interaction with social, political, economic and cultural relations, institutions and norms which exist in the respective societies. Though they "open" legal categories when investigating the relation between law and society, they nevertheless implicitly recognise the double aspect of the legal rule stressed by the theory of law. According to the strict conception of legal theory, the legal rule is conceived as a *norm* to which legal character is assigned by its *form*: the enaction of the norm by the competent authority according to a defined procedure conditions the legal nature of the norm and its enforcement as a legal rule in the society.

The originality of the study on "Sources of Law" consists in the fact that it explicitly accepts the categories of the theory of law and takes them as a central reference for the research. At the same time it challenges their formalism in submitting them to the techniques which are used in empirical sociological research.

1. DEFINITION OF THE RESEARCH OBJECT

Many research studies on law and institutions seem to encounter problems quite different from those of usual empirical sociological research. The latter often constructs the research object and defines the variables outside formally institutionalised categories in order to evaluate indirectly measurable phenomena, such as e.g. "job satisfaction" or "school achievement". This project, however, is based on categories that already exist in legal normative systems. We therefore have to define *within this binding framework* sociologically relevant relations between these categories which characterise their dynamics.

The first step in the study of legal normative systems in a comparative perspective must be the definition of a basically comparable structure. It is even more important when one compares Eastern and Western legal orders which are based on different social, political and economic systems.

In the Sources of Law project this problem was solved by selecting countries that belong to the same roman—germanic legal tradition of the "written law system".[1] Continental Eastern and Western European countries have adopted, although from different ideological and theoretical positions, the same principle of a legal normative system in which "sources of law" are elaborated, enacted and promulgated by the competent organs of the state in a written form. These sources of law are organised in a strict hierarchy which is constructed on the principle of the supremacy of normative acts emanating from the Legislative over those enacted by the Executive and the Administrative bodies. The basic standard categories of this hierarchy are, in order of decreasing importance, the Constitution, the constitutional laws, the statute laws (acts emanating from the Parliament as legislative body), the ordinances, decrees and all regulatory acts emanating from the Executive and the Administration. The provisions of all such normative acts have to be conform, or at least not contrary, to those of the superior categories (principles of constitutionality and legality). Normative acts on a lower level develop and detail the provisions of normative acts on a higher level in the application to particular fields. There are some variations in the individual legal systems with regard to these basic principles, particularly in some cases in the development in the present century of the regulatory power of the Executive up to an "autonomous" power. However, the common acceptance of this type of structure of the legal order in the selected countries enables us to compare the various systems for two reasons:

a. the legal normative systems to be compared are constructed according to similar principles and techniques;

b. the normative acts that are to be the basic data for the empirical research are officially published in the various countries.

In the Sources of Law project nine Eastern and Western European countries are participating: Austria, Federal Republic of Germany, France, German Democratic Republic, Hungary, Norway, Poland, Switzerland and Yugoslavia. These countries are selected according to the arguments mentioned above. Research teams from these countries agreed on the definition of the research object and adopted research methods to discover aspects of their legal normative systems which have been unexplored up till now.

[1] See, for example, for the classification of legal systems David, R. and Brierly, J. E. C. (1978): *Major Legal Systems in the World Today*. London (2nd ed.). First published in French: David, R.: *Les grands systèmes de droit contemporain*, Paris; Dalloz (5th ed.), 1973.

2. RESEARCH METHODS

2.1. Choice of the Quantitative Method

In legal research legal normative systems are thoroughly studied in a qualitative way, in particular because of the precise definition of their categories and elements and of their inter-relations. As an object of sociological research, these systems have also been submitted to qualitative reasoning, both in terms of their theoretical evaluation and in terms of their interaction with social phenomena.

The project participants, therefore, agreed with a proposal formulated by the research initiators[2] that the use of *quantitative methods* will give the best opportunity to discover new possibilities outside the existing patterns. They also agreed that this will at the same time secure the best possibilities for an objective comparison of phenomena of legal normative systems.

The quantitative analysis should be realised at two levels in order to highlight the concrete functioning of legal normative systems, their real flexibility and their capacity to adapt themselves to changing social situations.

a. first a *"static" analysis* evaluates the quantitative weight of the normative systems and of their elements at a given time;

b. second, a *"dynamic" analysis* should follow the evolution of the systems and of the relationships between the elements for each year. A ten-year period is considered to give a representative view of the aspects under study.

These two kinds of analyses should include the following items:

— quantitative measurement of each legal system as a whole in determining the number and volume of all generally binding normative acts that have emanated from central state authorities and are in force at the reference date (31 December, 1979 for the static analysis), or that were enacted during each year of the ten-year period (for the dynamic analysis);

— assessment of the "age" of the legal normative acts in force;

— the proportion of the "old", "new" and amended parts of the legal normative system;

— calculation of the respective weight of the different categories of sources of law within the whole system;

— the proportion between the normative acts that establish a basic reglementation and the acts providing an application reglementation. This should be calculated for the whole system as well as for various fields of social relations and should be completed by a distinction of the level, in the hierarchy of sources of law, at which the basic reglementation has been enacted (which may vary according to the covered field);

— assessment of the number and volume of normative acts which integrate international norms (international treaties and agreements) in the national legal orders;

— assessment of the number and volume of norms enacted in the form of normative acts that do not contain generally binding rules, but nevertheless have general consequences (e.g. creation of a public institution, dissolution of the Parliament etc.).

---

[2] Since then Prof. Imre Szabó (Hungary) and Prof. Erwin Melichar (Austria) have been co-directors of the research project.

2.2. Stages of the Research Work

a. It was decided that the stage of empirical investigation should be preceded by the preparation of national reports. These should serve as *background studies* and provide the necessary *qualitative* knowledge to enable the interpretation of the quantitative results to be compared later. It was *commonly agreed* that these reports should be conceived according to methods used in legal analysis and should contain the following elements:

- definition of the concept of "sources of law" in the national system;
- historical evolution of the national system of sources of law;
- elements of the current system: structure of the generally binding norms in relation to their enacting authority (normative acts emanating from central state authorities and, for the federal states, of one member-state chosen as a representative example; brief accounts on the local and regional normative acts; on the normative "autonomous" power; on the role of the Judiciary and the normative value of its decisions; on interpretation norms; on customary law); norms from international origin; specificity of the law concerning public enterprises; indications on normative acts emanating from non-state (social) organisations; control of the constitutionality and of the legality of normative acts; codification questions;
- development trends in the national system of sources of law.

b. With regard to the central stage of this project, the *quantitative analysis*, it was agreed that a questionnaire should be used. A draft questionnaire was elaborated by a restricted group of participants (two of them representing the Western system and two the Eastern system), according to concerns formulated by the whole research group. The final version of the questionnaire would be adopted with the agreement of all participants.

c. The last stage of the research project will be devoted to *comparison* and *interpretation of the quantitative results* obtained from the static and dynamic analyses. This will be facilitated by the qualitative "keys" provided by the national background studies which give the information on national contexts to which numerical and graphical data are to be related. This approach aims at avoiding the danger of an artificial comparability of only visible similarities and dissimilarities of the quantitative results. In such a way, the researchers hope to find, if not laws of concrete functioning of the written law systems, then at least the possible existence of regularities in addition to a better knowledge of the national systems studied.

3. PROBLEMS AND SOLUTIONS

In the present stage of the research project participants are collecting data to answer the questionnaire that was circulated in February 1980. At the same time the national background studies are being edited for publication.[3]

If one evaluates the difficulties already encountered in the project and how they were solved, two kinds of problems seem to be of interest for researchers engaged in cross-national comparative research:

[3]Ch. Kourilsky, A. Rácz and H. Schäffer (eds.) in press: *The Sources of Law. A Comparative Empirical Study*, Volume I: *The National Systems of Sources of Law*, Budapest: Akadémiai Kiadó.

— the scientific and organisational problems in the elaboration of the questionnaire items to be used for the quantitative study;

— the technical problem in finding a common terminology.

3.1. The Elaboration of the Questionnaire

3.1.1. Organisational steps

A working group was in charge of the elaboration of the questionnaire and met twice in 1979 to work out a draft questionnaire that could be qualified as "maximalist" in the sense that it integrated all the concerns that had been expressed by participants during the preceding general meeting of the project. This questionnaire will be answered by the participants themselves and by members of their research teams. A tri-lingual version of this draft questionnaire was sent out to all participants. They were asked, as a first step, to formulate criticism and proposals for modification. From the answers it became clear that they agreed in general with the character of the draft questionnaire but at the same time it was stressed that the final version should not be accepted without a general discussion.

The Vienna Centre then decided, with the agreement of the members of the working group, to ask the participants to apply the draft questionnaire in a national feasibility study during the months preceding the general meeting in January 1980. The final version was then worked out according to decisions taken at this meeting. Items and basic calculation criteria were re-elaborated in order to secure the most objectively comparable answers.

3.1.2. Specific difficulties of the quantitative research

In this description of the main scientific difficulties that were encountered in the elaboration of questionnaire items we will only mention those that seem to us of common interest for researchers in various fields of social sciences. For a proper understanding we have to turn again to the main constraints of the research project on sources of law:

— it investigates systems of legal norms the content of which is bound by their form;

— the material for the quantitative analysis is the codified structure of normative acts which are the formal expression of the legal norms.

In the translation of the qualitative concerns into quantitative items the following kind of difficulties had to be faced: To what extent can the evaluation of the volume of the normative legal systems be realised through the calculation of the number of legal norms they contain? How do national legislation techniques condition the formal response of normative legal systems to social change? And, if this formal response does not necessarily express the modification of the content of legal rules, which formal and substantial criteria can be used for quantitative measurement of stability or flexibility of a system or the capacity of renewing its content? Given the above-mentioned hierarchical principle of organisation of the sources of law system, which formal and substantial criteria separate normative acts enunciating basic norms and normative acts providing rules for their application (making the first category "operational")?

153

During the general discussion on the items of the questionnaire, it became clear that there was a wide diversity in the national evaluations of the change in content of normative acts. Finally, it led to the abandonment of the substantial criteria in most of the items in order to restrict the subjective margin of the various measurements. As a counterpart, the qualitative element was reintroduced by stressing the importance of the national comments on quantitative data. It was decided that the national answers to the questionnaire should take the form of directly readable reports relating numerical and graphical data to a qualitative framework of interpretation. The main points of this framework can be seen in the following issues:

a. the choice of the basic unit of calculation;

b. the "newness" of the normative acts; stability versus flexibility of the legal normative systems;

c. the distinction between normative acts enunciating basic norms and normative acts providing rules for their application.

a. The choice of the basic unit of calculation

The quantitative analysis is conditioned by the first measurement of the *number* and *volume* of all generally binding normative legal acts emanating from the state central authorities. It was decided that only normative acts published in Official Bulletins would be taken into consideration. For the static analysis those in force on December 31, 1979, were the basis; for the dynamic analysis those enacted each year of the ten-year period preceding this date were to be covered in the research project.

In the first stage of the project the participants had agreed that three methods of calculation of the *volume* of normative acts could be envisaged using the number of the following basic units of calculation:

— the smallest complete or independent subdivisions of the normative acts, e.g. the "articles" in French texts, the "paragraphs" in German and Austrian texts,

— the printed sheets of 40,000 letters or spaces (approximately 16 printed pages) and

— the norms contained in the normative acts.

The first two calculation units were considered less satisfactory because of their purely formal character and the inconvenience of additional variations due to the structure of various national languages. The third calculation unit was considered as ideal in the absolute. But a theoretical and operational definition of the legal norm where the diversity of the structure of norms could be taken into account was still to be found.

The research team from the German Democratic Republic proposed an experimental method to be applied. They suggested that the structure of the legal norm could be characterised by the following elements: (1) the description of social *conditions* to which actions of the juridical subjects, qualified as rights or obligations, are linked (called "section of the facts"); (2) the description of the *action* linked to the facts (called "section of the legal consequences"); (3) the *normative modality* expressed in various forms usually including the words "must", "are", "may", "will be", "shall not", "can" or "have the right" (called the "operator"), which specify whether the norm-receiver is authorised or obliged to accomplish the action in the determined conditions.

Some reservations were made by various participants with regard to the generally applicable character of these methods. The frequent link of legal norms to several branches

154

of law also made the application of the method complex. It was decided that the method would be applied optionally and as an experiment only to the civil code. In counterpart, the two first calculation methods (number of subdivisions and number of printed sheets) should both be used compulsorily for measuring the volume of the normative acts.

b. The "newness" of the normative acts; stability versus flexibility of the legal normative systems

The second element of the quantitative measurement of normative systems as a whole — the *number* of normative acts — raised a capital point that underlies several items of the questionnaire. It is the question of the "newness" of normative acts which was felt to be connected with the question of adaptability of legal systems to changing social conditions. Three items of the questionnaire touched upon these points at different levels:

1. the calculation of the number of normative acts in force, in which only normative acts introducing a new regulation were taken into account (modifications of these acts by more recent normative acts being considered as an integral part of the original text);

2. the assessment (number and volume) of normative acts in force according to their "age" (by year) in order to evaluate the degree of "modernity" of the legal systems;

3. the calculation of the proportion between normative acts introducing a new regulation and normative acts modifying an existing regulation. To determine the character of the normative acts (introducing a new reglementation or modifying an existing one) the working group proposed the criterion of "newness" of the acts in which formal and substantial elements were combined. Only normative acts introducing a "new" reglementation of specified social relationship, i.e. having both a new content and the form of an "independent" act, were considered as new. This procedure, however, would mean substantial differences in the amount of work to measure the number and volume of normative acts in force in Western and Eastern European legal orders. In the Western European systems normative acts that were adopted during the past centuries are still in force while in the socialist systems legal orders were almost completely renewed some decades ago. Therefore the working group proposed the following solution: participants would be free to limit the required measurements to a period of time that they would consider representative for their legal order (e.g. 50 or 100 years preceding 31 December 1979).

Since this measurement is dependent on the number of independent normative acts in force, each code is to be counted as a single normative act. This point stressed the difficulty of finding a common conception of normal and substantial newness of the normative acts. An illustration can be found in the legislation and codification techniques which vary from country to country.

In some Western countries even major reforms can be operated through normative acts introducing substantial changes "from inside" in the existing code, without touching their form in a way other than adding subdivisions. In socialist systems, on the contrary, the underlying principle of the constant adaptation of the law to social changes is reflected at the level of legislation technique in the relatively frequent adoption of new codes, though these codes can also integrate dispositions of the previous legislation that have proved to be well adapted to the field concerned. Therefore, the appreciation of the "newness" of the normative acts and of the "modernity" of the normative legal systems,

155

runs the risk of an unbalanced evaluation. A typical example may be quoted from the discussions in the project: fundamental reforms of the family laws were recently introduced in the majority of European countries. In the Western countries these were frequently operated only through modifications of the civil code, while in some socialist countries new family codes were adopted. The same can be said in other fields of legal reglementation. The proposed method leads to counting each code as a single normative act, even when it has been deeply transformed and to assess its "age" according to the year when it was enacted. The "physiognomy" of the legal order was therefore running the risk of a partial distortion.

As a solution, the following decisions were agreed upon:

1. To eliminate ambiguities, the criterion of "newness" was reduced to its formal aspect; the number of new normative acts depends on the legislator's will to create a formally independent reglementation or to introduce modifications in an existing normative act.

2. The measurement of the number of new normative acts as well as the assessment of their age will be extensively commented on by the respondents to the questionnaire. They will expose the legislation and codification techniques used in their national legal system and analyse the tendency of the legal order towards stability or change.

3. The calculation of the proportion between normative acts introducing a new reglementation and normative acts modifying an existing one would be restricted. It will only be applied to the particular fields covered by the constitution (and constitutional or organic laws) and by the civil code (and the family code).

c. The distinction between normative acts enunciating basic norms and normative acts providing rules for their application

As mentioned above, the hierarchy of sources of law in countries belonging to the written law system is constructed on the principle of the intrinsic superiority of the normative acts emanating from the Legislative on those enacted by the Executive. The latter must respect the principle of legality and are, in a general sense, entitled to develop and detail the basic provisions enacted by acts of superior level.

Two phenomena led the participants in the project to question the real functioning of these principles:

1. in the countries under study there exist variations in the hierarchy of sources of law in connection with the fact that legislating competence is vested either in the Executive power or in organs considered as emanations from the Legislative organs;

2. in many areas of economic and social life one may notice the increased intervention of the State, which has led to an increasing number of normative acts emanating from the Executive and the Administration and providing basic and application reglementation in the given fields.

In order to obtain clear results the complex character of these problems again led the participants to adopt also here a formal criterion to qualify normative acts as basic or application acts: the reference made by the application act to the original reglementation. Only when the specificity of a certain national legislation technique did not allow the application of this formal criterion, was the respondent allowed to use a substantial criterion that had to be justified in detail.

It was agreed among the participants of the project to measure these phenomena in a quantitative way by:

1. calculating the number and volume of normative acts in force according to their rank in the hierarchy of sources of law. In order to facilitate the comparison it seemed to be necessary for every respondent to define the function of each of these categories and to indicate their level compared to those existing in other countries (thus completing the information given in the background studies);

2. applying a distinction within these normative acts between those providing a basic regulation and those providing application rules (in using the criteria mentioned above). A comment should indicate the preferential level of adoption of basic acts for the various fields of legal regulation;

3. evaluating, as far as possible, the average number of application acts necessary to render "operational" a normative act which provides a basic regulation. This could provide a maximum of explanation of the legal regulation techniques existing in the participating countries. Additional information should be given in this respect about the power of interpretation of the law given to the judicial organs.

3.2. Finding a Common Terminology

In the national theroy of law the meaning of legal terms is precisely defined by concepts that closely relate to the specific system of legal and political institutions. The problem of finding an equivalent for these legal terms in a foreign language is very well known to all researchers in comparative law.

In the Sources of Law project the first solution to this problem was found by selecting participants from countries that belong to the written law system, and therefore have comparable institutions. Furthermore, as working languages for the project two continental languages were chosen: French and German. But this preliminary solution was only temporary. Another constraint was imposed upon the participants because they had to translate their reports into English for publication. Unfortunately, the English legal terminology is adapted to the basically different "common law" systems and makes it hardly possible to find equivalents to legal terms used in written law systems. Other solutions had therefore to be found.

The following two solutions are currently used in the project:

a. a special terminology was developed by a working group that was in charge of the elaboration of the questionnaire. This terminology should be as "neutral" as possible (e.g. "generally binding normative act", "normative act providing a basic regulation" or "normative act providing an application regulation"). In addition, examples were used giving an indicative hierarchy of sources of law to be adapted by the respondents to their system. All the necessary points were clarified by the working group with the participants during a general meeting preceding the final redaction of the tri-lingual questionnaire.

b. For the first publication of the project a provisional uniform terminology has been proposed to the participants by the co-editors, who are members of the previous working group. This terminology is somewhat different for Eastern and Western countries and relies on the principle of translating the same legal term in the original language by the same term in English, whatever the level of the hierarchy of sources of law is where the normative act is enacted. This system is currently discussed according to answers of participants. The final version of this terminology could be adopted to the second stage of the research project. In addition, it is considered to be necessary to quote the legal terms in their original language in the text of reports in order to avoid any misinterpretation.

4. CONCLUSIONS

It has often been stressed that qualitative and quantitative methods complement each other either in the different stages of the research work or in a combination of elements at the same stage. In this respect one may consider the Sources of Law project as a good example of this complementarity.

Qualitative approaches have been worked out at three stages:

1. the elaboration of national background studies that define the country system context of social phenomena under study;

2. the definition of the quantitative items of the questionnaire according to qualitative concerns;

3. the qualitative comments to the quantitative findings in order to obtain a correct interpretation.

The quantitative approach was at first characterised by the attempt to embrace a maximum of characteristics of the phenomenon of the sources of law (in defining both formal and substantial criteria for the various measurements). In a later stage the participants were confronted with the danger of too different national evaluations of the substantial criteria. They then realistically chose to limit themselves to the use of formal criteria more appropriate to secure objectively comparable data. At the same time they gave more importance to the qualitative comments to be asked from the respondents and created conditions for a richer interpretation of the national quantitative results.

In this respect these steps seem to be justified.

Problems of a Common Framework in Comparative Research: The Case of Inter-Cultural Comparative Investigation of the Situation of Women Working and Living in Rural Areas (FEM)

by Oskar Vogel

1. INTRODUCTION

The purpose of this contribution is to give a short overview of a research project. At the same time some central problems of theory and methodology are to be described which the social scientists from Poland, Federal Republic of Germany, Hungary, Sweden, France and Austria had to deal with in this comparative research. A detailed description of these and related problems will be provided by the research group in a forthcoming publication. The results of the project will be published in the Vienna Centre series in two volumes under the title "European Women in Rural Areas in a Changing World".

2. ON THE OBJECT AND AIM OF THE FEM PROJECT

This study is one of the first attempts in the field of rural sociology to carry out a comparative empirical research study with the cooperation of scholars from socialist and capitalist countries. It is characterised by the attempt to jointly draft the research documents, to have common methodological principles for the empirical investigations and to ensure the comparability of the results of the analysis of the empirical material.

How did the researchers proceed?

Closer contacts between the researchers had already existed before the group was actually formed. All of them had the strong desire to exchange empirical results and methodological experiences of their work. The group dynamics which emerged during the preliminary stage of the project (1976) were a decisive stimulus for the subsequent successful direct cooperation. It led to the idea of jointly planning a comparative empirical study and carrying it out.

Three considerations were of decisive importance for the definition of the research object:

1. the specific scientific interests of the participants had to be taken into account;

2. the research object should be of general sociological importance, but not yet dealt with on an emprical basis, so that there was no doubt about its scientific as well as socio-political topicality;

3. it should be easy to evaluate with emprical methods and to be analysed fairly independently from economic and political systems.

Women in rural areas fitted into these considerations. Based on shared assumptions with respect to the original situation and the socio-economic tendencies in the agriculture of the participating countries, as well as with respect to the evaluation of the situation of rural women in this developing process, the problem areas and research aim could be formulated.

2.1. The Problem Areas

The starting point was the assumption that the future development of the rural areas and of agriculture in the participating countries is highly influenced by the behaviour and activities of the women in these areas, their attitude towards work, household, family as well as towards their social environment.

Therefore the researchers were interested in:

— the present social and economic position of women;

— their tasks and position in the production process, on the farm, in the household and family;

— basic tendencies of their behaviour with regard to occupation, family and marriage;

— content and form of their social activity in rural communities.

Thus the following general questions were formulated to structure the empirical investigation:

1. which tasks and activities are carried out by women in the different domains of farm work, in the household and family as well as in areas outside the agricultural field?

2. in which domains do women participate in decision-making?

3. what is the absolute and relative amount of time spent by women in the domains of farm work, household/family and outside of the farm?

4. what is the relation between the time spent by women on agricultural or other work and the income of the farm and of the household?

5. what is the intermediary role of women in rural communities?

6. which personal, environmental and other objective factors determine

   — the amount and character of work in their occupation,

   — women's occupational attitude and behaviour, and

   — the social activities inside and outside the family.

As far as the empirical part of the investigation is concerned these general questions have been formulated in such a way as to avoid comparison of the socio-economic situation of women in rural areas between the countries investigated. Rather, it was more important to discover factors influencing the situation and attitude of women in rural areas with regard to their different spheres of life.

160

2.2. Aim of the Research

Some of the theoretical and scientific problems which the researchers encountered in connection with the aim of the research are briefly mentioned here: It is known that in the case of such a joint enterprise different approaches, the participants' different specialisations, their often differing understanding and experiences with regard to the aim of the research have to be integrated. The tasks should be determined in such a way that on the basis of a *common minimum programme* enough possibilities for specific evaluation per country still remain. Related to the scientific aim is the question of how and in which way the scientific potential of the group could be utilised in the process of the research.

Also one should consider whether all the realistic possibilities for carrying out such an investigation have been taken into account (political and cultural relationships between the countries, contacts between the scientific institutions, financial and personal conditions, different languages, etc.). It is also of importance whether practical relevance has been considered.

Decisive, however, is that by defining the general aim of the research, the possible increase of empirical and theoretical knowledge is pre-determined; similarly the range of the hypotheses and of the results will remain within the generally defined framework.

These and similar considerations played an essential role when the aim of the present project was formulated.

Firstly it was important to find a general framework of reference for the investigations. This was found in the rural communities (which are similar in the different countries). These communities were clearly defined with regard to their social, economic and space dimensions under the term "village". The researchers started from the theoretical presuppositions that the "village" is a fairly independent socio-cultural system. It was assumed that in this "system" the work and life processes of people in the investigated domains are rather independent of the socio-economic and political conditions in the various countries and that the intensity of these processes is influenced by the same or similar factors.

On this basis the following aim was formulated:

1. The factors which influence the social and economic situation of women in rural areas in different domains such as occupation, family, household and "village" as social environment should be investigated. Intensity and the direction these factors take should be studied.

2. The defined cultural systems, respectively the conditions and forms of life of women in rural areas should be "interculturally" compared.

This goal was to represent the general questions in a way comparable between the participating countries. Nevertheless, the empirical data collected according to standardised methods were used according to the specific interests and requirements of the various countries. These attempts should ensure comparability of the empirical results and at the same time maintain the freedom to evaluate and interpret the material for national research reports as well as for the intercultural comparison. The intercultural comparison aimed at the comparison of the cultural system "village" and led to the question: What is the influence of personal environmental and other objective aspects of the villages on the conditions of work and life of women in rural areas?

Though a clear-cut approach to this question would be interesting, this is not the purpose of this contribution. More general questions and problems relating to the research (especially with countries of different socio-economic systems) could, however, be of interest for our present discussion.

It was decided by the project participants to approach the comparative part of the joint study (the intercultural comparison) as a comparison of the social and economic situation of women in rural areas under the perspective of the system "village". General patterns and relationships influencing the system have been excluded. Possible problems arising from this decision can be indicated by the following questions:

— How to take social background into account in international comparative research?

— How to define it in such a way that it can be applied — at least in its most important points — in all participating countries?

— To what extent is it necessary — and possible — to concretely examine processess and phenomena and to take them out of their social context in order to be included in international comparison (e.g. economic situation of a farm, social status of women, etc.)?

— To what extent can one rely on abstractions in order to enable the international comparability of the research objects without running the risk of obtaining meaningless and uninteresting results from a sociological point of view?

All participants tried to base their research on a position of value neutrality in the research. So it was decided that only data referring to villages with different cultural structures should be compared. Some questions of general interest result from that:

Firstly, the general problem of any sociological research: no value judgement should appear in connection with sociological argumentation. It can be described as follows:

a. the sociological research is to give an objectively true picture of reality free of subjective evaluations;

b. however, the following factors are of decisive importance in this process: the purpose of the research, the pre-conception of the research object, the restriction of the area to be investigated both with respect to the theoretical interpretation of relationships and also with respect to the creative potentials of the researchers.

On this basis the following questions could be raised:

— What do we understand by value neutrality in international comparative research (especially if objects in different socio-economic systems are examined)?

— Is this value neutrality not very often just the expression of a value system on which the participants of the actual research project have agreed upon in order to exclude those problems which — at the time of the research — cannot be answered for various reasons?

— What are the repercussions of the intended value neturality on the unity of empirical and theoretical approach?

3. METHODOLOGICAL APPROACH OF THE INVESTIGATION AND ITS REALISATION

3.1. Methodological Attempts

The following parts of the work turned out to be most complicated and work-intensive for all participants: the respective research instruments, i.e. the elaboration of detailed and comparable aspects and their transformation into standardised questions.

To start with, the personal, environmental and other objective variables were determined.

Variables for the assessment of the environment are:

— size of the village, number of inhabitants;

— the socio-economic type of village, professional structure and percentage of inhabitants working in agriculture ("Agrarquote");

— extent of urbanisation and industrialisation, distance to the next town.

Variables with respect to objects:

1. within the domain of the farm: the size, the farming system, the specialisation of production, the technical and housing equipment, the economic situation;

2. within household and family: size of household, generation structure, size and equipment of the farm-house, technical equipment of the household, amount and structure of the income of the household.

In this way an attempt was made to define and determine the various fields on an empirical basis, independently of their respective specific national factors.

These above-mentioned *independent* variables, as they were defined, still had to be supplemented by variables referring to persons, since otherwise they would represent only a part of the influence carried out on the life conditions, task fulfilment, extent of work, attitudes and behaviour of women. It was assumed that the influence of the "environment" and "object" variables will be confounded, diminished or increased by person-related variables which were defined as follows: age, school education and occupational training, further education, contacts to the industrial-urban environment, occupation, social status (also of the husband), social background and social activity of the village.

In order to trace the respective factors influencing the situation of women in rural areas in the different spheres of life, variables also had to be developed for conditions, attitudes and behaviour of women in the mentioned problem areas. These *dependent* variables were determined as follows:

— women's perception of the tasks they have to fulfill on the farm and in the household,

— women's position in the decision structure,

— extent of work and its accomplishment,

— occupation of women and farm/household income,

— social activity,

— attitudes and behaviour patterns within family and marriage.

As a next step, the intercultural comparison required the operationalisation of the various variables in a comparable way for the participating countries to which the national teams had to adhere. It was especially difficult and time-consuming to develop comparable indicators and standardised questions.

What were the main problems at this stage of the cooperation?

On the basis of the general questions and of the variables, all national teams presented their suggestions together with detailed questions and answers with respect to the various problem areas.

The following questions had to be clarified:

1. The suggestions presented by the researchers contained a number of important aspects. It was impossible to include all of them in the investigation. It was therefore necessary to categorise and classify them. Conclusions and generalisations had to be made without exceeding the accepted framework for the investigation. How was it possible, for instance, to formulate a restricted number of questions to analyse the social activities out of the large number of single questions which had been suggested? What was the importance of questions and which ones should be accepted to measure the degree (the content) of the "social activities" of women in rural areas?

2. In order to operationalise the dependent variables, information on attitudes and behaviour patterns had to be collected. These, however, cannot be obtained directly. In order to obtain respective information, empirical indicators had to be found for these characteristics. These indicators still had to be tested for their validity and reliability in the participating countries. One can imagine that important differences exist in different countries between women in rural areas with regard to the attitudes in view of family and marriage, participation in the planning and management of the farm, or of sex education of the children.

3. Although an effort was made to limit the investigation to the problems connected to the cultural system "village" and to find common categories, a number of misunderstandings arose regarding the application of many necessary terms which could not be solved up to now:

– identical or similar terms are interpreted in different ways;

– identical or similar social phenomena and processes are conceptualised in different ways.

Terms like "social activity", "participation in planning and management", "competition" and "social structure" underline the problem. For instance, it was already difficult to clearly define "main profit farming" and "subsidiary profit farming" in all participating countries.

In my own opinion, these problems reflect to what extent the researchers are conditioned by the demands of the social practice in which they live and with which they are confronted every day. Influences of the different theoretical schools and ideologies become evident. Different points of view and opinions manifesting themselves in scientific thinking and having a historical background can neither be avoided in international comparative research.

4. It seems that the evaluation of the questionnaire formulations in international comparison is connected to a number of specific questions. The social facts existing in the various countries on different levels and in different relation to one another render it difficult to find an evaluation system which is valid for all countries to the same extent. For example: how can the different levels of education (high, medium and low) in the participating countries be definitely defined? What do the terms "weak, medium and well

164

developed" signify in intercultural comparison? What are the common ideas of the researchers with respect to the typical characteristics and threshold values for a small, medium or big farm? Positions which result from the different frameworks in the various countries affect the work on common measurement and evaluation in such a way that valid and objective access to social reality is threatened.

These few examples of the formulation and evaluation of common terms can only give a vague idea of the problems which must be paid attention to in international comparative research.

Due to problems which continuously arose within the present project the participating researchers were forced to make compromises. The reseachers stressed that their willingness to do so was one of the main causes for the success of the project. But what is the substance of compromises in scientific cooperation, what possibilties and limits are these compromises subject to in comparative research?

3.2. The Practical Realisation of the Investigation

The project began in autumn, 1976, with the formation of a working group consisting of the following participants:

FRG: Prof. Dr. Bernd van Deenen, University of Bonn
           Prof. Dr. Ulrich Planck, University of Hohenheim

Poland: Prof. Dr. Mikolaj Kozakiewicz, Polish Academy of Sciences
           Dr. Barbara Tryfan, Polish Academy of Sciences

Hungary: Dr. András Vágvölgyi, Hungarian Academy of Sciences
           Dr. Helga Répássy, Hungarian Economic Planning Institute

France: Mrs. Rosemarie Painvin, High School of Agriculture, Rennes
           Mrs. Martine Berlan, INRA, Paris

Sweden: Mrs. Rosemarie Andersson, Swedish University of Agricultural Sciences, Uppsala
           Mr. Nils-Erik Kasberg, Swedish University of Agricultural Sciences, Uppsala

Austria: Prof. Dr. Hans Bach, University of Linz

The collection of material, its preparation, evaluation and interpretation were carried out by various methods and in several research phases:

1. Evaluation of official statistics and available descriptive material concerning the situation of women in rural areas on the basis of a homogeneous organisation and presentation in the form of synoptic tables (1976—1977).

2. Selection of at least 4 villages to be investigated for each participating country and monographic description of the environment, i.e. "village", on the basis of a "community schedule and discussion instruction" worked out in common (1977). The criteria for the selection of the villages to be investigated was the degree of industrialisation (agricultural share) and urbanisation (distance to the next centre).

3. Questioning of married women (December 1977 — June 1979) in rural areas with a standardised and nationally adapted questionnaire. The questionnaire worked out by the working group contains eight problem areas:

1. structural data of family and household,
2. organisation and structural data of the farm,
3. technical-structural data of farm and household,
4. domestic economy,
5. working time required and division of tasks,
6. participation in decision making,
7. contacts outside the farm and the family,
8. family and marriage roles.

4. Preparation of the data for computer analysis (June 1978 — August 1979).

5. Evaluation of the empirical material on the basis of a standardised structure and a common evaluation plan (ongoing since 1978).

6. Interpretation of results and preparation of national reports according to the standardised structure (ongoing since 1979).

7. Intercultural comparison in a few selected spheres of life of women in rural areas (ongoing since March 1980). For example, selected topics are:

— socio-economic structures of rural households in six European countries,
— family and household structure of farms in six European countries,
— distribution of tasks and decision structure in rural families — comparison of six European countries,
— occupational activity of women in rural areas outside the farm in six European countries.

4. CONCLUSIONS

In this paper we presented some of the main features of a comparative study in the field of rural sociology. The participants in this project discussed during some seven meetings held until now the main problems mentioned in this contribution and agreed on their respective tasks in the project.

Although the questions that were discussed in this paper were related to a specific rural sociological project, one may consider these questions to be important for every comparative study.

Appendix

LIST OF PUBLICATIONS OF THE VIENNA CENTRE

1. *La délinquance juvénile en Europe.* Editions de l'Institut de Sociologie Solvay, Bruxelles, 1968, 192 pp.
2. *Regional Disequilibria in Europe. Backward Areas in Industrialized Countries.* Editions de l'Institut de Sociologie Solvay, Bruxelles, 1968, 614 pp.
3. *Foreign Aid to Newly Independent Countries. Problems and Orientations.* E. Boserup and I. Sachs (eds.), Mouton, The Hague, 1971, 184 pp.
4. *Le développement régional en Europe.* R. Petrella (ed.), Mouton, La Haye, 1971, 480 pp.
5. *Growth Poles and Regional Policies.* A. Kuklinski and R. Petrella (eds.) in collaboration with the United Nations Research Institute for Social Development, Geneva, Mouton, The Hague, 1972, 276 pp.
6. *Etudiants du Tiers-mode en Europe. Problèmes d'adaptation.* Une étude éffectuée en Autriche, en France, aux Pays-Bas et en Yougoslavie. O. Klineberg et J. Ben Brika, avec la collaboration de R. Eder, J. Goricar, B. van Ravenswaaij et M. Zavelloni. Mouton, La Haye, 1972, 236 pp.
7. *The Use of Time. A cross-national comparative survey of daily activities of urban and suburban populations in twelve countries.* A. Szalai and others (eds.), Mouton, The Hague, 1972, 868 pp.
8. *Le développement régional et les secteurs économiques.* R. Pötzsch and F. Voigt (eds.), Mouton, La Haye, 1972, 253 pp.
9. *Délinquance juvénile, famille, école et société.* H. Malewska et V. Peyre, en collaboration avec le Centre de Formation et de Recherche de l'Education Surveillée, Vaucresson, 1973, 213 pp.
10. *Délinquance juvénile et développement socio-économique.* Y. Chirol, Z. Jasovic, D. Lazarevic, B. Maroszek, V. Peyre, A. Szabo, avec la collaboration de H. Ornauer, Mouton, La Haye, 1975, 317 pp.
11. E. Almasy, A Balandier and J. Delatte: *Comparative Survey Analysis: An Annotated Bibliography.* 1967–1973. Sage Research Papers in the Social Sciences, Vol. 4, series No 90–028, Beverly Hills and London, Sage Publications, 1975, 93 pp.
12. *Law and Fertility in Europe.* M. Kirk, M. Livi-Bacci, E. Szabady (eds.) in collaboration with the International Union for the Scientific Study of the Population, Ordina Editions, Liège, 1976, 698 pp. in two volumes.
13. *Images of the World in the Year 2000.* Edited by H. Ornauer, H. Wiberg, A. Sicinski and J. Galtung, Mouton, The Hague, 1976, 729 pp.
14. *L'Etat et la politique agraire en Europe.* "Economies et Sociétés", Cahiers de l' I.S.M.E.A., Série AG, No 14, 1976, 309 pp.
15. H. Malewska and V. Peyre, *Juvenile Delinquency and Development: A Cross-national Study.* Sage Research Papers in the Social Sciences, Vol. 4, series No 90–031, Beverly Hills and London, Sage Publications, 1976, 40 pp.
16. E. Schach, *Reliability in Socio-medical Research: Implications for Cross-national Studies,* Sage Research Papers in the Social Sciences, Vol. 4, series 90–031, Beverly Hills and London, Sage Publications, 1976, 43 pp.

17. C. Barberis, H. Mendras (eds.): *L'avveniere delle campagne europee*. Rome, Franco Angeli, 1976, 215 pp.
18. *L'avenir des campagnes en Europe occidentale*. "Futuribles", numéro hors série sous la direction d'Henri Mendars, 1977, 205 pp.
19. *Aspects socio-politiques et démographiques de la planification familiale en France, en Hongrie et en Roumanie,* Institut National d'Etudes Démographiques (Paris), "Dossiers et recherches", No 2, février 1977, 247 pp.
20. *Cross-national Comparative Survey Research: Theory and Practice.* Edited by A. Szalai and R. Petrella in collaboration with S. Rokkan and E. K. Scheuch, Pergamon Press, Oxford, 1977, 498 pp.
21. *Papers of the International Conference on Information and Documentation in Social Sciences,* Institute of Scientific Information in Social Sciences, USSR, Academy of Sciences, Moscow 1977 (Vol. 1, 301 pp., Vol. 2, 138 pp.) Reprinted in: *Information Processing and Management.* Vol. 14, No 3/4 (Special Issue: Information Resources), Pergamon Press, Oxford—New York—Braunschweig, 1978, pp. 135—318.
22. *Public Policy in Temporal Perspective. Report on the Workshop on the Application of Time-Budget Research to Policy Questions in Urban and Regional Settings* (7—9 October 1975, Laxenburg, Austria). Edited by W. Michelson, Mouton, The Hague, 1978, 210 pp.
23. *Les services dans les pays de l'est et de l'ouest,* Revue d'études comparatives est—ouest, Economie, Planification et Organisation, Editions du Centre National de la Recherche Scientifique, Vol. X, No 1—2, mars—juin 1979, 372 pp.
24. *Consumption Patterns in Eastern and Western Europe. An Economic Comparative Approach – A Collective Study,* directed by V. Cao-Pinna and S.S. Chatalin, Pergamon Press, Oxford, 1979, 190 pp.
25. *Automation and Industrial Workers. A Fifteen Nation Study* (Vol. I, Part 1). Edited by J. Forslin, A. Sarapata, A. M. Whitehill in collaboration with F. Adler and S. C. Mills, Pergamon Press, Oxford, 1979, 250 pp.
26. *The Impact of Systems Change in Organisations. Results and conclusions from a multinational study of information systems development in banks.* Edited by N. Bjørn-Andersen, B. Hedberg, D. Mercer, E. Mumford and A. Solé, Sijthoff & Noordhoff, Alphen aan den Rijn (Netherlands), Germantown (Maryland, USA), 1979.
27. *The Socio-Economic Impact of Microelectronics.* Edited by J. Berting, S. C. Mills and H. Wintersberger, Pergamon Press, Oxford, 1980, 267 pp.
28. *Open Care for the Elderly in Seven European Countries.* Edited by A. Amann in cooperation with the European Centre for Social Welfare Training and Research, Vienna, Pergamon Press, Oxford, 1980, 228 pp.
29. *Rural Community Studies in Europe.* Vol. 1. Edited by J-L. Durand-Drouhin and L-M. Szwengrub in coll. with I. Mihailescu, Pergamon Press, Oxford, 1981, 332 pp.

BOOKS BEING PRINTED BY PERGAMON PRESS, OXFORD

The Location of Growing Industries in Europe. Edited by Penouil and Petrella.
Urban Europe: A Study of Growth and Decline (CURB Vol. 1). Edited by Van den Berg,
Drewett, Klaassen, Rossi and Vijverberg.
Rural Community Studies in Europe. Vol. 2. Edited by Durand-Drouhin and Szwengrub
in coll. with Mihailescu.
Automation and Industrial Workers. Vol. 1, Part 2. Edited by Forslin, Sarapata, Whitehill
in coll. with Adler and Mills.

BOOKS BEING PRINTED BY AKADÉMIAI KIADÓ, BUDAPEST

Comparative Research on Education. Edited by M. Nießen and J. Peschar.
The Sources of Law. A Comparative Empirical Study. Edited by Ch. Kourilsky, A. Rácz
and H. Schäffer.
Law and Dispute Treatment. Edited by M. Cain and K. Kulcsár.